Governing China in the 21st Century

Series Editors
Zhimin Chen
School of International Relations and Public Affairs
Fudan University
Shanghai, China

Yijia Jing
Institute for Global Public Policy & School
of International Relations and Public Affairs
Fudan University
Shanghai, China

Since 1978, China's political and social systems have transformed significantly to accommodate the world's largest population and second largest economy. These changes have grown more complex and challenging as China deals with modernization, globalization, and informatization. The unique path of sociopolitical development of China hardly fits within any existing frame of reference. The number of scientific explorations of China's political and social development, as well as contributions to international literature from Chinese scholars living and researching in Mainland China, has been growing fast. This series publishes research by Chinese and international scholars on China's politics, diplomacy, public affairs, and social and economic issues for the international academic community.

More information about this series at
http://www.palgrave.com/gp/series/15023

Lu Jiang

Beyond Official Development Assistance

Chinese Development Cooperation
and African Agriculture

Lu Jiang
Shanghai University of International
Business and Economics
Shanghai, China

Fudan Development Institute
Shanghai, China

ISSN 2524-3586   ISSN 2524-3594 (electronic)
Governing China in the 21st Century
ISBN 978-981-32-9506-3   ISBN 978-981-32-9507-0 (eBook)
https://doi.org/10.1007/978-981-32-9507-0

© The Editor(s) (if applicable) and The Author(s), under exclusive license to Springer Nature Singapore Pte Ltd. 2020
This work is subject to copyright. All rights are solely and exclusively licensed by the Publisher, whether the whole or part of the material is concerned, specifically the rights of translation, reprinting, reuse of illustrations, recitation, broadcasting, reproduction on microfilms or in any other physical way, and transmission or information storage and retrieval, electronic adaptation, computer software, or by similar or dissimilar methodology now known or hereafter developed.
The use of general descriptive names, registered names, trademarks, service marks, etc. in this publication does not imply, even in the absence of a specific statement, that such names are exempt from the relevant protective laws and regulations and therefore free for general use.
The publisher, the authors and the editors are safe to assume that the advice and information in this book are believed to be true and accurate at the date of publication. Neither the publisher nor the authors or the editors give a warranty, expressed or implied, with respect to the material contained herein or for any errors or omissions that may have been made. The publisher remains neutral with regard to jurisdictional claims in published maps and institutional affiliations.

Cover image: © Xinhua/Alamy Stock Photo

This Palgrave Macmillan imprint is published by the registered company Springer Nature Singapore Pte Ltd.
The registered company address is: 152 Beach Road, #21-01/04 Gateway East, Singapore 189721, Singapore

For my parents

Acknowledgements

This book is based on my Ph.D. project conducted during 2011–2016 at London School of Economics and Political Science (LSE) as well as follow-up research in the past few years. It cannot be completed without support and help from many in my academic and personal life.

I would like to give special thanks first to my Ph.D. supervisor, Professor Chris Alden, who provided me with constructive advices and constant encouragement during the Ph.D. years and guided me through the ten-month-long fieldwork in Africa.

I would express my gratitude to Dr. Sérgio Chichava (based in Instituto de Estudos Sociais e Económicos, Mozambique) and Ms. Angela Harding (based in Pretoria University, South Africa) for their tremendous help in facilitating my fieldwork in the two countries. Sincere thanks also to all the informants in Mozambique and South Africa for their time, as well as the invaluable information and opinions they shared with me.

I'm particularly grateful to Professor Julia C. Strauss (based in SOAS University of London) and Professor Tang Xiaoyang (based in Tsinghua University, China), who provided critical, detailed and constructive advices to help me improve the structure and arguments of this research.

I am also deeply indebted to my parents and Professor Xiao Jialing for their enduring love and support over the years. I'd like to thank in particular my husband, Wei, for his company, patience, encouragement and love that sustained me in the process of writing the book. I also want to say thanks to Maddalena Procopio, my colleague and dear friend in London, who provided me so generous support academically and emotionally.

I would like to give thanks to Mr. Ge Xinqiang and Chen Kaiyuan who funded my studies in London, and LSE who provided financial and intellectual support to my fieldwork. Last but not least, great thanks to Fudan University, my alma mater in China, who supports me to get the book published.

Contents

1 **Introduction** — 1
  1.1 *International Development Cooperation in the Transition* — 4
  1.2 *Chinese Development Cooperation in African Agriculture* — 18
  1.3 *Research Concerns, Methodological Notes and Book Structure* — 21
  References — 26

2 **Tracing the Root of China's Contemporary Agro-Development Cooperation with Africa: A Historical Review** — 35
  2.1 *'Pure Aid': The Earlier Stage (1960s–1970s)* — 36
  2.2 *A Momentum for Change: China's Foreign Aid Reforms* — 41
  2.3 *Consolidation and Transformation: The Transition Stage (1980s–1990s)* — 48
  2.4 *Time for Mutual Development: The Current Stage (2000s–Present)* — 52
  References — 59

3 China's Agro-Development Cooperation with Africa: The Innovative Agro-Aid Model   65
3.1   ATDC: The Flagship Project of China's Innovative Agro-Aid in Africa   66
3.2   Case Studies: Chinese ATDCs in Mozambique and South Africa   76
References   101

4 China's Agro-Development Cooperation with Africa: The Agribusiness Model   105
4.1   Chinese Agribusiness Investment in Africa   106
4.2   Case Studies: Chinese Agribusiness Investment Projects in Mozambique   132
References   174

5 Practical Challenges of Chinese 'Package' Model of Development Cooperation: A Public Policy Implementation Approach   181
5.1   Policy   182
5.2   Implementer   187
5.3   Environment   194
Reference   198

6 Conclusion   199
6.1   The Distinctive Mind-Set of 'Mutual Development': What the History Tells…   199
6.2   'Development Package' and Its Evaluation: The Case of Agriculture   202
6.3   China and the Transitioning Landscape of Global IDC   205
References   211

Appendices   213

Interviews   223

Bibliography   227

Index   263

Abbreviations

ATDC	Agriculture Technology Demonstration Centre
AU	African Union
BSFLR	Bureau of State Farms and Land Reclamation
CAADP	Comprehensive Africa Agriculture Development Programme
CAAIC	China-Africa Agriculture Investment Co., Ltd.
CACD	China-Africa Cotton Development Co., Ltd.
CADFund	China-Africa Development Fund
CAIDC	China Agriculture International Development Co., Ltd.
CDB	China Development Bank
CDC	Commonwealth Development Corporation
CNADC	China National Agricultural Development Group Co., Ltd.
CNFC	China National Fishery Co., Ltd.
COFCO	China National Cereals, Oils and Foodstuffs Corporation Co., Ltd.
CSFAC	China State Farms Agribusiness Co., Ltd.
DAC	Development Assistance Committee
DFI	Development Finance Institution
DFID	Department For International Development (UK)
DPA	Direcção Provincial de Agricultura
ECA	Economic Commission for Africa
FAO	Food and Agriculture Organization
FAOHB	Foreign Affair Office of Hubei Province
FDI	Foreign Direct Investment
FOCAC	Forum on China-Africa Cooperation
IDC	International Development Cooperation
LDC	Least Developed Country
M&A	Merger and Acquisition

MCT	Ministério de Ciência e Tecnologia
MINAG	Ministério de Agricultura
MOA	Ministry of Agriculture
MOC	Ministry of Commerce
MOF	Ministry of Finance
MOFA	Ministry of Foreign Affairs
NDRC	National Development and Reform Commission
NEPAD	New Partnership for Africa's Development
NGO	Non-Governmental Organizations
OECD	Organisation for Economic Co-operation and Development
PPI	Public Policy Implementation
PPP	Public–Private Partnership
PRC	People's Republic of China
SAE	State-owned Agricultural Enterprise
SOE	State-owned Enterprise
SSA	Sub-Saharan Africa
UK	United Kingdom
UN	United Nations
US	United States
USAID	United States Agency for International Development
WWII	World War II

List of Figures

Fig. 1.1 ODA by DAC donors in Total Aid, 1967–2017 (Unit: $ Million, at constant prices of 2017) (*Note* Total aid in the graph includes ODA provided by DAC donors, non-DAC donors, multilateral donors and private donors. *Source* OECD Statistics-Development-Aid [ODA] by sector and donor [https://stats.oecd.org/Index.aspx?DataSetCode=TABLE5, accessed 31 May 2019]) 5

Fig. 2.1 Chinese aid expenditure and its percentage in total fiscal expenditure (It is worth noting that, after the launch of two 'concessional loans' [see the last part of Sect. 2.2], the fiscal expenditure only covers the interest discount [i.e. difference between market interest and concessional interest] of the loans and thus the actual aid volume of China (insofar as grants and concessional loans are concerned) is much higher than the fiscal expenditure on aid as shown in this figure; *Source* The author based on CAITEC [2018, 88–90]) 43

Fig. 3.1 The ATDC in Mozambique, Boane, Maputo Province, 18 October 2013 77

Fig. 3.2 Vegetable fields and reservoir in the centre, Boane, 18 October 2013 79

Fig. 3.3 The Mozambican workers hired by the centre to grow rice. They were trained by the Chinese experts first and were now being able to work independently in the rice paddies. Boane, 28 October 2013 81

Fig. 3.4	People queuing to buy the produce from the ATDC and to sell on the local markets. Boane, 18 October 2013	84
Fig. 3.5	The ATDC in South Africa, Gariep Dam, Free State, 29 January 2015	87
Fig. 3.6	One of the six government-backed fish farms in Free State (left: the author, middle: Chinese fish expert, right: local fish farmer), 29 January 2015	89
Fig. 3.7	Fish hatchery of the centre, 29 January 2015	90
Fig. 3.8	Fish pond of the centre, 29 January 2015	91
Fig. 4.1	One of the farms under Wanbao project, Xaixai, 20 November 2013	134
Fig. 4.2	Wanbao project, Xaixai, 18 November 2013	135
Fig. 4.3	One of the lands allocated for training under Wanbao project, Xaixai, 21 November 2013	142
Fig. 4.4	The Chinese farm director (on the left) explained to the translator (in pink) and the three young Mozambican graduates (the three from the right) who were going to assist the Chinese agro-expert in training the local farmers. Xaixai, 21 November 2013	143
Fig. 4.5	The storage facilities under construction, Xaixai, 19 November 2013	144
Fig. 4.6	Local people queuing to buy rice directly from one of Wanbao's farms, Xaixai, 30 March 2013 (Taken by one of the accountants sent by CADFund to Wanbao)	145
Fig. 4.7	Wanbao rice sold in the Chinese supermarkets, Maputo, January 2015	146
Fig. 4.8	One of the 20 houses (among the 500 planned) Wanhao already built for the Mozambican workers working on their farm (exterior). Xaixai, 19 November 2013	150
Fig. 4.9	One of the 20 houses Wanhao already built for the Mozambican workers working on their farm (interior). Xaixai, 19 November 2013	150
Fig. 4.10	FONGA, Xaixai, 21 November 2013	151
Fig. 4.11	The base of Hefeng Company, Buzi, 15 January 2015	152
Fig. 4.12	The canteen used by the Chinese and Mozambican workers (left: exterior, right: interior), Buzi, 15 January 2015	153
Fig. 4.13	Land under Hefeng project, Buzi, 15 January 2013	155
Fig. 4.14	The simple processing facilities in the Hefeng base, Buzi, 15 January 2015	156
Fig. 4.15	The AAA rice produced by Hefeng, Buzi, 15 January 2015	157

List of Tables

Table 2.1	Selected Chinese-aided farms in Africa (1960–1980s)	38
Table 3.1	Chinese agriculture technology demonstration centres in Africa	67
Table 3.2	Evaluation indicators of the ATDC	72
Table 3.3	Initial plan of land use for the centre's future agribusiness (Unit: [ha])	83
Table 3.4	Governance structure for the South African ATDC	93
Table 4.1	Chinese agricultural FDI around the globe in/by 2016	107
Table 4.2	Chinese overseas agricultural FDI by Sector in/by 2016 (Unit: $ Million)	108
Table 4.3	Chinese overseas crop-farming FDI in 2016 (Unit: Thousand tons)	108
Table 4.4	China's 'Agriculture Going Out' policy	110
Table 4.5	Chinese agricultural FDI in Africa in/by 2016	117
Table 4.6	Top five SSA countries hosting Chinese agro-investment Firms	117
Table 4.7	Some of the sizable agribusiness projects invested by Chinese companies in Africa	118
Table 4.8	Policy and institutional developments of China's 'Agriculture Going Out' policy	123

CHAPTER 1

Introduction

As a student of international relations and development, the sixty years of Chinese engagement in African agriculture since the 1960s has been such an interesting story and wonderful case for me to investigate. It stems from a period when the People's Republic of China (PRC) itself was still a weak and vulnerable new-born regime and has since witnessed the ups and downs of China's development and reforms both at home and in its external relations. As of the turn of the 2020s, when China has now stood as the second largest economy and one of the major powers in the world, agricultural cooperation remains an integral part in China's relations with the African continent—though tremendous changes have taken place in terms of the motivations, priorities, actors and modalities involved in it.

Particularly, from the perspective of international development cooperation (IDC) that the book primarily adopts, the agro-cooperation of China with Africa not only serves as a perfect example of the evolution of Chinese external development cooperation in the past decades, but more importantly, the contemporary forms of it may indicate, or at least experiment with, a fresh model against the context of a transitioning IDC landscape globally. In a time when China, among other 'emerging' Southern development partners, has gained increasing significance and caught the eyes of the world, this book aims to explore the dynamics and modalities, among other key issues, as regards its contemporary development cooperation behaviours through examining the typical case of China's agro-cooperation with Africa. But to start with, I will firstly set the stage for the story of 'China-Africa agriculture' by outlining the development and current status of the IDC.

International development cooperation—as broadly understood as a form of collaborative activity among international community[1] that is aimed at assisting the achievement of commonly accepted development objectives[2] in the developing world—is largely a contemporary idea that emerged after the Second World War (WWII). Although the practice of IDC, since the very beginning in the 1940s, developed along two lines—that is IDC from the developed countries ('the North') to the so-called underdeveloped areas[3] ('the South') and IDC within the developing world (South-South cooperation)—the former had long possessed a dominant position on the global IDC landscape while the latter being largely sidelined in the twentieth century. Another common practice in IDC during the twentieth century was the overwhelming application of official aid, which is the case for both the Northern donors in the form of official development assistance (ODA) and the Southern actors through their external aid and technical assistance.

---

[1] Including primarily national states (both as development cooperation providers and recipients), but also international organizations, national/international non-governmental organizations (NGOs), and increasingly national/international private sector actors such as private foundations, private/state-owned enterprises (with state owned enterprises [SOEs] often treated as a broadly understood market force in practice) and multinationals.

[2] Most typical of them are the UN-proposed development objectives, first the Millennium Development Goals (MDGs) and since 2015 the Sustainable Development Goals (SDGs); most of these objectives concern the economic and social aspects of a country's development.

[3] As by President Truman of the United States in 'the fourth point' from his inaugural address (Truman 1949). This new type of distinction between developed and 'underdeveloped' countries has since been increasingly adopted, particularly by the Northern donors, and thus gradually replaced the old description of colonial powers and colonies. The shift of description, while reflecting the change of times, also demonstrates the efforts of the Northern countries to turn over a new leaf in dealing relations with their former colonies—as noted in Truman's address (1949), 'The old imperialism exploitation for foreign profit has no place in our plans. What we envisage is a program of development based on the concepts of democratic fair dealing'. This may partly explain, from a historical angle of their colonial past, why the Northern donors have always tried to draw a clear-cut line between aid and other profit-involving activities, whereas for Southern development partners like China, a combination of different cooperation forms in IDC does not seem to be any unacceptable issue, nor does it necessarily go against 'fair dealing'.

Changes, however, started to take place quietly towards the end of the last century. While the Northern ODA received widespread criticisms since the late 1990s (see, e.g., Hansen and Tarp 2000; Easterly 2003; Sachs 2005; Moyo 2010) and went through continual self-reflection and reforms,[4] the once low-profile Southern development partners—particularly China but also India, Brazil, and Turkey, just to mention a few—have rapidly developed into a non-negligible new polar in the world IDC arena. What further compound the situation are the divergent development cooperation models of the Southern actors from the North. While opening new opportunities for the cooperation recipient countries, some of the Southern actors' distinctiveness has seemed to get on the nerves of the traditional donors and impose a potential threat to the latter's long-held dominant status. The North–South divide within the development cooperation providers has hence become more visible in the current times.

More recently, another notable trend also started to emerge, that is the growing participation of global private sector actors in the IDC. Though still in its infancy, this new trend bears the potential not only to massively increase the development finances that can be mobilized, but also significantly change the ODA-dominating situation in IDC by incorporating more and diversified cooperation forms. The Public–Private Partnership (PPP) initiative that has been increasingly adopted in the Northern development cooperation circle is surely one embodiment of the trend. But perhaps a more forceful echo comes from some of the Southern development partners like China who have taken more open attitudes towards cooperation beyond mere official aid, and more essentially, cooperation that entails a 'mutual-development' mentality. 'Development package', as referred to in the book, is precisely such an experiment.

In a nutshell, it is fair to say that the global IDC is currently facing a turning point. And it may concern far beyond just a proliferation of actors, combination of modalities, or diversification of financial sources; but equally (if not more) important, a change of mind-set in terms of what on earth 'development cooperation' is, how we should treat it, and how much we can possibly expect from it.

---

[4]See, for instance, the High-level Fora on Aid effectiveness held by OECD-DAC in Rome (2003), Paris (2005), Accra (2008) and Busan (2011), and the corresponding agreements passed by the DAC members.

1.1 International Development Cooperation in the Transition

Growing North–South Divide

In 1947, the Secretary of State of the United States George C. Marshall launched the famous European Recovery Programme (1948–1952) through which more than $12 billion were funded by the US government to help with the reconstruction of the Western Europe (Department of State of the US). Many of the recipient countries, partly due to this external assistance, managed to recover from the ravages of war within a relatively short period of time. The great success of the 'Marshall Plan' thus ignited considerable enthusiasm and expectation for the prospects of helping other poorer countries in the world by means of external assistance (Führer 1996, 4; Hjertholm and White 2000, 61). The US, again, took a lead in this process through President Truman's 'Point Four Programme' proposed in 1949 (Truman 1949), and a number of newly recovered European countries soon joined the undertaking in the 1950s.[5]

Meanwhile, a series of development initiatives, funds and agencies were launched by multilateral international organizations such as the United Nations, World Bank and European Economic Community throughout the 1940s–1950s (Führer 1996, 4–7)—indeed, the UN Chapter (1945) was among the earliest in the post-WWII IDC history that explicitly called for an international collaboration of its member states to 'promote the economic and social advancement of all peoples'. In 1961, the Development Assistance Committee (DAC), an agency with specific mandates to promote economic development and people's welfare in the less-developed countries through providing development assistance, was formally created under the just established Organization for Economic Cooperation and Development (OECD). The OECD-DAC has since played a crucial role in guiding and coordinating the North-to-South development cooperation activities,

---

[5] In fact, foreign aid behaviours of both the US and some of the European countries (e.g. the UK, France and Netherlands) can be traced back even earlier to the nineteenth and the first half of the twentieth century, but mostly constrained to their neighbours (in the case of US) or colonies (in the case of European countries) and limited in scale—see, for instance, van Soest (1978, 31) and Hjertholm and White (2000, 60–61).

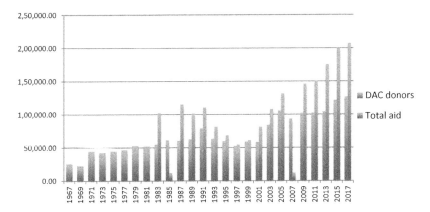

Fig. 1.1 ODA by DAC donors in Total Aid, 1967–2017 (Unit: $ Million, at constant prices of 2017) (*Note* Total aid in the graph includes ODA provided by DAC donors, non-DAC donors, multilateral donors and private donors. *Source* OECD Statistics-Development-Aid [ODA] by sector and donor [https://stats.oecd.org/Index.aspx?DataSetCode=TABLE5, accessed 31 May 2019])

especially that in the form of 'official development assistance (ODA)' (Hynes and Scott 2013).

The ODA offered by DAC members, or 'DAC donors' as what they often call themselves, has maintained an upward trend over the past six decades, increasing by about four times from $25.8 billion in 1967 to $126.8 billion in 2017 (Fig. 1.1). During most of the time, the DAC donors have contributed the bulk of the international aid—the proportion was particularly notable throughout the 1990s until the early 2000s when it reached up to 95% of the total (Manning 2006, 371; Fig. 1.1), thus establishing itself a dominant position in the global aid arena. Equally important, the DAC has over the years developed a comprehensive system of standards, rules and norms in terms of the provision of ODA, among other development modalities (Manning 2006, Bräutigam 2010, Hynes and Scott 2013), thereby further strengthening its leading status in the discourse and practice of IDC.

Despite the prominent role of the DAC donors, similar kinds of external development cooperation offered by national states towards other countries, particularly through aid-giving, were just common in the rest of the world. The single largest aid-giver outside the DAC community was surely the Soviet Union who had offered rather generous aid, including but not constrained to development-oriented assistance, to a large number of communist countries during the Cold War period. In Asia, India, for instance, started to commit itself to development cooperation with other developing countries almost concurrently with its gaining independence, thereby setting up a series of cooperation initiatives first with other Asian countries through the Asian Relations Conference in 1947 and 'Colombo Plan' in 1950, then African states through the Bandung Conference in 1955 (Chaturvedi et al. 2014). In a similar vein, China also started to provide foreign aid soon after the establishment of the PRC in 1949, first to its Asian neighbours in the 1950s and then Africa after the Bandung Conference. In Latin America, Brazil established its national system for IDC in 1969, with the main aim to better coordinate foreign assistance it received itself but meanwhile also to provide technical assistance to other developing countries, particularly in Latin America and Africa (Vaz and Inoue 2007). Even in Africa that usually served as the recipient end of development cooperation, the relatively better-off South African government also launched the Economic Cooperation Promotion Loan Fund in 1968 as a foreign policy instrument for various objectives (Besharati 2013).

These abovementioned countries, apart from the Soviet Union giant, were largely from what is commonly understood as 'the South'—among other things, many of them shared a colonial or semi-colonial history, gained independence not long and still faced tremendous challenges of developing their own economies at the time. Therefore, what they could possibly offer as external development assistance to other countries was rather limited; indeed, many of them were back then by themselves ODA recipients of the DAC donors. Their development cooperation and aid practice, often situated within the 'South-South Cooperation' framework, was thus largely incomparable to the DAC donors either in terms of volume or impacts. The development cooperation of the Southern countries was further reduced during the 1990s after the end of Cold War, when many of them shifted their focus back to their own domestic issues (Krugelund 2008).

Entering the new millennium, however, some of these Southern countries have gained an unprecedented momentum in economic growth, most notably the 'BRICS' (Brazil, Russia, India, China and South Africa) who are widely regarded as the forerunners among the developing world. With growing economic strength comes their increasing aspiration to have a greater say in the current international arena that is believed by them to be an 'unfair' system designed and dominated by the advanced countries. IDC, therefore, has become one of the platforms for them to project the image as emerging powers both regionally and globally. Lula's presidency during the 2003–2010, for instance, has marked a 'big leap' of Brazilian development cooperation inspired by the so-called solidarity diplomacy (Inoue and Vaz 2012). The budget speech made by Indian Finance Minister in 2003 signified a significant policy shift of India's IDC policy whereby it proclaimed to 'provide relief to certain bilateral partners' on the one hand and strengthen external support to other developing countries on the other (Government of India 2003). But most eye-catching among all these Southern 'donors' was definitely China, whose development cooperation particularly characterized by its 'development package' model has attained an unprecedented level since the new millennium, and especially notable in Africa.

It is against this context that former chair of the OECD-DAC Richard Manning (2006), among others, started to call attention to the phenomenon of the growing non-DAC donors, or the so-called emerging donors,[6] that occurred particularly since the 2000s. Among them, those from the 'Global South' as noted earlier—or referred to as the *Southern development partners*[7] in this book—are the most controversial and

---

[6] Manning (2006) divided the these 'emerging donors' into four groups, namely the non-DAC OECD members, the non-OECD new EU members, the Middle East and OPEC countries, and the remaining ones which include a diversity of countries such as Venezuela, Chile, Brazil, South Africa, Russia, Malaysia, Thailand, as well as the much discussed two 'heavyweights', India and China. For a practical use, the non-DAC donors can also be grouped to three broader categories: (1) the *DAC-like countries* who are often economically better off—and importantly—willing to align their own development cooperation practice to the DAC principles, including reporting their aid data to the OECD (Zimmermann and Smith 2011); (2) the *Gulf Arab countries* who, due to their unique historical, geopolitical and religious context, stand distinctively from others and form a separate development cooperation model (Villanger 2007; Shushan and Marcoux 2011; Momani and Ennis 2012; Turki 2014); and (3) the Southern development partners that are under discussion in this book.

[7] Typical examples and related research include, for instance, Brazil (Vaz and Inoue 2007; Xalma 2010; Inoue and Vaz 2012; Burges 2014; Cabral et al. 2014; Robledo 2015), India (Agrawal 2007; McCormick 2008; Chaturvedi 2008, 2012; Chanana 2009, 2010; Fuchs and Vadlamannati 2013; Chaturvedi et al. 2014), South Africa (Wolfe et al. 2008; Grimm 2011; Vickers 2012; Besharati 2013; Grobbelaar 2014), Turkey (Kulaklikaya and Nurdun 2010; Özkan and Akgün 2010; Rudincová 2014; Hausmann and Lundsgaarde 2015), and China (Lancaster 2007; Chin and Frolic 2007; Woods 2008; McCormick 2008; Opoku-Mensah 2009; Tan-Mullins et al. 2010; Bräutigam 2011; Haan 2011; Lengauer 2011; Chin 2012; Dreher and Fuchs 2015; Zhang et al. 2015; Dreher et al. 2016; Kilama 2016).

debated ones. These countries, though in a preceding position within the developing world, are still facing massive tasks and challenges in terms of economic and social development domestically, and some are yet to fully graduate from the aid-recipient list of the DAC donors until now. As a result, despite a rapid increase in the past two decades, aid provided by the Southern development partners is still rather limited compared to that of their DAC counterparts. In 2008, for instance, development cooperation provided by non-DAC donors in total averaged roughly at $12 billion, representing only about one-tenth of the DAC donors in the same year; the relative weight of the Southern development partners is even less (Smith et al. 2010, IDS online databases[8]).

Therefore, it is not really the *size* but rather the *modalities* of the Southern development partners that have triggered the heated debate in the academia and policy arena.[9] While some advocate that the distinct models of Southern development partners provide new alternatives and thus open policy space for developing countries that are in need of foreign assistance, many—especially those from the DAC community—have expressed considerable concerns about this new phenomenon and worry that their established rules and standards may be endangered. This is also where a growing divide between Northern donors and Southern actors starts to appear.

Some general differences between the two can be seen in the following aspects. First, in terms of *geographical distribution*, Southern development partners have provided most of their development aid to the UN-identified Least Developed Countries (LDCs), which demonstrates a similar pattern to the DAC donors. But different from the latter, the Southern development partners normally prioritize the LDCs that are

---

These Southern development partners are sometimes also referred to as 'providers of South-South Cooperation' (ECOSOC of the UN 2008; Zimmermann and Smith 2011).

[8] http://www.oecd.org/development/stats/idsonline.htm, accessed 31 May 2019.

[9] See, for instance, Manning (2006), Naim (2009), Woods (2008), Kragelund (2008), Six (2009), Paulo and Reisen (2010), Kim and Lightfoot (2011), Hann 2011, Zimmermann and Smith (2011), Chandy and Kharas (2011), Davies (2011), Sato et al. (2011), Chin and Quadir (2012), Mwase and Yang (2012), Quadir (2013), Roussel (2013), Kondoh (2015), Kilama (2016).

in close proximity to themselves, rather than extend to a global reach as many of the DAC donors do. For instance, India gave more than 85% of aid to its (South) Asian neighbours and Turkey around 83% to its (Central and South) Asian friends, while Brazil distributed the largest part of aid to its Latin American neighbours and a few Lusophone African countries who shared a common colonial past (ECOSOC of the UN 2008, 17–18). Exception of that is China whose aid has represented more a global allocation compared to other development actors from the South, with Africa receiving more than half (51.8%) of the Chinese aid, followed by Asia (30.5%), Latin America and the Caribbean (8.4%), among others (State Council of the PRC 2014).

As regards *targeted sectors*, Southern development partners have distributed a large proportion of their aid finance to economic sectors (e.g. economic infrastructure and productive sectors) compared to their OECD-DAC counterparts who have put more emphasis on social sectors (e.g. social infrastructure and human resource cooperation)[10] (Kragelund 2008, 2010; Walz and Ramachandran 2011; Mwase and Yang 2012). This feature is particularly visible in the case of China and India.[11] Take the former for example, about 50.4% of China's total aid funds was spent on economic sectors (44.8% in economic infrastructure and 5.6% in agricultural and industrial sectors) and 33.4% of that in social sectors (27.6% in social infrastructure and 5.8% in human resource cooperation) during the period 2010–2012 (State Council of the PRC 2014), whereas the DAC donors disbursed 23.9% of their ODA to economic sectors (16.6% in economic infrastructure and 7.2% in productive sectors) and 41.3% in social sectors in the year of 2012 (IDS online databases).

Similar to DAC donors, grants and loans are also widely used (e.g. in China, India, South Africa, Turkey) as the main *financing methods*,

---

[10] For the specific definition and scope of economic and social infrastructure, among other sectorial categories of aid, readers can refer to the OECD Statistics. China, for instance, has adopted a similar system as seen in its White Papers on foreign aid (State Council of the PRC 2011, 2014).

[11] This is, to a lesser extent, the case for other Southern development partners. For example, Brazil also puts much emphasis on social sector (Inoue and Vaz 2012), South Africa gives a special focus on peace-building and post-conflict development (Grobbelaar 2014) and Turkey on humanitarian aid (Hausmann and Lundsgaarde 2015).

or begin to emerge as a new trend (e.g. in Brazil) in the development partner countries from the South. That said, the proportion of the two (grants versus loans) in total aid differs greatly between the DAC and Southern actors. While grants have represented more than 80% of the total ODA among DAC donors in the past decade (IDS online databases), the figure is about 36.5% for China during 2012–2014 (State Council of the PRC 2014), and only 4% for India (in terms of its aid to Africa) during 2000–2014 (Chaturvedi et al. 2014). Furthermore, the concessional terms of the loans provided respectively by the DAC and Southern actors are also quite different from each other (see 'concessionality' below).

Concerning *cooperation forms*, while project aid is still overwhelmingly utilized among the Southern development partners, the DAC community has, since the 1980s, diverted increasing attention to programme aid or 'programme-based approaches (PBA)' as referred to in recent years, and particularly 'budget support' which stands as a major component of it (Mosley and Eeckhout 2000; Camara 2004). In 2015, for example, general programme aid represented 8% of DAC donors' total ODA in Africa (IDS online databases), whereas the Southern development partners normally do not provide significant programme aid to other developing countries. Exceptions may be seen in the use of budget support by South Africa and India, which however remains on a very limited scale in both cases (Besharati 2013; ECOSOC of the UN 2008, 12–13). Meanwhile, while technical assistance has traditionally occupied a special position and remained so in the aid practice for Southern development partners, the DAC donors have seemed to gradually shift towards the more broadly defined concept of capability building since the 1990s (Timmis 2018). For instance, India's famous Indian Technical & Economic Cooperation (ITEC) programme, which was launched in 1964, remains as an integral part of Indian contemporary aid. About $11 million was spent on ITEC every year, and the total disbursement mounted to almost 60% of the overall expenditure of Indian Ministry of External Affairs during 2012–2013 (Chaturvedi et al. 2014, 12–13). Brazil, as well, has had the tradition of providing technical assistance to other developing countries for decades, especially since 1978 when the Buenos Aires Action Plan was approved, whereby the Technician Cooperation among Developing Countries (TCDC) concept was increasingly integrated into Brazilian domestic system (Vaz and Inoue 2007, 5).

Apart from some of the general features and differences as mentioned above, a few other issues, particularly those around concessionality, conditionality and the typing status of aid, have made the Southern modalities of development cooperation even more controversial.

To 'ensure the benefits of the recipient developing countries', the DAC stipulates that ODA must be 'concessional in character' and uses 'grant element' as a yardstick to measure the *consessionality* of the ODA of DAC members (OECD 2008; OECD-DAC 2013). A minimum grant element of 25% is required for a loan to be qualified as ODA, calculated against a 10% reference rate of interest/discount that was adopted since the 1970s (Hynes and Scott 2013, 5–8). To LDCs, furthermore, the DAC demands even softer terms that the ODA should be essentially in the form of grants and as a minimum, the average grant element of all commitments from a given donor should either be at least 86% to each LDC over a period of three years, or at least 90% annually for the LDCs as a group (OECD 1978). In effect, the average grant element of total ODA by DAC donors is almost 96% (OECD 2016). By contrast, there isn't a strict stipulation among Southern development partners on the concessionality of their financial flows to the recipient countries. They apply varying rates of interest for their loans extended, which—while usually lower than market terms—still appear 'less concessional' than the DAC donors if measured by the OECD 'grant element' criteria. For instance, the grant element of Chinese loans is about 75.1% for the zero-interest government loan and between 24.2 and 67.6% for concessional loans provided by China's EXIM Bank, the figure for India is around 53.1–56.5%, and Turkey 26.6–80.8% (ECOSOC of the UN 2008, 24).

Conditionality is another long-held principle of the DAC donors particularly since the debt crisis in the 1980s. The ODA has become conditional on a wide range of economic, political, social and environmental policies, such as macroeconomic stabilization, privatization, 'good governance' and related reforms (Mold 2009). And despite the Paris Declaration emphasis on 'ownership', the DAC donors seem to have adopted an increasingly hands-on approach (Zimmermann and Smith 2011). Many of the Southern development partners, on the other hand, do not usually attach such economic or political conditions when giving aid to other developing countries, or at least to a far less extent than their DAC counterparts. China stands out greatly in this regard for its firmly held non-interference position (Tan-Mullins et al. 2010).

While the Southern actors usually invoke the core principles for South-South Cooperation as the rationale for their non-conditionality practice,[12] it is more often than not interpreted (particularly by the Northern donors) as merely a sort of political rhetoric (for commercial benefits) rather than being taken seriously.

Another important and hotly debated issue around development cooperation provided by Southern countries is *tied aid*, and more broadly, the '*development package*' model that often combines aid with other commercial activities (see in the next section). Tied aid is not formally prohibited—though subject to a series of rules concerning, for instance, the concessionality level (ECOSOC of the UN 2008, 22–23), the target countries as well as the developmental relevance—and used to be widely practiced among DAC donors for decades. However, given the common belief in the cost-inefficiency and reduced effectiveness of tied aid, the OECD-DAC made a Recommendation in 2001 for the donors to untie their ODA, especially that towards the LDCs. By the year of 2007, the proportion of fully untied bilateral aid of DAC donors rose from 46% in 1999–2001 to 76%, and for LDCs from 57 to 83% (Clay et al. 2009). In parallel with the efforts made by the DAC community—regardless of evident limitation at the same time[13]—many of the Southern development partners, however, still widely and frequently use tied aid. This has inevitably evoked great resentments and criticisms from the DAC donors (Manning 2006), though the actual effects of that remain largely unevaluated from either an efficiency or effectiveness perspective (Woods 2008; Clay et al. 2009).

---

[12] For instance, the principles of 'respect for the sovereignty and territorial integrity of all nations, abstention from intervention or interference in the internal affairs of another country, abstention by any country from exerting pressures on other countries' (Final Communiqué of the Asian-African conference of Bandung, 1955), and that of 'strict observance of national sovereignty, economic independence, equal rights and non-interference in domestic affairs of nations, irrespective of their size, level of development and social and economic systems' (Buenos Aires Plan of Action, 1978).

[13] According to Clay et al. (2009), technical cooperation and food aid were excluded from the Recommendation and both remain significant 'gray areas', with 30% and at least 50% respectively still reported as tied; meanwhile, there are large variations in the untying status of different DAC donors (e.g. the US and Japanese ODA were still heavily tied) and high level of non-reporting for technical cooperation and likely tied sectors (e.g. infrastructure, transport and energy), besides, statistical evidence also implied a considerable element of intended or unintended de facto tying that still widely exists in practice.

In sum, while it is quite normal for the Northern and Southern actors to have different approaches to development cooperation due to their distinctive histories, ideologies and development status, the problem is that they haven't been able to co-exist in a very harmonious way. Rather, the divide between the two seems to have widened, which is particularly evident from the attitudes of the Northern donors towards the Southern development partners. Given their long and rich practice in IDC, many of the Northern countries tend to observe and judge the Southern actors through the lens of their own DAC model. For instance, the Southern development partners are labelled as 'donors', which is largely influenced by DAC's accustomed mentality of the 'donor-recipient' logic. They are regarded as 'emerging' or 'new' actors due to DAC donors' more established and visible role in the IDC landscape. Their modalities of development cooperation—such as the financing methods, concessionality, conditionality and tying status of aid discussed above—are considered problematic and even 'rogue' for the obvious departure from the established DAC standards (Naim 2009; Paulo and Reisen 2010; Walz and Ramachandran 2011). They are hence invited to different sorts of 'dialogue', which however are often with an inexplicit intension of the DAC trying to converge the Southern actors and the underlying belief that DAC principles 'should be maintained' (Manning 2006, 384). Some scholars have further explored why it has been difficult for the Southern development partners to converge to the DAC guidelines (Kondoh 2015), and how possible—for instance, through policy dialogue and peer review—to achieve that goal (Paulo and Reisen 2010).

The development cooperation models of the Southern actors, therefore, tend not to be judged by what they are, but rather, what they are not (Kim and Lightfoot 2011); and this is so even when those rules and norms are neither fully complied by the DAC members themselves (Woods 2008; Tan-Mullins et al. 2010), nor have them been proved more productive or beneficial to recipient countries than the Southern models. Accordingly, what is relatively lacking in the academic and policy discussion is a more South-oriented perspective that is aimed to explore, for instance, how the contemporary modalities of development cooperation have been shaped by the Southern actors' respective histories and experiences in the past decades. To give some examples: the widely used financing method of loans in India's current external development cooperation is believed to have much to do with the influence of its own aid-receiving past, wherein the proportion of loans in the total aid received by India remained high and in fact increased from 81% in 1981–1982 to 93% in 2010–2011 (Chaturvedi 2012); and the principles of non-conditionality of Brazilian development cooperation were very much informed by the emerging ideals of horizontality in the 1970–1980s as well as its own experiences as an aid recipient (Leite et al. 2014). Therefore, as some have rightly pointed out, there may be some real obstacles to the mutual understanding between the DAC donors and Southern development partners, and it may thus be more realistic to have differentiated standards (Chandy and Kharas 2011).

The Emerging Public–Private Cooperation
There is not a particularly strict definition as to 'public private cooperation' in the IDC area, but rather a cluster of different arrangements that share some key common features: notably the expansion of participants from traditional public sector actors to private sector actors[14] and particularly the often (but not compulsory) incorporation of business model. The embracing of business model, and the acknowledgement of profit-seeking motives in particular, can be seen an innovative part for the current public–private cooperation compared to the more traditional model of private donations by some world-renown Foundations (e.g. the Gates Foundation). This emerging trend can be observed both in the practice of the Northern donors and that of the Southern development partners.

Over the decades, the Northern academic and policy circle of IDC has put an almost exclusive focus on ODA (Chandy 2011; Hynes and Scott 2013; Currie-Alder 2016). To get a hint of this, one just needs to take a glance at the annual Development Cooperation Reports produced by OECD in the past few decades, for instance, wherein all the documents were indeed only dealing with ODA-related issues. That said, there have seemed to be some signs of change in recent years—one notable case is the PPP model that starts to be adopted in the Northern development cooperation area. In the Northern countries, the PPP scheme was initially used domestically in the provision of public facilities and services (esp. infrastructure). It was then brought into the domain of IDC

[14] In practice (of both Northern donors and Southern development partners), it also expands to other market forces such as SOEs, research institutes and universities, as well as NGOs, among others.

('development PPP' hereinafter) since the late 1990s,[15] which has much to do with the growing role played by the global private sector in international financial flows.

With the end of Cold War and step-up of globalization, private financial flows grew rapidly and far surpassed ODA; indeed, by end of the 1990s, private flows had mounted to 82% of total global financial flows, representing more than 4 times of that of ODA (Ierley 2002). One of the major objectives of the Northern donors in initiating development PPP, therefore, is to mobilize the private sector resources, particularly capital funds but their specialized expertise as well. At the same time, many private sector actors were also seeking cooperation with the official donors with a view to benefiting from the latter's rich experiences, wide networks and good reputation, among others in the developing world (Binder et al. 2007; Ingram et al. 2016). These advantages were deemed valuable for the private actors either to improve their development-oriented efforts (e.g. out of social responsibility concern), or perhaps more importantly, to seek and expand business opportunities in the less-developed countries.

Against this background, the development PPP began to be widely adopted by a large number of DAC donors such as the US,[16] UK, the Netherlands, Germany, Sweden, Denmark, Canada, Australia and Japan (Troilo 2011; Devex 2011), and also publicly advocated by international organizations like the United Nations (Grahl et al. 2010; UNDP 2016). Recently, the concept of 'partnership' started to be raised also in the abovementioned OECD 'Development Cooperation Reports'; in their

---

[15] For instance, the flagship development PPP project of Germany, develoPPP.de, was launched in 1999.

[16] In the past two decades, the US has taken a leading role in creating public-private partnerships across the Northern development community—the USAID has signed over 1600 partnerships since 2001 with more than 3000 partners valued at nearly $20 billion (Devex 2011). The President Trump's Administration has recently established a new entity, the International Development Finance Corp. (IDFC), replacing the previous Overseas Private Investment Corp. (OPIC—the key financial institution of the US to mobilize private capital for development cooperation); and meanwhile doubled the budget for IDFC than OPIC to $60 billion. This is a move against the background of Trump Administration's recent proposal to massively cut aid budget and merge USAID to the Department of State, and thus reinforces the trend of the US to embrace diversified financing and cooperation forms (esp. by engaging the US private sector) in its overseas development cooperation practice.

2016 report, for instance, paid special attention and elaborated much on the potential positive role of 'business and private sector' (OECD 2016).

Specifically, there are at least three methods whereby the private sector actors are mobilized under the development PPP scheme—respectively 'grants model', 'LEGs model'[17] and 'risk-reducing model'. Under the 'grants model', the governments invite private sector actors to engage in development-oriented projects through providing a certain amount of 'free money'; a typical example of this is the widely used 'challenge funds' by many DAC donors (Pompa 2013). The 'LEGs model' indicates cases when the governments form partnership with private sector actors through providing the latter with loans, equities or guarantees in investment projects that are believed to bear important developmental impacts (ICAI 2015); this is mostly realized through the respective development finance institutions (DFIs) of the DAC donor countries, such as the CDC (UK), OPIC (US), Kfw-DEG (Germany), among others. The 'risk-reducing model' is utilization of risk-sharing mechanisms by the donors—such as in the form of advance market commitment (AMC) or catalytic first-loss capital (CFLC)—to encourage private actors to actively participate in certain development projects (Runde et al. 2011, 29–31); one of the typical application cases is the well-known Global Alliance for Vaccines and Immunization (GAVI) project.

At the current stage, the application of development PPP, despite a growing trend, is still in its infancy and largely outside the mainstream of the Northern development cooperation. Furthermore, similar to the practice of ODA but to a lesser extent, the Northern donors have also set up a series of standards for the use of PPP, including, for instance, the principle of additionality, neutrality, demonstration effect, shared interest and co-financing, among others (European Commission 2014, 5). Despite a good intention to safeguard the development impact of the PPP arrangement, there is inherent contradiction between the claimed neutrality and the accepted profit-seeking motives of private sector actors; it is also difficult to evaluate the additionality—that is whether the development PPP projects achieve increased development effects than ODA or pure private development projects. Lastly, whether this new type of cooperation will be scaled up in the future may depend also on what the Northern donors determine to do in the face of the challenges of

---

[17] This name is borrowed from the ICAI report (2015).

ODA—to continue with its reform path as shown in the Paris and Busan Declarations; or, more radically, to embrace a broader, more flexible methods of development cooperation (Alonso 2012, 30–32).

For the Southern development partners, similar public–private cooperation (that features private engagement and business model) also exists; and indeed, the practice of blending commercial and charitable elements in IDC is believed to be even more fluid for the Southern actors (Chandy 2011, 10). Linked to 'tied aid' discussed earlier (Sect. 1.1), development cooperation provided by Southern development partners is also often associated with their broader economic interactions (e.g. trade and investment) with the recipient countries (Manning 2006; Alden 2007; Woods 2008; Paulo and Reisen 2010; Kragelund 2010; Mwase and Yang 2012). In contrast to the DAC donors who always prefer to deal with ODA in a very independent, 'neutral' way, the Southern actors are believed to have 'taken account of wider political and economic interests' (Manning 2006, 376). In fact, this has constituted a marked feature of the way the Southern development partners engage with Africa—particularly typical in the case of China and India (Goldstein et al. 2006; McCormick 2008), and to a lesser extent, Brazil, Turkey and South Africa—with a oft-claimed objective for mutual benefits. This is referred to as '*development package*' in the book, indicating the mix of cooperation modalities with a clear view to achieving development objectives for both recipient countries and the development partner countries themselves.

There are actually plenty of similarities between the Northern development PPP and Southern development package. Take China as an example—the Chinese development package and Northern development PPP follow the same basic logic of public–private cooperation in terms of co-investing resources and sharing benefits and risks, among others, between the public and (broader) private actors. Both utilize financial leverage—particularly that of grants, loans, equities and guarantees[18]—to attract and mobilize private and particularly corporate actors to engage in IDC. Both allow and indeed encourage corporate actors to bring in business models to IDC, that is, in other words, to promote development by means of investment. And the one largest distinction between

---

[18] Risk-reducing facilities have not yet been utilized in China's development package model.

the two[19] seems to be the objectives of utilizing the public–private cooperation: while China, as always, upholds 'mutual development' in applying the development package model, the Northern donors have tried to emphasize the recipient-oriented developmental impact over the self-interest pursuing aspect of the PPP through applying certain rules such like additionality and neutrality as mentioned above. As will be shown in the rest of the book, China's more open-minded mentality makes its external development cooperation in more flexible forms and at a larger scale as well, which may potentially serve as a source of comparison and reflection for the Northern donors in their future application of their development PPP model.

1.2 Chinese Development Cooperation in African Agriculture

Chinese contemporary development cooperation with Africa, which has attracted great attention in the global academic and policy circle, should be understood against the context of a changing global IDC landscape just described.

Among a wide range of areas that the bilateral development cooperation covers, furthermore, agriculture merits special consideration and examination for at least two important reasons.

First of all, agriculture has always played a significant part in African development, either for the continent's economic growth or for its people's welfare. Agriculture, until now, still constitutes the backbone of most African economies. In the bulk of them, agricultural sector stays among the largest contributors to the countries' GDP, and a main generator of savings, tax revenues and hard currency earnings. With nearly two-thirds of the manufacturing value-added based on agricultural raw materials, the sector also serves as a significant boost to the continent's industrial development (NEPAD 2003). Meanwhile, conventional wisdom also supports a strong and positive role of agriculture in addressing the hunger and poverty problems that still prevail across the continent

---

[19] Some other (minor) differences include, for instance, a larger extent of SOE in China's development package model than that in Northern PPP, and a lack of specialized financial institutions (such like the DFIs of Northern countries) in China—instead, the national development bank (China Development Bank) and export credit agency (EXIM Bank of China) take charge of relevant issues.

(Diao et al. 2010). With some 70–80% of the total population—including 70% of the continent's extremely poor and undernourished—living in rural areas and depending mostly on agriculture for their livelihood, the agricultural sector is believed to have the potential to enhance food security and uplift people on a mass scale more than any other sector (NEPAD 2003; ECA of the UN 2007). For that reason, African agriculture has long been the focal point and emphasis of the international development community throughout the past decades (Eicher 2003), including that of China which can be traced back to the late 1950s (Bräutigam 1998; see also Chapter 2 of the book).

Second and more pertinently (to this book's concern), among various development cooperation fields, agriculture has effectively become the frontier area for China to apply or experiment with its innovative 'development package' model with Africa. The nature of agriculture being inherently a productive sector—different from other IDC fields such as health and education—makes it more ready to embrace some other market-oriented cooperation modalities (e.g. agribusiness) than merely relying on traditional development assistance. China, for instance, has launched a series of policy measures—far beyond only aid—to boost its agro-development cooperation with Africa since the 2000s, particularly under the Forum on China-Africa Cooperation (FOCAC) framework. Just to mention a few, the Chinese government has pledged:

(*technical assistance and capability building*)

- to send 100 Chinese agro-experts (FOCAC 2006), 50 agro-technical teams (with a view to training 2000 agro-technicians in Africa) (FOCAC 2009, 2012), 30 senior agro-technical teams (to provide technical, managerial and vocational training) (FOCAC 2015) and 500 senior agro-experts (FOCAC 2018);
- to send teams of teachers and help Africa to establish agricultural vocational education systems (FOCAC 2012);
- to establish 10 Agriculture Technology Demonstration Centres (ATDCs) in Africa (FOCAC 2006)—the number was further increased to 20 (FOCAC 2009, 2012), and plans concerning the upgrade of ATDCs were made (FOCAC 2015);
- to establish and improve the '10+10' cooperation mechanism between Chinese and African agricultural research institutes (FOCAC 2015, 2018);

- to promote experts exchange and technology transfer in areas such as molecular detection and identification of plant diseases, pest risk analysis, seed health testing/certification, and management of quarantine containment facilities for high-risk materials with biosecurity levels (FOCAC 2018);

(*infrastructure, aid in cash and kinds, and multilateral cooperation*)

- to support agro-infrastructure construction and help African countries develop water conservancy and irrigation projects in Africa (FOCAC 2015);
- to provide humanitarian food aid to Africa (FOCAC 2015)—the value pledged was ¥1 billion in 2018 (FOCAC 2018);
- to implement the project of "Agriculture Leads to Prosperity" in 100 African villages (FOCAC 2015);
- to support the Africa-initiated 'Comprehensive African Agriculture Development Programme (CAADP)' through policy dialogue and collaboration (FOCAC 2015);
- to set up China-African Union (AU) agriculture cooperation commission and hold China-Africa Agricultural Cooperation Forum regularly (FOCAC 2018);
- to support cooperation with African countries under the framework of the UNFAO's Special Program for Food Security (SPFS) and donate $30 million to the SPFS (FOCAC 2006, 2009, 2012, 2015);

(*trade and investment*)

- to encourage and support Chinese companies to conduct agribusiness investment in Africa (FOCAC 2003, 2006) and provide technical assistance through cooperation projects in grain planting, storage, sanitary and requirements, animal husbandry, agro-processing capacity, forestry, and fisheries, in order to create a favourable environment for African countries to realize long-term food security that is supported by their own national agro-production and processing (FOCAC 2015);
- to encourage Chinese financial institutions to support cooperation between Chinese and African companies in agricultural planting,

processing of agricultural products, animal husbandry, fishery and aquaculture (FOCAC 2012);
- to strengthen cooperation in specific fields including cotton, sugar, agro-processing, among others (FOCAC 2018);
- to promote agricultural trade between China and Africa, particularly Africa's agro-export to China (FOCAC 2012, 2015).

1.3 Research Concerns, Methodological Notes and Book Structure

Research Concerns

Out of abovementioned considerations, the agro-cooperation between China and Africa can serve as a good angle for observers to take so as to investigate Chinese contemporary development cooperation. More specifically, the book attempts to tackle the following questions.

While more often than not being discussed (and at times criticized) in comparison with the traditional donors, the current model of China's external development cooperation has surely a deep-rooted domestic origin. This, however, tends to be unfairly downplayed sometimes when people simply regard the Chinese—or more broadly the Southern—models as erratic and even try to converge them to the Northern 'normal' (Sect. 1.1). Hence the *first* issue the book wants to deal with is the evolution logic of China's agro-development cooperation behaviours; in other words, how the current modalities (esp. the 'development package' model) have been shaped by China's decades-long history of aid-giving and reforms, and particularly by some of the evolving mentalities that underpin this historical trajectory.

The *second* and also a core cluster of questions the book is going to examine are concerning the characteristic 'development package' per se. That is, how exactly the package model has been played out on the ground—and especially how the innovative commercial elements (e.g. business actors and mechanisms) have been incorporated and utilized in China's agro-development cooperation with Africa? What the results, though still at an initial stage of its practice, of the package model have been so far? Last but not least, why certain 'implementation gaps' (between the policy expectation and realities) exist in the practice of China's current agro-development cooperation with Africa?

Lastly, based on the in-depth investigation of the case of agro-cooperation with Africa, the book will also provide a reflection of Chinese contemporary development cooperation model against the transitioning global IDC background. Questions are asked revolving, for instance, what 'new', if any, China has offered to the global IDC thinking and practice? What makes the differences between the 'new' development cooperation of China and the more traditional manners of the Northern donors? and whether it is necessary and possible for these 'new' elements to develop into common practice in the global IDC community.

Methodological Notes

This is essentially a qualitative piece of work that endeavours more to provide a rich description, in-depth explanation and critical reflection concerning the research topic in question, instead of generating any abstract, universally applicable statement. It is thus based on methods of materials collection that is 'both flexible and sensitive to the social context in which data are produced, rather than rigidly standardized or structured, or entirely abstracted from 'real-life' contexts', and methods of materials analysis that 'involves understandings of complexity, detail and context' rather than 'surface patterns, trends, and correlations' (Mason 2002, 2–3).

A mix of qualitative methods is adopted in researching the subject. For instance, historical process-tracing method is used in tracking the evolution and changes of Chinese agro-development cooperation with Africa with a view to explaining why certain mentality (e.g. 'mutual development) and modality (e.g. 'development package') have come into being against the context of Chinese external development cooperation. In addition, comparative case study method is utilized in examining the commonalties and differences between Chinese 'innovative agro-aid model' and 'agribusiness model' applied in Africa, as well as that within each of the two models. Specifically, Mozambique is chosen as the primary case country for its typicality in China's contemporary agro-cooperation with Africa, while South Africa is used as a comparison counterpart mainly in the scenario of Chinese Agriculture Technology Demonstration Centres (ATDCs). Meanwhile, a few ATDC and agribusiness projects that share basic common background but also display comparable distinctions from each other are selected in the two case countries.[20]

Furthermore, in order to base the analysis and argument on a more solid foundation, in-depth project-level fieldwork was conducted in a number of locations within Mozambique and South Africa during the period of 2013–2015.[21]

With the great assistance of my colleagues in the two countries,[22] I managed to investigate nine projects in total (five in Mozambique and four in South Africa) but kept only five of them in the book—given their particular representativeness and relevance to the research[23]; they are the ATDCs in Mozambique and South Africa, the Wanbao, Hefeng and CAAIC agro-investment projects in Mozambique. Two specific methods were used in the fieldwork process: qualitative interviewing[24] and participant observation. In terms of the former, I talked with dozens of informants through formal and informal interviews.[25] The informants roughly fall into three categories: (1) officials from both Chinese and Mozambican sides related to the projects; (2) company staff (Chinese and Mozambican), including the heads, managers, technicians, as well as

[20] For the detailed rationale for selecting these specific project cases, see Chapters 3 and 4, respectively.

[21] Including Maputo (the capital city), Boane (in Maputo province), Xaixai (in Gaza province) and Buzi (in Sofala province) in Mozambique; and Gariep Dam (in Free State), Bizana (in Eastern Cape), Umzimkhulu (in Kwa-Zulu Natal) and Val de Vie estate (in Western Cape) in South Africa.

[22] They are Dr. Sérgio Chichava from the Instituto de Estudos Sociais e Económicos based in Maputo, Mozambique and Ms. Angela Harding from Pretoria University in South Africa.

[23] The three projects of Chinese agro-investment in South Africa under fieldwork, for instance, are not included in this book (for the still early status of the projects and their very different investment modalities compared to those in Mozambique, among other reasons). They are separately discussed in another book chapter, see Angela Harding, Lu Jiang, et al. 'Between Promise and Profit: Chinese Agro-Investment and the Challenges of Operating in South Africa', in HSRC ed., *South African Industry Policy Handbook*, Pretoria: Human Sciences Research Council (HSRC), 2018.

[24] *Qualitative interviewing* refers to 'in-depth, semi-structured or loosely structured forms of interviewing', with a few distinctive characteristics such as 'the interactional exchange of dialogue', 'a relatively informal style', and 'a thematic, topic-centred, biographical or narrative approach' (Mason 2002, 62–63).

[25] See the 'Interviews' listed at the end of the book.

workers and farmers working on the projects; and (3) Mozambican farmers living near the project sites and local NGOs.[26]

The participant observation[27] was realized in two ways. The first is through working and living together with the company staff being researched. During the work time, I went with the staff to the paddies and observed their production and processing models, the agro-technology training process (between the Chinese technicians and Mozambican farmers), and the co-working models (between Chinese and Mozambican farmers), among others. During lunch and dinner break, semi-structured interviews (formal) or causal talks (informal) were conducted with different people on the sites. Second, the participant observation is also realized through frequent site visits and informal inquiries. For example, I visited different supermarkets and convenience stores of both Chinese and local brands to check and compare the prices, ask the shopkeepers about the sales (and problems, if any) and consumers about their feedback as to certain Chinese brand rice, in order to gain a better understanding of the rice sales of the Chinese companies being researched.

Book Structure
The book consists of six chapters in total. The current chapter of Introduction (this chapter) has set up the research background of the transitioning IDC—in particular the deepening divide between the traditional Northern donors and the 'emerging' Southern development partners, as well as the growing trend of public–private cooperation in IDC. It has then situated the research topic of China-Africa agro-development cooperation into the broader picture of global IDC and hence developed a cluster of research concerns while introducing the methods adopted to address these concerns.

Chapter 2 of the book will offer a historical review of Chinese agricultural development cooperation with Africa since the late 1950s, in

---

[26] Most of the interviews were done face-to-face with the interviewees in the field; a few follow-up interviews, however, were conducted over phone or in a third city after I left the field.

[27] *Participant observation* refers to 'methods of generating data which entail the researcher immersing herself or himself in a research "setting" so that they can experience and observe at first hand a range of dimensions in and of that setting' (Mazon 2002, 84).

order to help readers to better understand how the contemporary models have come into being. It will go through the three historical phases—respectively the earlier period in the 1960–1970s, the transition period during the 1980–1990s, and the current period from the 2000s until the present time—which are characterized by different motives, modalities and institutional structures. The chapter will also give a special focus on China's foreign aid reforms, taking place between the 1980s and 1990s, which have significantly informed the practice of China's contemporary external development cooperation. In the end of the chapter, it identifies three specific models embraced in China's contemporary 'development package' of agricultural cooperation with Africa, namely the 'traditional agro-aid', 'innovative agro-aid' and 'agribusiness' models.

Chapter 3 endeavours to investigate the 'innovative agro-aid model' of Chinese development cooperation with Africa, particularly through examining the flagship project of Chinese ATDCs on the continent. It will first introduce the objectives, actors and mechanisms of the ATDCs, along with their general developments since 2006, and then provide detailed case studies on two of the ATDCs, in Mozambique and South Africa, respectively. Based on the comparative case studies, the chapter will give a preliminary analysis as to the actual results of the ATDCs, mostly drawing on the fieldwork-based observations from the two cases but also combining other ATDC cases according to the author's primary and secondary sources.

Chapter 4 will follow on to look at another representative model that is currently adopted in Chinese agro-development cooperation with Africa, the 'agribusiness model'. Similarly, the chapter will first introduce the model by exploring its motives, actors and modalities and then further unpack the model by examining four fieldwork-based case studies of Chinese agribusiness projects in Mozambique. These four cases bring to light different types of company actors (e.g. private/state-owned/mixed), governmental relations (both with the Chinese and Mozambican), investment fields (e.g. rice/cotton) and modalities (in terms of financing, production and processing). At the same time, they share, to varying degrees, similarities with each other, and thus provide a good basis for a comparative integrated analysis. In the end of the chapter, there will be a preliminary analysis concerning the results until recently, and especially certain problems of the 'agribusiness model'.

Based on the historical and empirical studies, the last two chapters (Chapters 5 and 6) attempt to respond to the research concerns raised in the Introduction. Chapter 5 will provide a synthesized explanation as to the problems appearing in the process of Chinese agro-development cooperation with Africa, particularly in terms of the 'innovative agro-aid model' and 'agribusiness model' (Chapters 3 and 4). Adopting a public policy implementation (PPI) approach, the explanation develops at three levels, respectively policy, implementer and environment. While the three sets of factors all play an indispensible role, the 'implementer' element appears to act prominently in explaining the policy results (esp. the 'gaps') as observed in the case of China-Africa agro-development cooperation; and this is mostly due to the proactive role or agency that the implementers could exert to remedy imperfect policies and counter unfavourable environments in this particular PPI situation.

The last chapter (Chapter 6) will first conclude from the historical trajectory of Chinese agro-cooperation with Africa that how the status of being as a developing country (along with other historical experiences) has shaped China's 'mutual-development' mind-set in external development cooperation. It will then summarize the three models of China's contemporary development cooperation in African agriculture and explain the logic of 'development package' behind as well as its link with the 'mutual-development' mentality. The last section of the chapter will bring China back into the global IDC landscape, reflecting the 'new' elements involved in Chinese development cooperation and comparing that with the Northern practice. It thus calls for a broadening understanding for IDC that can allow win-win ideology and embrace diversified cooperation forms beyond the traditional ODA or pure aid.

REFERENCES

Agrawal, S. 2007. 'Emerging Donors in International Development Assistance: The India Case'. Working Paper. International Development Research Centre, Canada.

Alden, Chris. 2007. *China in Africa: Partner, Competitor or Hegemon?* London: Zed Books.

Alonso, José. 2012. 'From Aid to Global Development Policy'. Working Paper No. 121. United Nations Department of Economic and Social Affairs (UNDESA). http://www.un.org/esa/desa/papers/2012/wp121_2012.pdf.

Besharati, Neissan Alessandro. 2013. 'South African Development Partnership Agency (SADPA): Strategic Aid or Development Packages for Africa?' (SAIIA) South African Institute of International Affairs.

Binder, Andrea, Markus Palenberg, and Jan Martin Witte. 2007. 'Engaging Business in Development'. GPPi Research Paper Series No. 8. Global Public Policy Institute, Berlin.

Bräutigam, Deborah. 1998. *Chinese Aid and African Development: Exporting Green Revolution.* New York: Palgrave Macmillan.

———. 2010. 'China, Africa and the International Aid Architecture'. Working Paper 107. African Development Bank Group. https://www.afdb.org/fileadmin/uploads/afdb/Documents/Publications/WORKING%20107%20%20PDF%20E33.pdf.

———. 2011. 'Aid "with Chinese Characteristics": Chinese Foreign Aid and Development Finance Meet the OECD-DAC Aid Regime'. *Journal of International Development* 23 (5): 752–764.

Burges, Sean. 2014. 'Brazil's International Development Co-operation: Old and New Motivations'. *Development Policy Review* 32 (3): 355–374.

Cabral, Lídia, Giuliano Russo, and Julia Weinstock. 2014. 'Brazil and the Shifting Consensus on Development Co-Operation: Salutary Diversions from the "Aid-Effectiveness" Trail?' *Development Policy Review* 32 (2): 179–202.

Camara, Morro. 2004. 'The Impact of Programme Versus Project Aid on Fiscal Behaviour in The Gambia'.

Chanana, D. 2009. 'India as an Emerging Donor'. *Economic and Political Weekly* 44.

———. 2010. 'India's Transition to Global Donor: Limitations and Prospects'. *Real Instituto Elcano* 123.

Chandy, Laurence. 2011. 'Reframing Development Cooperation'. In *The 2011 Brookings Blum Roundtable Policy Briefs.* Washington, DC: The Brookings Institute. https://www.brookings.edu/wp-content/uploads/2016/07/2011_blum_reframing_development_cooperation_chandy.pdf.

Chandy, Laurence, and Homi Kharas. 2011. 'Why Can't We All Just Get Along? The Practical Limits to International Development Cooperation'. *Journal of International Development* 23 (5): 739–751.

Chaturvedi, Sachin. 2008. 'Emerging Patterns in Architecture for Management of Economic Assistance and Development Cooperation: Implications and Challenges for India'. Working Paper.

———. 2012. 'India's Development Partnership: Key Policy Shifts and Institutional Evolution'. *Cambridge Review of International Affairs* 25 (4): 557–577.

Chaturvedi, Sachin, Anuradha Chenoy, Deepta Chopra, Anuradha Joshi, and Khush Lagdhyan. 2014. 'Indian Development Cooperation: The State of the Debate'. Working Paper No. 95. Evidence Report. IDS (Institute of Development Studies), Sussex.

Chin, Gregory. 2012. 'China as a "Net Donor": Tracking Dollars and Sense'. *Cambridge Review of International Affairs* 25 (4): 579–603.

Chin, Gregory, and B. Michael Frolic. 2007. 'Emerging Donors in Development Assistance: The Case of China'. Working Paper. International Development Research Centre, Canada.

Chin, Gregory, and Fahimul Quadir. 2012. 'Introduction: Rising States, Rising Donors and the Global Aid Regime'. *Cambridge Review of International Affairs* 25 (4): 493–506.

Clay, Edward, Matthew Geddes, and Luisa Natali. 2009. 'Untying Aid: Is It Working? An Evaluation of the Implementation of the Paris Declaration and of the 2001 DAC Recommendation of Untying ODA to the LDCs'. DIIS (Danish Institute for International Studies), Copenhagen.

Currie-Alder, Bruce. 2016. 'The State of Development Studies: Origins, Evolution and Prospects'. *Canadian Journal of Development Studies* 37 (1): 5–26.

Davies, Joanne. 2011. 'Washington's Growth and Opportunity Act or Beijing's "Overarching Brilliance": Will African Governments Choose Neither?' *Third World Quarterly* 32 (6): 1147–1163.

Devex. 2011. 'Bilateral Donor Agencies Open for Partnerships: A Closer Look at 5 Leaders in Development Partnerships'. https://pages.devex.com/rs/685-KBL-765/images/Devex_Reports_Biateral_Donor_Agencies_A_Closer_Look_at_5_Development_Leaders.pdf.

Diao, Xinshen, Peter Hazell, and James Thurlow. 2010. 'The Role of Agriculture in African Development'. *World Development* 38 (10): 1375–1383.

Dreher, Axel, and Andreas Fuchs. 2015. 'Rogue Aid? An Empirical Analysis of China's Aid Allocation'. *Canadian Journal of Economics* 48 (3): 988–1023.

Dreher, Axel, Andreas Fuchs, Roland Hodler, Bradley Parks, Paul Raschky, and Michael J. Tierney. 2016. 'Aid on Demand: African Leaders and the Geography of China's Foreign Assistance'. Working Paper. AidData.

Easterly, William. 2003. 'Can Foreign Aid Buy Growth?' *Journal of Economic Perspectives* 17 (3): 23–48.

ECA of the UN (Economic Commission for Africa of the United Nations Economic and Social Council). 2007. 'Africa Review Report on Agriculture and Rural Development'. https://sustainabledevelopment.un.org/content/documents/eca_bg2.pdf.

ECOSOC of the UN. 2008. 'Background Study for the Development Cooperation Forum: Trends in South-South and Triangular Development Cooperation'. United Nations Economic and Social Council.

Eicher, Carl. 2003. 'Flashback: Fifty Years of Donor Aid to African Agriculture'. https://rmportal.net/framelib/donor-aid-to-african-agriculture.pdf.

European Commission. 2014. 'A Stronger Role of the Private Sector in Achieving Inclusive and Sustainable Growth in Developing Countries'. http://ec.europa.eu/transparency/regdoc/rep/1/2014/EN/1-2014-263-EN-F1-1.Pdf.

FOCAC (Forum on China Africa Cooperation). 2003. 'The Forum on China-Africa Cooperation Addis Ababa Action Plan (2004–2006)'. Ministry of Foreign Affairs of the People's Republic of China, Beijing. https://www.focac.org/eng/zywx_1/zywj/t606801.htm.
———. 2006. 'The Forum on China-Africa Cooperation Beijing Action Plan (2007–2009)'. Ministry of Foreign Affairs of the People's Republic of China, Beijing. https://www.focac.org/eng/zywx_1/zywj/t280369.htm.
———. 2009. 'The Forum on China-Africa Cooperation Sharm El-Sheikh Action Plan (2010–2012)'. Ministry of Foreign Affairs of the People's Republic of China, Beijing. https://www.focac.org/eng/zywx_1/zywj/t626387.htm.
———. 2012. 'The Forum on China-Africa Cooperation Beijing Action Plan (2013–2015)'. Ministry of Foreign Affairs of the People's Republic of China, Beijing. https://www.focac.org/eng/zywx_1/zywj/t954620.htm.
———. 2015. 'The Forum on China-Africa Cooperation Johannesburg Action Plan (2016–2018)'. Ministry of Foreign Affairs of the People's Republic of China, Beijing. https://www.focac.org/eng/zywx_1/zywj/t1327961.htm.
———. 2018. 'The Forum on China-Africa Cooperation Beijing Action Plan (2019-2021)'. Ministry of Foreign Affairs of the People's Republic of China, Beijing. https://www.focac.org/eng/zywx_1/zywj/t1594297.htm.
Fuchs, Andreas, and Krishana Vadlamannati. 2013. 'The Needy Donor: An Empirical Analysis of India's Aid Motives'. *World Development* 44: 110–128.
Führer, Helmut. 1996. *The Story of Official Development Assistance: A Story of the Development Assistance Committee and the Development Co-operation Directorate in Dates, Names and Figures*. Paris: OECD Publishing.
Goldstein, Andrea, Nicolas Pinaud, Helmut Reisen, and Xiaobao Chen. 2006. 'China and India: What's in It for Africa?' Report. OECD Development Centre. http://www.oecd.org/development/pgd/36259343.pdf.
Government of India. 2003. 'Budget 2003–04: Speech of Jaswant Singh, Minister of Finance'.
Gradl, Christina, Subathirai Sivakumaran, and Sabha Sobhani. 2010. 'The MDGs: Everyone's Business—How Inclusive Business Models Contribute to Development and Who Supports Them'. UNDP (United Nations Development Programme).
Grimm, S. 2011. 'South Africa as a Development Partner in Africa'. Policy Brief 11. Centre for Chinese Studies, Stellenbosch.
Grobbelaar, Neuma. 2014. 'Rising Powers in International Development: The State of the Debate in South Africa'. IDS (Institute of Development Studies), Sussex. https://www.google.com.hk/url?sa=t&rct=j&q=&esrc=s&source=web&cd=2&ved=0ahUKEwi_49jAzNDUAhXOLlAKHVq8B-0wQFgguMAE&url=https%3a%2f%2fopendocs%2eids%2eac%2euk%2fopendocs%2fbitstream%2f123456789%2f4305%2f1%2fER91%2520Rising%2520Powers%2520in%2520International%2520Dev

elopment%2520The%2520State%2520of%2520the%2520Debate%2520in%2520South%2520Africa%2epdf&usg=AFQjCNFsE7Gc4j-5_TZwO9Rlmvw6ODqAGg.
Haan, Arian. 2011. 'Will China Change International Development as We Know It?' *Journal of International Development* 23: 881–908.
Hanson, Henrik, and Finn Tarp. 2000. 'Aid Effectiveness Disputed'. *Journal of International Development* 12 (3): 375–398.
Harry S. Truman. 1949. 'Truman's Inaugural Address'. https://www.trumanlibrary.org/whistlestop/50yr_archive/inagural20jan1949.htm.
Hausmann, Jeannine, and Erik Lundsgaarde. 2015. 'Turkey's Role in Development Cooperation'. Working Paper. Centre for Policy Research at United Nations University.
Hjertholm, Peter, and Howard White. 2000. 'Foreign Aid in Historical Perspective: Background and Trends'. In *Foreign Aid and Development: Lessons Learnt and Directions for the Future*, 59–77. London: Routledge.
ICAI. 2015. 'Business in Development'. ICAI (Independent Commission for Aid Impact). https://icai.independent.gov.uk/wp-content/uploads/ICAI-Business-in-Development-FINAL.pdf.
Ierley, Doug. 2002. 'Private Capital Flows as a Springboard for World Bank Reform'. *Journal of International Law* 23 (1).
Ingram, George, Anne E. Johnson, and Helen Moser. 2016. 'USAID's Public-Private Partnerships: A Data Picture and Review of Business Engagement'. Brookings. https://www.brookings.edu/wp-content/uploads/2016/07/WP94PPPReport2016Web.pdf.
Inoue, Cristina, and Alcides Vaz. 2012. 'Brazil as "Southern Donor": Beyond Hierarchy and National Interests in Development Cooperation?' *Cambridge Review of International Affairs* 25 (4): 507–534.
Kilama, Eric. 2016. 'The Influence of China and Emerging Donors Aid Allocation: A Recipient Perspective'. *China Economic Review* 38: 76–91.
Kim, Soyeun, and Simon Lightfoot. 2011. 'Does "DAC-Ability" Really Matter? The Emergence of Non-DAC Donors: Introduction to Policy Arena'. *Journal of International Development* 23 (5): 711–721.
Kondoh, Hisahiro. 2015. 'Convergence of Aid Models in Emerging Donors? Learning Processes, Norms and Identities, and Recipients'. Working Paper. JICA Research Institute, Tokyo.
Kragelund, Peter. 2008. 'The Return of Non-DAC Donors to Africa: New Prospects for African Development? Peter Kragelund, 2008'. *Development Policy Review* 26 (5): 555–584.
———. 2010. 'The Potential Role of Non-traditional Donors' Aid in Africa, International Centre for Trade and Sustainable Development'. Issue Paper 11. International Centre for Trade and Sustainable Development.

Kulaklikaya, Musa, and Rahman Nurdun. 2010. 'Turkey as a New Player in Development Cooperation'. *Insight Turkey* 12 (4): 131–145.

Lancaster, Carol. 2007. 'The Chinese Aid System'. Centre for Global Development.

Leite et al. 2014. 'Brazil's Engagement in International Development Cooperation: The State of the Debate'. Evidence Report No. 59. Institute of Development Studies, Brighton.

Lengauer, Sara. 2011. 'China's Foreign Aid Policy: Motive and Method'. *Culture Mandala* 9 (2).

Manning, Richard. 2006. 'Will "Emerging Donors" Change the Face of International Co-operation?' *Development Policy Review* 24 (4): 371–385.

Mason, Jannifer. 2002. *Qualitative Researching*. 2nd ed. London: Sage.

McCormick, Dorothy. 2008. 'China & India as Africa's New Donors: The Impact of Aid on Development'. *Review of African Political Economy* 35 (115): 73–92.

Mold, Andrew. 2009. 'Policy Ownership and Aid Conditionality in the Light of the Financial Crisis: A Critical Review'. OECD Publishing. http://www.keepeek.com/Digital-Asset-Management/oecd/development/policy-ownership-and-aid-conditionality-in-the-light-of-the-financial-crisis_9789264075528-en#.WPWLnhJ95E4.

Momani, Bessma, and Crystal Ennis. 2012. 'Between Caution and Controversy: Lessons from the Gulf Arab States as (Re-)Emerging Donors'. *Cambridge Review of International Affairs* 25 (4): 605–627.

Mosley, Paul, and Marion J. Eeckhout. 2000. 'From Project Aid to Programme Assistance'. In *Foreign Aid and Development: Lessons Learnt and Directions for the Future*, 101–119. London: Routledge.

Moyo, Dambisa. 2010. *Dead Aid: Why Aid Is Not Working and How There Is Another Way for Africa*. London: Penguin Press.

Mwase, Nkunde, and Yongzheng Yang. 2012. 'BRICs' Philosophies for Development Financing and Their Implications for LICs'. Working Paper. IMF.

Naim, Moises. 2009. 'Rogue Aid'. *Foreign Policy*. https://foreignpolicy.com/2009/10/15/rogue-aid/.

NEPAD (New Partnership for Africa's Development). 2003. 'Comprehensive Africa Agriculture Development Programme 2003'.

OECD. 1978. *Recommendation on Terms and Conditions of Aid (from the 1978 DAC Chair Report on Development Co-operation)*. OECD.

———. 2008. 'Is It ODA?' www.oecd.org/dac/stats.

———. 2016. *Development Co-operation Report 2016: The Sustainable Development Goals as Business Opportunities*. Paris: OECD Publishing. http://dx.doi.org/10.1787/dcr-2016-en.

OECD-DAC. 2013. 'Converged Statistical Reporting Directives for the Creditor Reporting System (CRS) and the Annual Dac Questionnaire—Addendum 2'. OECD. http://www.oecd.org/dac/stats/documentupload/DCD-DAC(2013)15-ADD2-FINAL-ENG.pdf#page=5.

Opoku-Mensah. 2009. 'China and the International Aid System: Challenges and Opportunities'. Working Paper. Aalborg University: Research Centre on Development and International Relations.

Özkan, M., and B. Akgün. 2010. 'Turkey's Opening to Africa'. *The Journal of Modern African Studies* 48 (4).

Paulo, Sebastian, and Helmut Reisen. 2010. 'Eastern Donors and Western Soft Law: Towards a DAC Donor Peer Review of China and India?' *Development Policy Review* 28 (5): 535–552.

Pompa, Claudia. 2013. 'Understanding Challenge Funds'. London: Overseas Development Institute. https://www.odi.org/sites/odi.org.uk/files/odi-assets/publications-opinion-files/9086.pdf.

Quadir, Fahimul. 2013. Rising Donors and the New Narrative of 'South–South' Cooperation: What Prospects for Changing the Landscape of Development Assistance Programmes? *Third World Quarterly* 34 (2): 321–338.

Robledo, Carmen. 2015. 'New Donors, Same Old Practices? South-South Cooperation of Latin American Emerging Donors'. *Bandung: Journal of Global South* 2 (3).

Roussel, Lauren. 2013. 'The Changing Donor Landscape in Nicaragua: Rising Competition Enhances Ownership and Fosters Cooperation'. *Journal of International Development* 25 (6): 802–818.

Rudincová, Kateřina. 2014. 'New Player on the Scene: Turkish Engagement in Africa'. *Bulletin of Geography* 25.

Runde, Daniel, Holly Wise, Anna Saito Carson, and Cleanor Coates. 2011. 'Seizing the Opportunity in Public-Private Partnerships: Strengthening Capacity at the State Department, USAID, and MCC'. Center for Strategic & International Studies. https://csis-prod.s3.amazonaws.com/s3fs-public/legacy_files/files/publication/111102_Runde_PublicPrivatePartnerships_Web.pdf.

Sachs, Jeffrey. 2005. *The End of Poverty: Economic Possibilities for Our Time*. New York: Penguin Press.

Sato, Jin, Hiroaki Shiga, Takaaki Kobayashi, and Hisahiro Kondoh. 2011. '"Emerging Donors" from a Recipient Perspective: An Institutional Analysis of Foreign Aid in Cambodia'. *World Development* 39 (12): 2091–2104.

Shushan, Debra, and Christopher Marcoux. 2011. 'The Rise (and Decline?) of Arab Aid: Generosity and Allocation in the Oil Era'. *World Development* 39 (11): 1969–1980.

Six, Clemens. 2009. 'The Rise of Postcolonial States as Donors: A Challenge to the Development Paradigm?' *Third World Quarterly* 30 (6): 1103–1121.

Smith, Kimberly, Talita Fordelone, and Felix Zimmermann. 2010. 'Beyond the DAC—The Welcome Role of Other Providers of Development Co-operation'. DCD Issues Brief. OECD. https://www.oecd.org/dac/45361474.pdf.
Soest, Jaap van. 1978. *The Start of International Development Cooperation in the United Nations 1945–1952*. Assen: Van Gorcum Press.
State Council of the PRC (People's Republic of China). 2011. 'China's Foreign Aid'. State Council of the People's Republic of China. http://news.xinhuanet.com/english2010/china/2011-04/21/c_13839683.htm.
———. 2014. 'China's Foreign Aid'. State Council of the People's Republic of China. http://english.gov.cn/archive/white_paper/2014/08/23/content_281474982986592.htm.
Tan-Mullins, May, Giles Mohan, and Marcus Power. 2010. 'Redefining "Aid" in the China-Africa Context'. *Development and Change* 41 (5): 857–881.
Timmis, Hannah. 2018. 'Lessons from Donor Support to Technical Assistance Programmes'. K4D Helpdesk Report. Institute of Development Studies, Brighton, UK. https://assets.publishing.service.gov.uk/media/5ab0e81140f0b62d854a9bc5/Lessons_from_donor_support_to_technical_assistance_programmes.pdf.
Troilo, Pete. 2011. 'PPPs in the Developing World'. Devex. https://www.devex.com/news/ppps-in-the-developing-world-76370.
Turki, Benyan. 2014. 'The Kuwait Fund for Arab Economic Development and Its Activities in African Countries, 1961–2010'. *Middle East Journal* 68 (3): 421–435.
UNDP. 2016. 'Strategy Note: UNDP's Private Sector and Foundations Strategy for the Sustainable Development Goals 2016–2020'. UNDP (United Nations Development Programme).
Vaz, Alcides, and Cristina Inoue. 2007. 'Emerging Donors in International Development Assistance: The Brazil Case'. Working Paper. International Development Research Center, Canada.
Vickers, Brendan. 2012. 'Towards a New Aid Paradigm: South Africa as African Development Partner'. *Cambridge Review of International Affairs* 25 (4): 535–556.
Villanger, Espen. 2007. 'Arab Foreign Aid: Disbursement Patterns, Aid Policies and Motives'. *Forum for Development Studies* 34 (2): 223–256.
Walz, Julie, and Vijaya Ramachandran. 2011. 'Brave New World: A Literature Review of Emerging Donors and the Changing Nature of Foreign Assistance'. Working Paper 273. Centre for Global Development, Washington, DC.
William Hynes, and Simon Scott. 2013. 'The Evolution of Official Development Assistance: Achievements, Criticisms and A Way Forward'. OECD Development Co-operation Working Papers No. 12. OECD Publishing, Paris.

Wolfe, Braude, Pearl Thandrayan, and Elizabeth Sidiropoulos. 2008. 'Emerging Donors in International Development Assistance: The South Africa Case'. Working Paper. International Development Research Center, Canada.

Woods, Ngaire. 2008. 'Whose Aid? Whose Influence? China, Emerging Donors and the Silent Revolution in Development Assistance'. *International Affairs* 84 (6): 1205–1221.

Xalma, C. 2010. 'Report on South-South Cooperation in Ibero-America'. SEGIB Studies No. 5. Madrid.

Zhang, Yanbing, Jing Gu, and Yunnan Chen. 2015. 'China's Engagement in International Development Cooperation: The State of the Debate'. IDS (Institute of Development Studies).

Zimmermann, Felix, and Kimberly Smith. 2011. 'More Actors, More Money, More Ideas for International Development Co-operation'. *Journal of International Development* 23 (5): 722–738.

CHAPTER 2

Tracing the Root of China's Contemporary Agro-Development Cooperation with Africa: A Historical Review

As noted in the Introduction, China (as well as other development partners from the South) has a parallel historical trajectory and as rich experience of engaging in international development cooperation as that of the Northern donors. This history—especially some essential continuities and shifts, and key guidelines that have been gradually established over the past half-century—has left an indelible imprint on the mentality and modality of China's contemporary development cooperation practice, explaining a lot about the much-debated distinctions between the Northern donors and Southern counterparts. However, one of the notable shortcomings of existing research on development cooperation from the South, including that of China, is precisely a lack of a historical dimension. In light of this, the primary objective of the present chapter is to provide a historical review of Chinese development cooperation with Africa through the typical case of agriculture, thereby shedding some light on how the current modalities, and the 'development package' model in particular, have come into being.

China's agro-development cooperation with Africa dates back to the late 1950s and can be divided roughly into three phases: the 'earlier stage' in the 1960–1970s, the 'transition stage' in the 1980–1990s and the 'current stage' from the 2000s until the present time. The three phases of development cooperation are featured by different political and/or economic driving forces, diverse cooperation forms and evolving institutional structures in terms of management and implementation.

© The Author(s) 2020
L. Jiang, *Beyond Official Development Assistance*,
Governing China in the 21st Century,
https://doi.org/10.1007/978-981-32-9507-0_2

Particularly important in this historical process are the foreign aid reforms starting from the 1980s, which have greatly informed the practice of Chinese development cooperation in the 'transition' and particularly the current stage. This chapter is going to unfold along this line and elaborate respectively on the three historical phases as well as the change-provoking event of China's foreign aid reforms.

2.1 'Pure Aid': The Earlier Stage (1960s–1970s)

Chinese agricultural engagement with Africa can be traced back to the late 1950s, and the first wave of it covers roughly the period from the 1960s to 1970s. That could be fairly regarded as a form of development cooperation and indeed a more ODA-like, or 'pure aid' type of development cooperation—as referred to by some Chinese scholars (e.g. Yun 2000a)—in the sense that it was official aid, highly concessional, and with a primary aim to boost the underdeveloped agricultural sector of many African countries. That said, there were also strong political motivations behind China's outward development cooperation, not only in the agricultural arena. The 1950–1960s was a time of the newly established People's Republic of China (PRC) fighting hard for the regime survival and international recognition. China was then confronted with tremendous challenges and difficulties in the face of the comprehensive blockade imposed by the West against the Cold War background. In particular, with the deterioration of foreign relations with the Soviet 'brother' since the late 1950s, building a broad alliance with African and other Third-World[1] countries gradually developed into an integral part of China's diplomatic strategy in order to counter the threats from both the Soviet and Western blocs (Fu 2008, 97–98).

It is within this broader context that China-Africa agro-development cooperation started to unfold. China began to develop diplomatic relations with African countries and provided aid to the continent after the Bandung Conference in 1955 (State Council of the PRC 2011). Agricultural aid, due to its widespread popularity among African leaders (Jiang 2013, 31–34), soon became an important and widely adopted

---

[1] The 'Third World' here is used in the sense of Mao Zedong's Three Worlds theory, indicating the majority of African, Asian (except for Japan, including China itself) and Latin American countries during the period of Cold War, whereas the First World referring to the

instrument in China's dealings with African relations. In 1959–1960 China donated 15,000 tons of rice to Guinea at the request of the Guinean president, which signified the start of Chinese agro-aid towards Africa. This deserves attention given the fact that China itself was suffering a severe famine during 1959–1961 and thus further demonstrates the urgency and significance of expanding international space to the Chinese government at that time. In October 1959, the two countries established formal diplomatic relations and Guinea became the first state in the sub-Sahara Africa that recognized the PRC (Tang 2002, 13; Meng 2013). In 1964, a new agency, the Bureau of Foreign Affairs, was set up under the Chinese Ministry of Agriculture (MOA) to take specific charge of the country's foreign agricultural aid issues, indicating the beginning of the institutionalization of agro-aid in China (Jiang 2013, 31; Tang et al. 2014). Throughout the 1960s, there were about seven countries[2] in Africa who had received agro-aid from China (Shi 1989, 146; Bräutigam 1998, 43–47; Jiang 2013, 31).

Entering the 1970s, the scale of Chinese agro-aid in Africa was massively increased. Apart from the consideration of solidarity and alliance with African states that was still at work, another key factor at play was the competition with Taiwan in Africa. With the help of the United States, Taiwan had conducted rather successful agro-aid programmes in a number of African countries during the 1960s. As a result, many of these countries felt hesitant to expel the Taiwanese 'farming teams', as requested by the Chinese government during the negotiation process for establishing diplomatic relations with the PRC. To overcome this obstacle, Chinese then Premier Zhou Enlai assured the African leaders that China would take over all the agro-aid projects left by Taiwan and do even better than the latter. This led to the so-called replacement aid

---

Soviet Union and United States—the superpowers at the time, and Second World then secondary powers including European countries, Canada, Australia, Japan (MOFA of the PRC, n.d.). This usages is different from some other Western tradition of categorizing, for instance, that regards the United States and its NATO allies as the First World, the Soviet Union and its communist allies (including China) as the Second World, and those unaligned, often with colonial pasts, such as many of the African, Latin American, Asian and Oceanian countries as the Third World (see e.g. Sauvy 1952). The latter usage is also adopted in the following section of this chapter (2.2).

[2] Guinea, Mali, Mauritania, Congo-Brazzaville, Tanzania, Zambia and Somalia.

Table 2.1 Selected Chinese-aided farms in Africa (1960–1980s)

Country	Project (year of establishment)
Tanzania	Wubenjia and Lufu farm (late 1960s); Mubalali Farm (1977)
Mali	Two sugarcane farms and sugar refineries (1970, 1976)
Mauritania	Mupoli rice farm (1972)
Uganda	Qibenba farm (1976)
Congo-Brazzaville	Gongbei farm (1976)
Zaire	Two sugarcane farms and sugar refineries (late 1970s)
Sierra Leone	A sugarcane farm and sugar refinery (1981)
Guinea	Keba sugarcane farm (1982)
Togo	Aniye sugarcane farm and sugar refinery (1986)
Somalia	Feinuoli farm (1987)

Note Due to the lack of and difficult access to some historical documents, especially those from the respective African countries, the names of the farms are presented uniformly in pinyin according to their transliteration in Chinese rather than in their respective original languages

Source The author based on Shi (1989), Yun (2000b) and Jiang (2013)

(*dingti yuanzhu*) which involved 18 African countries[3] and lasted for 13 years during the period 1970–1983. By the time the 'replacement aid' ended, China had replaced almost all the agro-aid projects left by Taiwan except for those in Côte d'Ivoire and Malawi (Shi 1989, 146–147; Jiang 2013, 46).

All through the first two decades of Chinese agro-development cooperation with Africa, complete projects (*chengtao xiangmu*)[4] such as farms (Table 2.1), agro-technology experiment and extension stations, irrigation and other agro-infrastructure were the most common modalities. In total, China aided around 25 African countries with 90 or so agro-complete projects, with approximately 43,400 hectares of farmland reclaimed (mostly for food crops and sugarcane) (Yun 1998, 96). Meanwhile, thousands of Chinese agricultural experts and technicians

[3] Sierra Leone, Ruanda, Ghana, Togo, Congo-Kinshasa, Senegal, Benin, Gambia, Chad, Mauritius, Gabon, Nigeria, Niger, Madagascar, Central Africa, Liberia, Botswana, Burkina Faso.

[4] 'Complete project' is a term used by Chinese government to refer to the type of foreign aid project that involves project engineering and construction, equipment and facilities provision, and post-construction service (MOC of the PRC 2015). China started to include complete projects into its development cooperation portfolio since 1954; before that, the mostly adopted aid modalities were donation (both in cash and in kind) and technical assistance (see CAITEC 2018, 12).

were dispatched alongside the different projects to provide the locals with technical support and training (Jiang 2013, 30). In addition, China also offered large donations of foodstuff and agricultural materials.

Most of these abovementioned types of agro-aid were provided by Chinese government via grants or interest-free loans, and rarely associated with other profit-seeking economic activities (e.g. trade or investment). This 'pure aid', therefore, bore close similarity to the Northern concept of ODA considering, for instance, its official nature, concessionality and non-tying feature—except for one significant distinction, the non-conditionality principle that was first proposed by Premier Zhou Enlai in 1964[5] and has since been upheld by the Chinese government in its external development and economic cooperation activities.[6] The only condition implicitly attached at the time was the recognition of the PRC as the *one and only* legitimate representative of China. This sole condition, and to certain extent the 'purity' nature[7] (e.g. the high concessionality and free from commercial motives, among others) of China's aid in the early days, demonstrates how the development status and priorities—a new-born regime struggling for survival and recognition against the gloomy context of the Cold War—had informed the application of the country's external development cooperation.

From an institutional perspective, these earlier agro-aid programmes were all financed and deployed by the central Chinese government, particularly through the MOA, and implemented by the Departments of Agriculture at the provincial level alongside their government-affiliated institutions (Yun 2000a; Tang et al. 2014). Entering the 1970s, with a

---

[5] Zhou Enlai proposed eight principles for external economic and technical assistance in 1963–1964 during his visit to a dozen of Asian and African countries, which established the foundation for China's development cooperation (and foreign aid more generally) until now. Non-conditionality is one of the eight principles. For the full content of the eight principles, see Bräutigam (2009, 313).

[6] According to the authors' interviews with several Chinese elderly diplomats in Africa, the long-held 'non-conditionality' principle is deeply rooted in Chinese government's respect for the UN Chapter and the Bandung Spirit in terms of respecting other countries' sovereignty. Apart from that, the unpleasant experience with Soviet Union trying to intervene Chinese domestic affairs in the late 1950s did not only directly lead to the 'breakup' of the two countries but also reconfirm the 'non-interference' principle in PRC's diplomatic thinking and practice (Niu 2010).

[7] This is also related to the prevailing ideology of proletarian internationalism in China at the time.

sharp increase in agro-aid projects due to the 'replacement aid' initiative, provincial governments were mobilized and incorporated into the aid implementation process on a much larger scale (Shi 1989, 81–82; Xiao and Zhang 2002). Overall, Chinese foreign aid, including agro-aid, in this early stage during the 1960–1970s was delivered overwhelmingly by government agencies—central and provincial—through a strict top-down chain of command, which is largely in accordance with the country's then centrally planned economy system in general. With little management autonomy and a tightly controlled budget (thus little economic incentives), the front-line implementing staff tended to demonstrate limited proactivity in their daily work, which was believed to be responsible for the often-seen low efficiency of aid projects in that period (Shi 1989, 89).

China's earlier agricultural aid in Africa did help increase the food supply and boost the local economy in many of the recipient countries. The Mubalali Farm in Tanzania, for instance, used to produce one quarter of the whole country's rice supply by itself during the 1970–1980s (Shi 1989, 565–569; Table 2.1). In Mali where China began to provide agricultural aid since 1961, the Chinese indeed started the country's history of producing and processing tea and sugarcane on its own, thus helping providing local employment, increasing government revenue and saving foreign exchange of the country that is used to import sugar (Han 2011); the sugarcane factories, as to be picked up again later (Sect. 2.3), are still currently operational after almost six decades. However, one of the major problems concerning China's earlier agricultural aid in Africa is that most of those aid projects were not sustainable. As observed by Yun (2000a), while almost all the agro-projects achieved initial success upon completion, they could barely survive for long after being transferred to the recipient governments (see also Li et al. 2010, 219). In the case of Sierra Leone, for example, only two years after the Chinese experts left, all the ten farms were flourishing with weeds (Bräutigam 2009, 237). Other similar cases were common at that time (Shi 1989, 221; also see Sect. 2.3).[8] On top of others, the lack of technical, managerial and financial capability on the African (government) side was believed to be a main reason. Besides, the mechanized

---

[8] It is worth noting that this 'non-sustainability' problem was not only seen in Chinese agro-aid projects in Africa, but indeed a common problem that was also widely observed in other Western countries' aid efforts in African agricultural sector (Eicher 2003).

farming modality required by some of the Chinese-aided farms was also considered beyond the actual economic and productivity level of the African countries (Cai 1992; Sun 1996; Zhou and Wang 1997).

2.2 A Momentum for Change: China's Foreign Aid Reforms

After three decades of efforts, especially with the re-entry into the United Nation and the normalization of relations with the United States in the 1970s, the external environment of the PRC could been seen as much improved, either compared to the rather vulnerable period as a newly formed regime in the 1950s or the most hostile decade of the 1960s when it had to 'fight on two fronts' with both the Soviet Union and the US. By the end of 1979, China had established formal diplomatic relations with 120 countries around the world, including those from the Soviet, Western blocs and the non-aligned Third World[9] (MOFA of the PRC), and thus became an increasingly recognized and matured player in the international arena. The strategic needs for providing foreign aid, especially in exchange for international political support as conducted in the earlier period of 1950–1960s, was hence relatively reduced.

What is equally, if not more important, is the launch of the Reform and Opening-Up policy in 1978. With the end of the disastrous 'Cultural Revolution', the Communist Party of China (CPC) finally shifted its domestic policy priority from 'class struggle' to the country's economic development, which was regarded, as put by Deng Xiaoping (1980), 'the principal condition for solving all the problems [of China] both at home and abroad'. The 'domestic economy' factor, accordingly, also began to be put onto China's diplomatic agenda and has since gained increasing weight for itself. This can be seen, starting from the 1980s until now, from both the diplomatic efforts carried out with the aim of creating a peaceful and favourable external environment to

---

[9]The 'Third World' here, different from that in the context of Mao's 'Three Worlds' theory (Sect. 2.1), is used in the Western tradition of categorizing that regards the United States and its NATO allies as the First World, the Soviet Union and its communist allies (including China) as the Second World, and those unaligned, often with colonial pasts, such as many of the African, Latin American, Asian and Oceanian countries as the Third World (e.g. see Sauvy 1952).

guarantee China's domestic economic development, and more importantly, the growing number of economic issues and commercial objectives that have entered the country's foreign policy agendas, including that of Chinese foreign aid (Sect. 2.4).

Furthermore, the Chinese foreign aid per se was also facing problems. The increasingly overstretched trend of aid-giving in the 1960–1970s, strongly informed by the political needs and communist ideology of proletarian internationalism, and ironically, the diplomatic setbacks and relation deterioration with some socialist 'brother countries' who had been receiving large amount of Chinese aid for decades, caused the Chinese government to reflect upon its earlier aid practice (Xiao and Zhang 2002; Zhou 2008; Shu 2009). Meanwhile, some practical problems, such as the lack of efficiency, profitability[10] and sustainability of Chinese aid projects, were also being gradually acknowledged to the realization that change was needed (Shi 1989, 64–69; Yun 2000a).

Against all these factors, a series of reform measures started to be introduced first in the 1980s and then in the mid-1990s by the Chinese government. Some of the most relevant policy changes, especially those that would help understand the evolving practice of Chinese agricultural development cooperation with Africa under discussion, will be presented as follows, namely the normalization of aid scale, the improvement of aid performance, and the emphasis on mutual development.

Normalization of Aid Scale
While still acknowledging the strategic significance of aiding the Third-World countries and deciding to continue on aid provision, a broad consensus was finally achieved among the Chinese leadership around the early 1980s that aid should be given according to China's own actual strengths (Shi 1989, 71). As commented by Deng Xiaoping (1978),

> We are still very poor and cannot do much in terms of proletarian internationalism at the moment. We may be able to contribute more to mankind, especially the Third World, when we realize the Four Modernizations and have a stronger national economy in the future.

---

[10] Here, the 'profitability' refers mostly to the ability of the aid projects to bring economic benefits to *the African locals*, which is different from the more *self-interested* profit-seeking motive as growingly seen in the Chinese aid practice later on (particularly from the 1990s on) after the foreign aid reform.

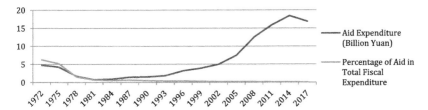

Fig. 2.1 Chinese aid expenditure and its percentage in total fiscal expenditure (It is worth noting that, after the launch of two 'concessional loans' [see the last part of Sect. 2.2], the fiscal expenditure only covers the interest discount [i.e. difference between market interest and concessional interest] of the loans and thus the actual aid volume of China (insofar as grants and concessional loans are concerned) is much higher than the fiscal expenditure on aid as shown in this figure; *Source* The author based on CAITEC [2018, 88–90])

In line with this, the Chinese government made a series of cost-effective adjustments to the aid-giving practice, particularly around the early 1980s (1979–1982) when the government had a rather tight budget.[11] These adjustments included, for instance, increasing medium-/small-sized social sector-oriented projects (e.g. agricultural demonstration bases, hospitals and schools) and symbolic projects (e.g. conference centres, stadiums), and accordingly reducing large-scaled productive projects (Shi 1989, 71–72; Zhou 2008, 38; State Council of the PRC 2011). As a result, the aid scale was dragged back to a more acceptable level, with the share of aid in the government fiscal expenditure falling from the record high of 6–7% in the early 1970s to below 1% during the 1980s (Fig. 2.1).[12] This also enabled China to expand its development cooperation partners to a much broader range and especially to the least development countries (LDCs); for example, during the 1980s China increased 24 new aid receivers from the previously 64 and aid to the LDCs increased by 63% during 1984–1988 compared to that of 1979–1983 (CAITEC 2018, 11–12).

---

[11] This is largely due to tremendous capital investment required to recover the national economy after the ten years of political turmoil caused by the 'cultural revolution'.

[12] Even with a dramatic increase of foreign aid in absolute terms in the past two decades (1990s–present), the proportion of that to the total government fiscal expenditure has remained reasonably under 1% over the same period (Li and Wu 2009; State Council of the PRC 2014).

This aid scale readjustment, driven partially by the constrained economic power of China at that time but more importantly by the changes of the country's strategic needs behind, shows how its identity as a developing country would affect its external development cooperation behaviours: the limited resources it possesses would have to be balanced towards the more urgent policy priority—for China in the 1980s, the domestic economic development accordingly. At least at that stage, China by no means possessed the necessary strengths to keep an independent development cooperation agenda as that of the Northern donors which was claimed to be more recipient-oriented and less influenced by donors' self-interests.

Improvement of Aid Performance
Despite the efforts trying to reduce the aid scale, it did not suggest, as noted already, a downplaying of the role of aid in China's foreign strategy. Nor did it by any means demonstrate less care of China about its aid effectiveness; rather, the aim was to 'use the limited foreign aid funds to achieve the best results' (MOFET of the PRC 1983). Particularly, in the face of the problems that came increasingly to the government's awareness (e.g. the efficiency, profitability and sustainability deficiency of China's earlier aid projects), specific measures were taken with an express purpose of enhancing the aid performance. Two of them are notably relevant: that is, the introduction of 'contract and responsibility system (CRS)',[13] and the strengthening of post-construction engagement.

The CRS was introduced to the foreign aid and development cooperation area from 1983. Different from the previous wholly government-dominated approach, aid projects were now contracted to state-owned enterprises (SOEs) and government-affiliated institutions (*shiye danwei*) to carry through, while the government agencies were only in charge of the macro-planning and project supervision. By separating aid decision-making and implementation, in particular through allowing for more autonomy and economic incentives of the implementing entities, the CRS was believed to have increased the operational efficiency (and economic viability) of Chinese foreign aid projects (Shi 1989, 89–90). That said, it is worth noting that at this stage the

---

[13] The 'contract and responsibility system' was first adopted in the rural reforms of China since the late 1970s and later gradually extended to other areas of the Reform.

aid work contracted to SOEs or government institutions was still largely revolving around infrastructure *construction* of the projects; post-construction engagement (discussed below), on the other hand, was developed on a rather limited scale. It is from the late 1980s and early 1990s that the contracted aid-implementing agencies became more actively involved in the project *operation*.

In order to 'consolidate the aid effects' (MOFET of the PRC 1984), or in other words, to cope with the lack of sustainability problem, the Chinese government also started to place more emphasis onto the post-construction engagement. The Chinese aid workers had, until then, showed great caution in engaging with post-construction operation, especially in terms of project management, for fear of being considered as intervening in the internal affairs of the aid recipient countries. Confronted with the oft-seen unsustainability problem, however, the Chinese government began to realize that it was necessary to step up the post-construction engagement, both in the form of *technical* and *managerial* cooperation—which, as reassured by the then Premier Zhao Ziyang, should 'not be taken as intervention, but to help them [African countries] achieve self-dependence' (Zhao 1982, cited in Shi 1989, 224–225).

Specifically, the *technical cooperation*, which had been practiced since the 1960s, normally involved provision of technical support and training to the locals, and at times establishment of technical and management regulations and/or systems required by the aid projects, with the assistance of the dispatched Chinese experts. This type of cooperation generally took place after the project construction was completed and lasted one to two years unless being requested by the recipient countries for a longer period. The *managerial cooperation*, on the other hand, was a new trend in China's aid practice, starting only after 1983 (Shi 1989). It required, to varying degrees, participation of the Chinese staff in the day-to-day management of the aid projects. This involvement manifested itself under different forms, such as managing aid projects on behalf of recipient countries, lease management and joint ventures (State Council of the PRC 2011). In practice, these two methods were often combined together; that is, the Chinese agro-expert groups would provide both technical and managerial support to the recipient countries.

It is worth noting that, although the abovementioned reforms in aid modalities were initially introduced mostly for the consideration of aid performance enhancement, measures such as incorporating company actors and encouraging post-construction engagement also smoothed the way for further, more commercially oriented aid reforms forthcoming in the mid-1990s. As to be shown in the following sections, with the 'mutual-development' idea gaining more confirmation from the leadership and being increasingly applied in the real development cooperation practice, a number of aid projects that incorporated post-construction engagement, especially that of management cooperation, naturally transformed to agribusiness projects (often in the form of joint venture) in the 'transition period' (Sect. 2.3) and finally converged into the so-called agribusiness model in the 'new era' after 2000 (Sect. 2.4).

Emphasis on Mutual Development
Indeed, the principle of 'equality and mutual benefit' was proposed as early as Premier Zhou Enlai visited Africa in 1964, whereby it was already attenuated that 'China never regards aid as an one-sided donation, but rather that, aid is reciprocal' (Zhou 1964). Apparently, however, there was little space for China to receive reciprocal aid from African countries back then; nor did China explicitly make its own development and benefit, especially in economic terms, a major pursuit when providing aid to Africa in the 1960–1970s.[14] Against the background of foreign aid reforms in the early 1980s, China's then Premier Zhao Ziyang proposed a new 'Four Principles of Conducting Economic and Technical Cooperation with African Countries',[15] which while reinforced Zhou's statement by emphasizing reciprocal benefits and mutual development, also demonstrated the pragmaticism entailed by Deng Xiaoping's reform spirit by highlighting the necessity of adopting diverse forms and pursuing actual effects. Ten years later in 1994, with the deepening of Chinese reform process, Wu Yi, the then Minister of Commerce of China, further introduced the 'Grand Economic and Trade Development (*da shangmao*)' policy that aimed to boost the domestic economy through combining diverse types of economic activities—such as international trade,

[14]Apart from the fact that political (rather than economic) development was deemed more urgent in China's foreign strategy at the time, the relatively backward economic development status on both China and Africa also limited the space for profound and profitable economic cooperation—beyond the unilateral 'pure aid' from the former to the latter—to take place.

[15]Include 'equality and reciprocal benefits', 'pursuing actual effects', 'diversity of cooperation forms' and 'mutual development'. For more details, see Bräutigam (2009, 314).

foreign investment, overseas project contracting and labour cooperation, utilization of external capital, as well as foreign aid—and seeking a synergetic effect among them. Until then, the self-development dimension and thus the mutual-development role of aid, could be seen as having gradually acknowledged and established by the Chinese leadership.

A very important progress occurring at this time was the emergence of so-called development package at mid-1990s. That is, China intentionally started to promote the combination of aid, trade, investment and other possible economic forms with an express mutual-development objective to boost both the economies of recipient countries and that of China itself (Liang and Wang 1995). This marks the moment when Chinese development cooperation began to go beyond mere aid but to embrace all possible forms that could effectively promote development (esp. economic development), and importantly, the development of both sides including China as the aid provider per se. To give one example, Chinese aid projects were in most cases contracted to Chinese companies and accompanied by export of Chinese equipment and labour, thus paving the way for the 'Going Out' strategy launched in 1995. This sort of 'tied aid', however, is precisely what the Northern donors have been trying to reduce in their aid-giving practice in the past two decades, despite varying performances among the donors (Clay et al. 2009).

In tandem with the 'development package', China also started to increasingly mobilize and channel market capital into the development cooperation area. From 1995, China started to provide the *Government Medium/Long-term Concessional Loan* to aid-recipient countries via the newly established Export-Import Bank of China (EXIM Bank) (State Council of the PRC 2011). Later, since the 2000s, the EXIM Bank also began to offer *Preferential Export Buyers' Credit*. Both of them are made 'concessional' through their lower-than-market rates of interest, the loss of which is offset to the EXIM Bank by the fiscal expenditure of the government. These two facilities are often referred to together as the 'two concessional loans (*liangyou*)' and have since played a significant role in supporting Chinese companies' foreign investment, and particularly their overseas project contracting, in developing countries. According to the EXIM Bank (2013), the 'two concessional loans' had increased dramatically since 1995, with a particularly notable growth rate of over 30% per annum during 2006–2011. In addition, through different types of 'managerial cooperation' over aid projects in the 1980–1990s and burgeoning

FDI from the 2000s on, the self-owned capital of Chinese companies has become another important financing source for China's external development cooperation.

2.3 Consolidation and Transformation: The Transition Stage (1980s–1990s)

With the completion of the 'replacement aid' phase and the launch of the foreign aid reforms, from the early 1980s onward, Chinese agro-development cooperation with Africa entered what can be termed, notably in retrospect, as a 'transition stage'. It is so called partly because of the less explicit motives (either strategically or development-oriented) behind the cooperation compared to the earlier or following period; and equally important, of the transitional feature of the cooperation forms from unilateral 'pure aid' to cooperation that places increasing emphasis on mutual benefit, particularly in commercial terms.

While the aid reforms had brought the idea of 'reciprocal benefit and mutual development' more clearly into China's foreign aid and development cooperation arena, a few factors effectively constrained this from being put into practice in the transition period. China's external economic interactions with Africa were still in a rather moderate and unbalanced state given its constrained national power and limited degree of 'opening' at the time. China's 'opening' before mid-1990s concentrated more on inward resource flows—that is, 'introducing in (*yin jinlai*)' different sorts of foreign resources, notably capital (either in the form of FDI or aid) and technology, but less on outward resource movement especially in terms of financial flows. The major economic partners of trade, investment as well as aid (with China as the FDI and aid recipient) then were largely developed countries from the North; the Southern countries—and Africa, in particular, that was hit by the debt crisis and stuck in the 'structural adjustments'—could offer relatively less to China. Indeed, the economic drivers of Chinese development cooperation with Africa, including that in the agricultural area, did not become very evident until the turning of the new millennium (Sect. 2.4).

Against this context, Chinese agro-development cooperation with Africa, while largely following the general aid reform directions (i.e. scale reduction, performance enhancement and commercial orientation), also did not experience much radical or rapid change. Rather, consolidation and gradual transformation of the earlier aid projects seemed to constitute the main themes of Chinese agro-aid practice in Africa in the transition period. Accordingly, except for a handful of cases—such as the sugarcane farms and sugar refineries in Guinea, Sierra Leone, Zaire, Madagascar respectively, and irrigation and farming projects in Ghana (Shi 1989, 76), there were not many newly launched agro-aid projects or programmes during the 1980–1990s.

In terms of *consolidation*, as mentioned in the earlier section, the Chinese government started to strengthen the more traditional technical cooperation and meanwhile introduce a new method, namely managerial cooperation, in the post-construction phase, in order to cope with the commonly experienced project unsustainability problem (Sect. 2.2). For example, at the request of the African side, the Chinese government sent back agro-expert teams to some of the previously established farms— such as that in Mali, Mauritania and Congo-Brazzaville (Table 2.1)— in the 1980s. The aim was to help deal with the degradation problems that occurred after the Chinese experts left and try to reinvigorate those aged projects through the provision of technical (and at times managerial) support. In Tanzania, for instance, in the case of the Chinese-aided Mubalali Farm (Table 2.1), immediately after the completion of the project construction in 1977, an eight-year-long technical cooperation (1977–1985) agreement was signed with a view to consolidating the aid effects. Compared to the more common one-two-year technical cooperation, this project entailed a much longer period of time, adopted a wide range of consolidation measures (e.g. technical support, human resource training, co-management, etc.) and proved to be rather successful by the late 1980s (Shi 1989, 222–223). As to managerial cooperation, some African governments—for example, Mali, Congo-Brazzaville and Sierra Leone—while re-inviting Chinese experts to go back to the previously built farms, also asked them to play a leading role in the project management, taking care of the day-to-day operation from production, sales, finances to labour management of the farms. The African governments, instead, played more a secondary or supporting role in this process (Shi 1989, 224–228).

Entering the 1990s, with the deepening of both market-oriented reforms at home and aid reforms in the foreign arena, China's agro-development cooperation with Africa started to experience a gradual transformation. This mainly took two forms. The first form is the emergence of a few newly launched agribusiness projects through utilizing the 'two concessional loans'. This trend began in the 1990s but developed only on a very limited scale at that time compared to that occurred in the new millennium, particularly after 2006 (Chapter 4). Examples of these newly built agribusiness projects are, for instance, the sisal and rice farms set up in Tanzania and Guinea respectively in the 1990s by the state-owned company, China State Farms Agribusiness Corporation (CSFAC).[16]

The second form is the transformation of previous agro-aid projects into agro-investment projects. A typical example of this can be seen in the case of the sugarcane project in Mali. Mali was among the earliest in Africa that received agro-aid from China. After successfully testing the growing of sugarcane in Mali in 1962, China then helped Mali to build two sugarcane farms (1970, 1977) and two sugar mills (1966, 1976) and conducted several rounds of 'technical cooperation' with the country. However, the projects fell into degradation after the Chinese agro-technical team left. The Malian government, therefore, re-invited the Chinese experts in 1982 to come back to Mali and help revive the sugarcane projects. Soon after that (in 1984), the Malian government decided to combine the two sugarcane farms and two mills so to establish a unified state-owned enterprise, wherein the Chinese agro-experts were employed as the enterprise managers (i.e. 'managerial cooperation'). This move proved to be very effective, not only greatly enhancing the project productivity and profitability but also contributing to the job creation and people's welfare in the local neighbourhood (Shi 1989, 582–587). One decade later, in 1996, the enterprise was further transformed into a joint venture, the Complexe Sucrier Du Kala Superieur SA, with the Chinese state-owned CLETC[17] holding 60% of the share and taking the major responsibility of the company's management, and the Malian government holding 40% of the company's stake (CLETC). By then, the three-decade-long Chinese agro-aid projects had finally developed into jointly owned agribusiness projects between China and Mali. And based on that practice, CLETC invested in another sugar joint venture, the New Complexe Sucrier Du Kala Superieur SA, with Malian government in 2009 (CLETC).

We could observe at least two lines of change in this process: first, the change of project-implementing agencies from Chinese government

---

[16] For more details about this company and the relevant projects, see Sect. 4.1.2.

[17] CLETC is short for China Light Industrial Corporation for Foreign Economic and Technical Co-operation, which was established in 1983 and from then started to take over the agro-aid projects in Mali that had used to be undertaken by the then China's Ministry of Light Industry in the 1960–1970s.

(China's Ministry of Light Industry) to Chinese companies (CLETC), and accordingly, the change of motivations lying behind from a more politically driven to an increasingly business-oriented approach.[18] In a similar vein, the Chinese-aided sugarcane projects in Sierra Leone, Togo and Madagascar (Table 2.1) were also converted into agribusiness projects starting in the 1990s. These three, however, operated on a lease management basis (Sect. 2.2) by COMPLANT,[19] another Chinese state-owned enterprise.

Different from the 1960–1970s when government agencies took a predominant role in the implementation process, with the introduction of the 'contract and responsibility system' (Sect. 2.2), from the 1980s onwards aid projects started to be contracted to company entities who thus gained increasing implementing power—first in the construction, later also in the operation phase. The government agencies, on the other hand, played more a supervising and coordinating role. The abovementioned CSFAC, for instance, was established under the then Ministry of State Farms and Land Reclamation (which later merged to form the MOA) and took charge of a number of aid projects. At provincial levels, many Foreign Economic and Technical Cooperation Companies were established under provincial governments and mandated to carry out aid, including agro-aid projects, in other developing countries. That said, during the 1980–1990s, only *state-owned* enterprises were allowed to participate in the delivery of government aid projects.

In terms of aid performance in this transition period (1980–1990s), despite the measures taken in line with the aid reforms, the thorny problem of project unsustainability still persisted. The 'success story' of the Mubalali Farm in Tanzania noted earlier did not continue after the eight-year-long technical and managerial cooperation came to an end, but gradually fell into disrepair as the Chinese agro-experts and

---

[18] This latter change was a more progressive process. That is to say, the change of implementing agencies did not immediately bring about the change of motivations, for the former was a more direct reflection of the functional separation of government agencies and enterprises as required by the domestic market-oriented reforms, but the latter grew more evidently only as the reforms deepened and thus the companies, especially those state-owned enterprises, truly gained more autonomy and discretion over company operation matters rather than acting merely as a government instrument.

[19] COMPLANT is short for China National Complete Plant Import & Export Corporation, which was established in 1959 and had since played a predominant role in implementing Chinese government aid projects abroad.

workers left. The Mubalali Farm, together with Lufu, another Chinese-aided farm (Table 2.1), was finally sold out by the Tanzanian government in the early 2000s (ECCO in Tanzania 2004a, b). A similar case is the agro-technology experiment station in Guinea, which was transferred to the Guinean government in 1982 but could not sustain on its own. In 1989, the Chinese government started to re-inject funds and re-send agro-experts in order to rehabilitate the station. These renewed efforts, however, only managed to sustain the station for another ten years—it shut down almost immediately after the Chinese left in 1999 (Yun 2000b).

2.4 Time for Mutual Development: The Current Stage (2000s–Present)

Over the years from the 1980s till the present time—from Deng Xiaoping through Jiang Zemin, Hu Jintao to Xi Jinping– the CPC has stuck firmly to its outward-oriented economic development policies and the efforts to restore China's global status. The 'Reform and Opening-Up' policy, accordingly, remained among the top agenda of Chinese domestic and foreign policies, and grew even more profoundly in the 1990s featured by an increasing proactive posture in participating international economic dealings and finally the launch of 'Going Out' strategy around the 2000.[20] At the same time, though at a lesser pace, the African continent had also achieved steady economic growth and recovery particularly since the new millennium, thus positioning itself a better economic cooperation partner in the international arena. The past two decades, therefore, have witnessed a dramatic development

---

[20] In 2001 the 'Going Out' strategy was formally proposed and written into the country's 10th Five-year Plan of the National Economy and Social Development, which was further enriched in the 11th and 12th Five-year Plans in 2006 and 2011, respectively (People's Congress of the PRC 2001, 2006, 2011). Specifically, by promoting the 'Going Out' strategy, the Chinese government actively encourages and supports the Chinese enterprises to conduct foreign project contracting and labour services cooperation; exploit foreign resources that are domestically lacked; conduct processing and trade abroad, create international marketing networks and brands; set up overseas Research & Development (R&D) agencies and design centres; conduct transnational operation and develop towards transnational companies. The core objectives of the 'Going Out' strategy, therefore, are largely to gain access to foreign resources, markets and technology through primarily conducting FDI but also other modalities.

of bilateral relations between China and Africa, with China's African policy acquiring, in particular, an unprecedented economic dimension compared to all its earlier engagement with the continent through the twentieth century. Moreover, the establishment of FOCAC (Forum on China-Africa Cooperation) since the year of 2000 has become a significant milestone in contemporary China-Africa relations and served as an effective catalyst—through its continual proposals and follow-up mechanisms on a three-year basis—to push forward an all-round and sustained cooperation between the two sides.

From the agricultural perspective, more specifically, different from the previous two stages (Sects. 2.1 and 2.3), two factors have opened opportunities for China and Africa not only to carry on with, but to further deepen their bilateral development cooperation. First, China's domestic agricultural sector has achieved a widely renown success, while ensuring food security of a population of 1.3 billion also uplifting millions of people from the extreme poverty (Huang 2010; Li et al. 2013). This success story of Chinese own agriculture has put China in a welcome position in conducting agro-development cooperation with Africa; furthermore, the existence of relatively more similarity and closer gap in terms of agricultural development between China and Africa[21] may to certain extent facilitate the transfer of agro-technology and development experiences.[22] Second, though helping boost Africa's underdeveloped agro-sector per se remains a key concern for the Chinese government, its agro-development cooperation with Africa has started to be growingly intertwined with China's own agricultural development agenda—notably its foreign agricultural strategy. Given a number of development challenges at home and some long-term pursuits globally,[23] China's agricultural sector has been increasingly opening up to the external world, welcoming and encouraging exchange of products, capital, technology, and human

---

[21] Compared, for instance, to that between some of the agriculture-based advanced countries from Europe, Oceania, or North America, and Africa.

[22] That said, Chinese scholars have clearly realized that the success story and experiences cannot be simply copied by African states without proper adjustment and localization process due to the latter's distinct historical, cultural and policy environments, among other factors (Li et al. 2013).

[23] For instance, to alleviate the agricultural resource bottleneck, upgrade China's domestic agro-industry, climb up the global agribusiness value chain and cultivate competitive agricultural multinational corporations, among others.

resources with other countries. After entering the WTO and opening its agricultural trade in 2001, Chinese government further launched the 'Agriculture Going Out' policy in 2006 with a primary aim to utilize the overseas agricultural resources (Sect. 4.1.1).

Against this context, the past two decades since the new millennium have witnessed a fresh and high wave of agro-development cooperation between China and Africa, especially compared with the rather moderate, more 'consolidation'-oriented interactions during the 1980–1990s. At the policy level, agricultural cooperation measures with Africa started to be detailed at the Beijing Summit of the 3rd FOCAC (2006). Since then, they have been modified and strengthened at every FOCAC (2009, 2012, 2015, 2018), including the specific forum on agriculture (FOCAAC 2010). Particularly, the 'mutual-development' idea as entailed in the four principles set up by Premier Zhao Ziyang in the early 1980s (Sect. 2.2) finally began to be substantialized given a more mature point of time in the new century. In line with the 'mutual-development' mentality, China's agro-development cooperation with Africa, while maintaining certain continuity, has undertaken a great change since the 2000s. Most notable is the so-called development package (Chapter 1) applied in the agricultural area. There are three distinct models within the 'development package', respectively the '(technology-centred) traditional agricultural aid model', the 'innovative agricultural aid model' and the 'agribusiness model'.

Traditional Agro-Aid Model
In the first place, many traditional forms, often grant-funded types of agricultural aid as practiced in the 1960–1990s, still remain and constitute a significant part of China's contemporary agricultural development cooperation with Africa. Having said that, there has seen an important shift of focus from more 'complete project' type of aid (Sect. 2.1) to that of increasingly 'technical assistance' centred (Li et al. 2010, 219–220). This has much to do with Chinese own experience in agricultural development in the past few decades. China established a comprehensive agro-technology extension system from as early as the 1950s, and by the year 2015 technological advances had contributed more than 55% to the growth of China's agriculture (Yu and Wang 2015). It is widely acknowledged that the utilization and dissemination of agro-technology have played an essential role in transforming the country's agricultural sector (Huang 2010). In light of this, *technical assistance* has also

been established as the cornerstone of China's current agricultural aid to Africa, which further takes a number of specific forms.

First, the Chinese government has launched a new round of expert dispatch. At the Beijing summit of FOCAC in 2006, China pledged to assign 100 senior agro-experts specializing in diverse areas to assist African countries with agricultural development (FOCAC 2006); the number was further increased to 500 in 2018 (FOCAC 2018). In 2009 and 2015, China promised respectively to send 50 and 30 agro-technical teams to the continent (FOCAC 2009, 2015). The main task of the different forms of expert dispatch, as explained by the MOA,[24] is to 'participate in the formulation of aid-recipient countries' agricultural development plan, assist with the establishment of agricultural technology extension system, offer technological consulting and services for their agricultural production, and eventually enhance the capabilities for agricultural macro-control and self-development' (MOA of the PRC 2008). By the year of 2018, China had dispatched 71 groups—involving in total 724—of agro-experts, technicians and teachers to 37 African countries (Han 2018).[25]

There have also been constant exchange and training programs launched by Chinese MOA for a wide range of African recipients, including farmers, technicians, students, officials and others, either in China or in the related African states. While the ATDCs can serve a good example that involves programmes targeting at African smallholder farmers and local agro-technicians (Chapter 3), China has also trained a large number of young students through vocational education cooperation with Africa. The China-Ethiopia Agricultural Vocational Education Programme, for instance, is one of the flagship projects and success stories in this regard. From 2001 to 2010, China had sent more than 300 teachers to Ethiopia while around 66,000 local students been trained under the program; more importantly, this programme has helped Ethiopia to establish from scratch its own agricultural vocational education system, building up in total about 28 training institutions all over the country (Li 2010, 9;

---

[24] The ministry was renamed Ministry of Agriculture and Rural Affairs (MOARA) since March 2018. To avoid confusion, this book still refers to it as MOA uniformly.

[25] For a discussion on the sustainability issue of Chinese decades-long programme of agro-expert dispatch, see Lu et al. (2015).

Bräutigam and Tang 2012, 7). In 2012, furthermore, the Chinese government proposed to facilitate the setup of agro-vocational education systems all across the African continent (FOCAC 2012). At officials level, more than 20 different training programs in agro-technology and management are held every year (MOA of the PRC 2010). And it is estimated that around 10,000 African officials were trained each year, through either bilateral or multilateral channels (Tugendhat and Alemu 2016).

In addition, China also provides technical support to African countries under diverse multilateral cooperation frameworks. For instance, China has played, since 1996, an active role in the South-South Cooperation (SSC) program, one of the Supporting Programs for Food Security launched by the Food and Agricultural Organization (FAO) of the UN. In 2008, a further partnership was established between China and FAO whereby China pledged to offer 30 million USD trust fund and dispatch 3000 agro-technicians and experts between 2006 and 2012 to support the SSC program, with a prioritized focus on Africa (i.e. Ethiopia, Mauritania, Ghana, Nigeria, Mali, Sierra Leon, Gabon) (Han 2011). Also, China has been working together with the Northern donors, especially the DAC under the OECD. In 2009, for instance, a study group between China and OECD-DAC was set up with a primary goal of facilitating mutual learning on poverty reduction among developing countries (China-DAC 2009). In the agricultural sector specifically, the group has conducted a series of research with a view to transferring the successful experience of agricultural development in China to the African continent (China-DAC 2011).

Despite a particular focus on technical assistance, other more traditional forms such as *infrastructure and materials support* remain an integral part of Chinese agricultural aid to Africa. For example, in terms of agricultural infrastructure, by the end of 2009, China had helped build 215 agricultural 'complete projects', including 168 general agro-projects (such as farms and technology extension stations) and 47 irrigation projects, in different developing countries. Most of these projects were located in Africa, with a large part of them being built during the early years between the 1960 and 1990s though (State Council of the PRC 2011; Li 2010). Some more recent examples include, for instance, the Chinese-aided grain barns in Zambia and the rice-processing factories in Mozambique. On a yearly basis, the Chinese government also earmarks a certain amount of funds for purchasing agricultural materials for African countries, including agro-inputs such as seeds, fertilizers and pesticides, as well as small- and medium-sized farm implements and some agro-processing equipment. This sort of materials donation is often provided alongside other Chinese agro-aid projects, or separately upon request from the aid-recipient countries. Besides, China is also an important humanitarian aid-giver to Africa. At the FOCAC summit in 2018, for instance, Chinese President Xi Jinping offered to provide ¥ one billion emergency food aid to African countries that suffered from poor harvest; and according to the UN-affiliated World Food Program, China has been one of the leading contributors in the developing world (WFP 2015).

Innovative Agro-Aid Model
The second model of Chinese contemporary agricultural development cooperation in Africa is termed as '*innovative agro-aid model*' in this book. It is so called because of its inherent dualistic nature; that is, on the one hand, it still resembles the 'traditional agro-aid model' in many respects and so that is often regarded as Chinese aid projects, but on the other hand, it has effectively brought in the idea of 'mutual development' to the practice of China's agricultural development cooperation through introducing some innovative mechanism design. Most typical of this would surely be the ATDCs (Agricultural Technology Demonstration Centres), the flagship project of China's agricultural development cooperation with Africa in the new millennium.

The ATDCs have been launched for more than one decade since the Beijing Summit of the 3rd FOCAC in 2006. As will be elaborated in Chapter 3, the ATDCs, at the first glance, are a combination of all the abovementioned agro-aid forms (agro-technology assistance, infrastructure support and materials donation). However, the incorporation of corporate actors as project-implementing agencies and accordingly the expected commercial operation model in the mid-/long term makes them essentially distinct from projects under the 'traditional agro-aid model'. This special design is very much in line with the 'mutual-development' idea, with both developmental and commercial implications. By 2012, there had been in practice at least 23 Chinese-funded ATDCs all over the African continent, with the first batch of 14 centres having finished construction and been transferred to the host governments, while 9 others still in the process of completing the feasibility study or construction.

Agribusiness Model

Lastly, there is also the '*agribusiness model*' that features tapping into the potential of agribusiness investment in promoting the development of African agriculture. The developmental impact of agribusiness could be exerted in two ways. First, through the natural, spill-over effect of the development of agribusiness, particularly in terms of enhancing food security (when grain crops are concerned), boosting job creation and accordingly promoting poverty reduction. Second, through intentional, extra efforts that are made either by governments (through the PPP mechanism) or by companies themselves (out of CSR consideration) to further strengthening the developmental impact of agribusiness, such as the scaling up of projects through financial support from government or national banks or free training programs for agro-technology transfer provided spontaneously by companies. In line with the overarching guideline of pursuing mutual development and reciprocal benefits, the 'agribusiness model' also fits well in China's 'Agricultural Going Out' strategy that was launched in mid-2000s and with a clear view to stimulating Chinese companies' overseas agro-investment. Chinese companies' agribusiness engagement in Africa has stepped up quickly in the past decade or so. China's agro-FDI stock in Africa was about $289 million in 2009 (MOC of the PRC 2010), which has increased to $1.27 billion by the end of 2016; and it is estimated that around 108 Chinese companies were involved in agro-investment in Africa by the same year (MOA of the PRC 2017, 25).

Summary

As already shown above, from an institutional perspective, both the management and operational mechanism of Chinese agricultural development cooperation projects in the 'new era' (2000s–present) have undergone important changes. This is particularly notable at the operational level wherein an increasing diversity of non-governmental actors, especially companies, starts to actively engage in the enterprise of Chinese international development cooperation. However, despite the general image of greater efficiency and important financer that is often associated with corporate actors, their disparate motivations, capabilities, discretions and cooperative tendencies all potentially impose great challenges to their implementation results. Even at the management level, due to the growing agency awarded to non-governmental actors and some market-based mechanisms adopted such as that under the 'innovative agro-aid' and 'agribusiness model', it is becoming more and more challenging for Chinese government to exert effective control over the actual implementation and thus the ultimate outcomes of the new 'development package'. No less importantly, given the typical 'trial and error' nature of Chinese policy making, the country's development cooperation strategy per se is still largely a policy *in the making* and thus will no surprisingly suffer from certain loopholes and immaturity.

The questions, then, are how will the new and supposedly different (from the DAC-donors) 'package' model of China's development cooperation perform? To what extent is it going to be more, or less, effective? And how will it be constrained by the aforementioned potential challenges? All these questions will be examined in the next two empirical chapters (Chapters 3 and 4) and synthesized in the chapter that follows (Chapter 5).

References

Bräutigam, Deborah. 1998. *Chinese Aid and African Development: Exporting Green Revolution*. New York: Palgrave Macmillan.
———. 2009. *The Dragon's Gift: The Real Story of China in Africa*. Oxford: Oxford University Press.
Bräutigam, Deborah, and Xiaoyang Tang. 2012. 'An Overview of Chinese Agricultural and Rural Engagement in Ethiopia'. Discussion Paper 1185. IFPRI (International Food Policy Research Institute). https://deborahbrautigam.files.wordpress.com/2014/02/ifpri-ethiopia-dp.pdf.
Cai, Lingming. 1992. 'Woguo Dui Feizhou de Nongye Yuanzhu (China's Agricultural Aid to Africa)'. *Guoji Jingji Hezuo* (International Economic Cooperation) 2: 43–44.
CAITEC (Chinese Academy of International Trade and Economic Cooperation). 2018. *Guoji Fazhan Hezuo Zhilu: 40 Nian Gaige Kaifang Dachao Xia de Zhongguo Duiwai Yuanzhu* (Road of International Development Cooperation: China's Foreign Aid in the Four-Decade Waves of Reform and Opening-Up). Beijing: China Commerce and Trade Press.
China-DAC (The China-DAC Study Group). 2009. 'The China-DAC Study Group: Sharing Experiences and Promoting Learning About Growth and Poverty Reduction in China and African Countries'. http://www.oecd.org/china/44390151.pdf.
———. 2011. 'Economic Transformation and Poverty Reduction: How It Happened in China, Helping It Happen in Africa'. http://www.oecd.org/officialdocuments/publicdisplaydocumentpdf/?cote=DCD(2011)4&docLanguage=En.

Clay, Edward, Matthew Geddes, and Luisa Natali. 2009. 'Untying Aid: Is It Working? An Evaluation of the Implementation of the Paris Declaration and of the 2001 DAC Recommendation of Untying ODA to the LDCs'. DIIS (Danish Institute for International Studies), Copenhagen.

Deng, Xiaoping. 1978. 'Shixian Sihua, Yongbu Chengba (Realise the Four Modernasation, Never Be the Hegemon)'. In *Deng Xiaoping Wenxuan* (The Selected Works of Deng Xiaoping). Vol. 2. http://cpc.people.com.cn/GB/64184/64185/66611/4488666.html.

———. 1980. 'Muqian de Xingshi He Renwu (The Current Situations and Tasks)'. In *Deng Xiaoping Wenxuan* (The Selected Works of Deng Xiaoping). Vol. 2. http://cpc.people.com.cn/GB/64184/64185/66611/4488647.html.

ECCO in Tanzania (Economic and Commercial Counsellor's Office of the Embassy of the People's Republic of China in Tanzania). 2004a. 'Tan Zhengfu Gongkai Zhaobiao Chushou Lufu Shuidao Nongchang (Tanzanian Government Invites a Bid for Lufu Rice Farm)'. http://tz.mofcom.gov.cn/aarticle/jmxw/200408/20040800261893.html.

———. 2004b. 'Tan Zhengfu Gongkai Zhaobiao Chushou Mubalali Nongchang (Tanzanian Government Invites a Bid for Mubalali Farm)'.

Eicher, Carl. 2003. 'Flashback: Fifty Years of Donor Aid to African Agriculture'. https://rmportal.net/framelib/donor-aid-to-african-agriculture.pdf.

EXIM Bank of China. 2013. 'Zhongguo Jinchukou Yinhang "liangyou" daikuan Yewu Jieshao ("Two Preferential Loans" of the EXIM Bank of China)'. http://www.chinca.org/cms/html/files/2013-12/16/20131216102948872930302.pdf.

FOCAAC (Forum on China-Africa Agricultural Cooperation). 2010. 'Zhongfei Nongye Hezuo Luntan Beijing Xuanyan (Beijing Declaration of Forum on China-Africa Agricultural Cooperation)'. http://www.moa.gov.cn/ztzl/zfnyhzlt/ltdt/201008/t20100813_1618055.htm.

FOCAC (Forum on China Africa Cooperation). 2006. 'The Forum on China-Africa Cooperation Beijing Action Plan (2007–2009)'. Ministry of Foreign Affairs of the People's Republic of China, Beijing. https://www.focac.org/eng/zywx_1/zywj/t280369.htm.

———. 2009. 'The Forum on China-Africa Cooperation Sharm El-Sheikh Action Plan (2010–2012)'. Ministry of Foreign Affairs of the People's Republic of China, Beijing. https://www.focac.org/eng/zywx_1/zywj/t626387.htm.

———. 2012. 'The Forum on China-Africa Cooperation Beijing Action Plan (2013–2015)'. Ministry of Foreign Affairs of the People's Republic of China, Beijing. https://www.focac.org/eng/zywx_1/zywj/t954620.htm.

———. 2015. 'The Forum on China-Africa Cooperation Johannesburg Action Plan (2016–2018)'. Ministry of Foreign Affairs of the People's Republic of China, Beijing. https://www.focac.org/eng/zywx_1/zywj/t1327961.htm.

———. 2018. 'The Forum on China-Africa Cooperation Beijing Action Plan (2019–2021)'. Ministry of Foreign Affairs of the People's Republic of China, Beijing. https://www.focac.org/eng/zywx_1/zywj/t1594297.htm.

Fu, Xiaohan. 2008. '"Duiwai Jingji Jishu Yuanzhu de Baxiang Yuanze" juece de Cengci Fenxi (Level Analysis of the Decision-Making On "the Eight Principles of Foreign Economic and Technical Assistance")'. *Lishi Jiaoxue* (History Teaching) 2: 95–98.

Han, Changfu. 2018. 'Tuidong Zhongfei Nongye Hezuo Zaishang Xin Taijie (Step Up China-Africa Agricultural Cooperation)'. Ministry of Agriculture and Rural Affairs of the People's Republic of China, 1 September. http://www.moa.gov.cn/xw/zwdt/201809/t20180901_6156672.htm.

Han, Yan. 2011. 'Fazhan Huli Gongying de Zhongfei Nongye Hezuo (Develop Reciprocal China-Africa Agricultural Cooperation)'. *Guoji Jingji Hezuo* (International Economic Cooperation) 5: 33–37.

Huang, Jikun. 2010. 'Liushinian Zhongguo Nongye de Fazhan He Sanshinian Gaige Qiji (Sixty Years of Chinese Agricultural Development and Thirty Years of the Reform Miracle)'. *Nongye Jishu Jingji* (Agro-Technology Economy) 1: 4–18.

Jiang, Huajie. 2013. 'Nongji Yuanfei (1971–1983): Zhongguo Yuanfei Moshi Yu Chengxiao de Gean Yanjiu (Agricultural Technological Aid to Africa 1971–1983: A Case Study of the Modalities and Effectiveness of Chinese Aid to Africa)'. *Waijiao Pinglun* (Foreign Affairs Review) 1: 30–49.

Li, Jiali. 2010. 'Sino-Africa Agricultural Cooperation Experience Sharing'. Foreign Economic Cooperation Center of Chinese Ministry of Agriculture, Beijing. http://www.iprcc.org/userfiles/file/Li%20Jiali-EN.pdf.

Li, Xiaoyun, Gubo Qi, Lixia Tang, and Jin Wu. 2010. *Xiaonong wei jichu de nongye fazhan: zhongguo yu feizhou de bijiao yanjiu* (Smallholder-Based Agricultural Development: A Comparative Analysis of Chinese and African Experiences). Beijing: Shehui kexue wenxian chuban she (Social Sciences Academic Press).

Li, Xiaoyun, Lixia Tang, Gubo Qi, and Haimin Wang. 2013. 'What Can Africa Learn from China's Experience in Agricultural Development'. *IDS Bulletin* 44 (4): 31–41.

Li, Xiaoyun, and Jin Wu. 2009. 'Zhongguo Duifei Yuanzhu de Shijian Jingyan Yu Mianlin de Tiaozhan (A Study on China's ODA to Africa)'. *Zhongguo Nongye Daxue Xuebao Shehui Kexue Ban* (China Agricultural University Journal of Social Sciences Edition) 26: 45–54.

Liang, Hongyu, and Cheng 'an Wang. 1995. 'Woguo Kaishi Gaige Duiwai Yuanzhu Fangshi (China Starts to Reform the Modalities of Foreign Aid)'. *Guoji Shangbao* (International Business Daily), 6 June.

Lu, Jixia, Qian He, and Xiaoyun Li. 2015. 'Zhongguo Yuanfei Nongye Zhuanjia Paiqian Xiangmu de Kechixuxing Chutan (Sustainability of Chinese Agro-Expert Dispatch Programme)'. *Shijie Nongye* (World Agriculture) 432 (4).

Meng, Qingtao. 2013. 'Zhongguo Yuanzhu Feizhou Yiwang (Recalling the History of Chinese Aid in Africa)'. *Qingxi Zhonghua* 2. https://www.qxzh.zj.cn/magazine/article/876.html.
MOA of the PRC (Ministry of Agriculture of the People's Republic of China). 2008. 'Nongyebu Bangongting Guanyu Xiezhu Xuanba Dierpi Yuanfei Gaoji Nongye Zhuanjia de Han (Ministry of Agriculture On Assisting to Select the Second Batch of Senior Agricultural Experts)'.
———. 2010. 'Capability Building'. http://www.moa.gov.cn/ztzl/zfnyhzlt/zhongguo/201008/t20100806_1613799.htm.
———. 2017. 'Report on Chinese Overseas Agricultural Investment and Cooperation'. Ministry of Agriculture, Beijing.
MOC of the PRC (Ministry of Commerce of the People's Republic of China). 2010. 'Zhongguo Yu Feizhou Jingmao Guanxi Baogao (China-Africa Economic and Trade Relations Report)'.
———. 2015. *Duiwai Yuanzhu Chengtao Xiangmu Guanli Banfa (Shixing)* (Regulations on Foreign Aid Complete Projects). http://www.scio.gov.cn/xwfbh/xwbfbh/wqfbh/33978/34188/xgzc34194/Document/1469217/1469217.htm.
MOFA of the PRC (Ministry of Foreign Affairs of the People's Republic of China). n.d. 'Chairman Mao Zedong's Theory on the Division of the Three World and the Strategy of Forming an Alliance Against an opponent'. https://www.fmprc.gov.cn/mfa_eng/ziliao_665539/3602_665543/3604_665547/t18008.shtml.
MOFET of the PRC (Ministry of Foreign Economy and Trade of the People's Republic of China). 1983. 'Diliuci Quanguo Yuanwai Gongzuo Huiyi Wenjian (The Sixth National Conference on Foreign Aid)'. Beijing.
———. 1984. 'Guanyu Gonggu Jiancheng Jingyuan Chengtao Xiangmu Chengguo de Yijian (On Consolidating the Effects of Complete Projects of Foreign Economic Aid)'. Beijing.
Niu, Jun. 2010. *Zhonghua Renmin Gongheguo Duiwai Guanxi Shi Gailun, 1949–2000* (Introduction to History of Foreign Relations of the People's Republic of China, 1949–2000). Beijing: Peking University Press.
People's Congress of the PRC. 2001. 'Guomin Jingji Yu Shehui Fazhan Wunian Jihua (Five-Year Plan of the National Economy and Social Development)'.
———. 2006. 'Guomin Jingji Yu Shehui Fazhan Wunian Jihua (Five-Year Plan of the National Economy and Social Development)'.
———. 2011. 'Guomin Jingji Yu Shehui Fazhan Wunian Jihua (Five-Year Plan of the National Economy and Social Development)'.
Sauvy, Alfred. 1952. 'TROIS MONDES, UNE PLANÈTE'. *L'Observateur*, 14 August.
Shi, Lin, ed. 1989. *Dangdai zhongguo de duiwai jingji hezuo* (Foreign Economic Cooperation of Contemporary China). Beijing: Zhongguo shehui kexue chubanshe (China Social Science Press).

Shu, Yun. 2009. 'Jiuzheng Yu Guoli Bufu de Duiwai Yuanzhu: Zhongguo Waiyuan Wangshi (Correcting the Aid-Giving That Is Incompatible with the State Strength: Memories of Chinese Foreign Aid)'. *Tongzhou Gongjin* 1: 40–44.

State Council of the PRC (People's Republic of China). 2011. 'China's Foreign Aid'. State Council of the People's Republic of China. http://news.xinhuanet.com/english2010/china/2011-04/21/c_13839683.htm.

———. 2014. 'China's Foreign Aid'. State Council of the People's Republic of China. http://english.gov.cn/archive/white_paper/2014/08/23/content_281474982986592.htm.

Sun, Yihou. 1996. 'Shilun yingxiang nongye yuanzhu xiangmu xiaoyi de zhuyao yinsu (Main Factors Affecting the Effectiveness of Agricultural Foreign Aid Projects)'. *Guoji jingji hezuo* (International Economic Cooperation) 7: 54–56.

Tang, Lixia, Xiaoyun Li, and Gubo Qi. 2014. 'Zhongguo Dui Feizhou Nongye Yuanzhu Guanli Moshi de Yanhua Yu Chengxiao (Evolution and Effectiveness of the Management Modalities of Chinese Agricultural Aid to Africa)'. *Guoji Wenti Yanjiu* (International Studies) 6: 29–40.

Tang, Zhengping. 2002. 'Qianjing Guangkuo de Zhongfei Nongye Hezuo (China-Africa Agricultural Cooperation Has Bright Prospects)'. *Xiya Feizhou* (West Asia and Africa) 2: 13–17.

Tugendhat, Henry, and Dawit Alemu. 2016. 'Chinese Agricultural Training Courses for African Officials: Between Power and Partnerships'. *World Development* 81 (May): 71–81.

WFP (World Food Programme). 2015. 'Contributions to WFP: Comparative Figures and Five-Year Aggregate Ranking'. http://documents.wfp.org/stellent/groups/public/documents/research/wfp232961.pdf.

Xiao, Zongzhi, and Derong Zhang. 2002. 'Zhongguo Wushi Duonian Lai de Duiwai Jingji Jishu Yuanzhu Pingxi (On China's Economical & Technical Assistance to Foreign Countries During 50 Years or More)'. *Beijing Keji Daxue Xuebao Kehui Kexue Ban* (Journal of University of Science and Technology Beijing/Social Sciences Edition) 18 (4): 80–83.

Yu, Wenjing, and Yu Wang. 2015. 'The Contribution Rate of Technology Advances to Agricultural Development Is to Be Above 56% (Woguo Nongye Jishu Jinbu Gongxianlv Jiang Chaoguo 56%)'. *Xinhua News Agency*, 27 December. http://news.xinhuanet.com/fortune/2015-12/27/c_1117592182.htm.

Yun, Wenju. 1998. 'Zhongfei hezuo kaifa nongye de zhanlue xuanze (Strategic Choices of China-Africa Agricultural Cooperative Development)'. *Zhongguo ruan kexue* (China Soft Science) 12: 96–102.

———. 2000a. '21 shiji de zhongfei nongye hezuo (Sino-Africa Agricultural Cooperation in the 21st Century)'. *Xiya Feizhou* (West Asia and Africa) 5: 38–42.

———. 2000b. 'Cong guoji yuanzhu de fazhan kan zhongguo duifei nongye yuanzhu (The Development of International Aid and China's Agricultural Aid to Africa)'. *Xiya Feizhou* (West Asia and Africa) 2: 17–23.

Zhou, Enlai. 1964. 'The Eight Principles of Foreign Economic and Technical Cooperation'. In *Selected Works of Zhou Enlai in Diplomacy*. Beijing: Central Party Literature Press.

Zhou, Hong. 2008. 'Zhongguo Duiwai Yuanzhu Yu Gaige Kaifang 30 Nian (China's Foreign Aid and 30 Years of Reform)'. *Shijie Jingji Yu Zhengzhi* (World Economics and Politics) 11: 33–43.

Zhou, Jianjun, and Qiang Wang. 1997. 'Xin Xingshi Xia Dui Feizhou Nongye Yuanzhu de Tantao (Agricultural Aid to Africa Under the New Circumstances)'. *Guoji Jingji Hezuo* (International Economic Cooperation) 3: 9–11.

CHAPTER 3

China's Agro-Development Cooperation with Africa: The Innovative Agro-Aid Model

In the previous chapter, I have outlined the historical trajectory of Chinese half-century-long agricultural cooperation with Africa with the hope to demonstrate the roots and logics for its contemporary practice. I have also briefly introduced the three distinctive models of China's current development cooperation in African agriculture and already expanded on the 'traditional agro-aid' model. The present chapter and the one that follows will examine, respectively, the 'innovative agro-aid' and the 'agribusiness' models that feature most prominently in the current phase of China-Africa agricultural cooperation. To start with, this chapter is going to first investigate the 'innovative agro-aid' model, and specifically, China's flagship Agriculture Technology Demonstration Centre (ATDC) project that stands out as the very epitome of this model.

As distinct from the earlier 'pure aid' period (1960–1970s) and transition period (1980–1990s), the agricultural cooperation in the new century entails more clearly the 'win-win, mutual-development' concept, combines both development and commercial objectives and activities, and accordingly involves a diversity of public and private actors. That said, as noted in Chapter 2, the evolution of Chinese international development practice has not only been a response to the changing priorities of the government's foreign policy in different time periods, but also a reflection of the more internally driven process of China's foreign aid reforms. In this regard, the ATDCs, while clearly demonstrating certain

© The Author(s) 2020
L. Jiang, *Beyond Official Development Assistance*,
Governing China in the 21st Century,
https://doi.org/10.1007/978-981-32-9507-0_3

historical continuity through a hybrid of agro-aid forms adopted before (e.g. farms, agro-technology demonstration/extension stations, experts dispatch), involve as well some of the mechanisms are intentionally designed to avoid problems experienced in the past few decades.

The ATDCs also differ from the 'agribusiness model' that is to be discussed in Chapter 4 where the corporate actors take a more proactive part while the government only an assisting role. The ATDCs, however, are still largely regarded as government aid projects, especially in the early stage of the centres, considering the evident financial and supervision responsibilities borne by the government, and the Chinese companies involved in theory only the implementing agencies. In line with this, the 'development' dimension is supposed to overweigh the 'commercial' one for the ATDCs; as will be shown later in more detail, the commercial gains are moderate in the near term, only in terms of business introduction, and even in the long run when the centres enter into fully commercial operations they are nonetheless still expected to perform 'public-interest functions'.

There are two parts in this chapter. The first part (Sect. 3.1) will introduce the objectives, actors and mechanisms of the ATDCs, along with their general developments since 2006. The second part (Sect. 3.2) will flesh out the ATDC story by providing a detailed case study on one of the earliest and highly ranked (by Chinese government) centres—the one in Mozambique. It will examine and evaluate the actual performance of the Mozambican ATDC in terms of the three key dimensions—respectively the technical transfer, business introduction and project sustainability—against the objectives set for the ATDCs by the Chinese government.

3.1 ATDC: The Flagship Project of China's Innovative Agro-Aid in Africa

The project of Agricultural Technology Demonstration Centre ('ATDC' hereinafter) was first proposed at the Beijing Summit of the 3rd FOCAC in 2006. The Chinese government pledged to build 10 ATDCs in different African countries (FOCAC 2006). The number was then increased to 20 during the 4th FOCAC in 2009 (FOCAC 2009). By 2012, there had been in practice around 25 Chinese-funded ATDCs on the African continent, with the first batch of 14 centres having finished construction and been transferred to the host governments (Table 3.1).

Table 3.1 Chinese agriculture technology demonstration centres in Africa

No.	Host country	Chinese implementing agent(s)	Operational stages	Area (ha)	Cooperation fields
The first batch of 14 ATDCs					
1	Benin	China National Agricultural Development Group Co., Ltd.	C: 2009–2010 T: 2010–2013 B: 2014–now	51.6	Grains (e.g. maize), vegetables, livestock (e.g. chicken)
2	Cameroon	*Shanxi province* Shanxi State Farms and Land Reclamation Group Co., Ltd. *[TS: Northwest Agriculture and Forestry Technology University]*	C: 2009–2010 T: 2013–now	100	Rice, etc.
3	Republic of Congo	Chinese Academy of Tropical Agricultural Sciences	C: 2009–2011 T: 2012–2015 B: 2015–now	59	Grains (e.g. maize, cassava), vegetables, livestock (e.g. chicken); fodder production and processing; agricultural mechanization
4	Ethiopia	*Guangxi province* Guangxi Bagui Agricultural Science and Technology Co., Ltd. *[TS: Guangxi Agricultural Vocational College]*	C: 2010–2012 T: 2012–now	52	Grains, vegetables, and livestock (e.g. pigs, cows and chicken)
5	Liberia	*Hunan province* Longping High-tech Agriculture Co., Ltd.	C: 2009–2010 T: 2010–2014 B: 2014–now	32.6	Hybrid rice, etc.
6	Mozambique	*Hubei province* Lianfeng Overseas Agricultural Development Co., Ltd.	C: 2009–2010 T: 2012–2015 B: 2015–now	52	Grains (e.g. maize and rice), vegetables, livestock (e.g. pigs); agro-processing
7	Rwanda	*Fujian province* Fujian Agriculture and Forestry University	C: 2009–2011 T: 2011–2014 B: 2014–now	22.6	Grains, mulberry plantation and silkworm keeping; juncao cultivation, water-conservancy

(continued)

Table 3.1 (continued)

No.	Host country	Chinese implementing agent(s)	Operational stages	Area (ha)	Cooperation fields
8	South Africa	China National Agricultural Development Group Co., Ltd. [TS: Chinese Academy of Fishery Sciences]	C: 2009–2011 T: 2014–2017	0.47	Freshwater aquaculture
9	Sudan	Shandong province Shandong International Economic and Technical Cooperation Group Co., Ltd. [TS: Shandong Academy of Agricultural Sciences]	C: 2009–2011 T: 2012–2015 B: 2015–now	65	Grains (e.g. wheat, maize), vegetables, cotton, peanuts; water-conservancy
10	Tanzania	Chongqing Municipality Chongqing Seed Group Co., Ltd. [TS: Chongqing Academy of Agricultural Sciences]	C: 2009–2010 T: 2011–2014 B: 2015–now	62	Grains (e.g. rice, maize, soybeans), vegetables, flowers, livestock (e.g. chicken)
11	Togo	Jiangxi province Huachang International Economic and Technical Corporation	C: 2009–2011 T: 2012–2015 B: 2015–now	10	Rice, maize, etc.
12	Uganda	Sichuan province Huaqiao Fenghuang Group, Co., Ltd.	C: 2009–2010 T: 2011–2014 B: 2015–now	0.3	Freshwater aquaculture
13	Zambia	Jilin province Jilin Agriculture University	C: 2010–2011 T: 2012–2015 B: 2015–now	120	Grains (e.g. wheat, maize, soybeans), vegetables; agricultural mechanization
14	Zimbabwe	Chinese Academy of Agricultural Mechanization Sciences (Menoble)	C: 2009–2011 T: 2012–2015 B: 2015–now	109	Agricultural mechanization and irrigation

(continued)

Table 3.1 (continued)

No.	Host country	Chinese implementing agent(s)	Operational stages	Area (ha)	Cooperation fields
The second batch of 11 ATDCs					
15	Angola	Xinjiang Production and Construction Corps	Construction completed and transferred to Angola since 2019		
16	Central Africa Republic	Shanxi International Company	Memorandum of Understanding signed in 2012 *(has been postponed due to the domestic political turmoil)*		
17	Democratic Republic of the Congo	ZTE Energy	Under technology cooperation		
18		Zhejiang Huayou Guye Co., Ltd.	Feasibility to be conducted		
19	Equatorial Guinea	Ganliang Co., Ltd.	Under technology cooperation		
20	Malawi	China-Africa Cotton Co., Ltd.	Under technology cooperation		
21	Mali	Zijinhua Co., Ltd.	Agreement signed in 2012 *(has been postponed)*		
22	Mauritania	Mudanjiang Yanlinzhuanyuan Technology	Under technology cooperation		
23		Ningxia Jinfulai yangchanye Co., Ltd.	Under technology cooperation		
24	Nigeria	COVEC	Feasibility to be conducted		
25	Zimbabwe	Anhui State Farms and Land Reclamation Group Co., Ltd.	TBC		

Source The author based on media reports and fieldwork, updated by May 2019
(C: Project Construction, T: Technology Cooperation, B: Business/Commercial Operation, TS: Technical Support)

3.1.1 Objectives: A Strong Mutual-Development Feature

In line with the 'core spirit' of China's contemporary development cooperation with Africa (Sects. 2.2 and 2.4), the ATDCs have carried an evident feature of pursuing mutual-development objectives through the implementation of the projects. According to the key official document that guides the practice of the ATDCs ('ATDC Guidance' hereinafter), issued jointly by China's Ministry of Commerce (MOC) and Ministry of Agriculture (MOA), the purposes of the ATDCs were explained as follows (MOC and MOA of the PRC 2011):

I. To serve China's foreign strategy and promote bilateral relations with the recipient countries;
II. To help increase grain production, improve agricultural technology and enhance food security of the recipient countries;
III. To provide a platform for Chinese companies to develop business in Africa and promote China's 'Agriculture Going Out' policy;
IV. To build the ATDC into a base for agro-technology experiment and research, demonstration and extension, human resources training and display.

There is, first and foremost, a clear Africa-oriented development objective involved in the ATDCs. The limited input as well as the low level of agro-technology has been one of the biggest hindrances to the productivity enhancement of African agriculture, whereas in China the success story of agricultural development in the past decades has been greatly attributed to the rapid advancement of agro-technology underpinned by the government's accentuated efforts to strengthen agro-technology education, research as well as extension system across the country (Huang 2010). An important objective of the ATDCs, therefore, is to promote the transfer of Chinese advanced agricultural technology to Africa through the realization of the four tasks designed for the centre, namely demonstration, training, research, and display[1] (Objective IV),

---

[1] Among the four tasks, demonstration and training, mostly targeted at agricultural producers and technicians, are more central to the technology transfer purpose and therefore the main focus of the ATDCs. Research is more a supportive function that is often carried out alongside and closely serves the aim of demonstration and training. And display, open to the broader public, usually involves a general introduction to Chinese agro-technology and experience, among others (MOC and MOA of the PRC 2011; Interview 8 November 2013).

with an ultimate aim to help increase the grain production and thus enhance the food security of the recipient countries (Objective II). It is also hoped that by achieving these ends, the bilateral diplomatic relations between China and African countries could meanwhile be bolstered (Objective I). This dimension, therefore, is termed by the Chinese government as the 'public-interest function' of the ATDCs, for all the activities in this line are supposed to be non-commercial and purely for the developmental benefits of the recipient countries.

Particularly worth noting here is also Objective III, which differentiates ATDCs from those more traditional forms of Chinese agro-aid in Africa (Sect. 2.4), that is the intention of the project designers trying to make the ATDCs in the meantime a platform for Chinese agro-companies to 'go out' and conduct agribusiness abroad. The ATDCs, therefore, also serve the function of introducing Chinese companies to Africa and facilitating their agribusiness on the continent. This dimension, termed as 'business introduction' in the book, explicitly demonstrates the self-oriented development agenda entailed in the ATDC project; that is, more specifically, the seeking of business opportunities for Chinese companies. In addition to that, similar to the practice of other Chinese aid projects nowadays, the ATDCs are accompanied by, and also expected to promote, export of Chinese agro-equipment and materials,[2] among other things (MOC and MOA of the PRC 2012).

A last dimension that is not shown in the statement of purposes of the ATDCs but surely bears considerable significance in terms of the pursuits of the centres is the project sustainability concern. The sustainability issue derives from China's decades-long practice of agricultural aid on the continent (Chapter 2) and has been widely observed by practitioners and scholars (Shi 1989; Cai 1992; Sun 1996; Zhou and Wang 1997; Yun 2000; Bräutigam 2009). Almost all the Chinese earlier agro-aid projects could not escape the cycle that, no matter how successful the initial period of the project proved to be, the project would soon fall into disrepair once the Chinese team left.[3] In most cases, the reason for this

---

[2] Most of these equipment and materials are donated by the Chinese government, and in most cases exempt from tariffs due to their aid nature.

[3] Few exceptions exist, for instance, in Mali and Sierra Leone, where the Chinese-aided agro-projects during the early years are still operational now; however, in these two countries, the projects have since been managed by the Chinese whereas the host governments act only as shareholders.

Table 3.2 Evaluation indicators of the ATDC

Diplomatic influence	Improvement of the agricultural development and food security of the host country	Promotion of China's 'agriculture going-out and inviting-in' policy	Sustainable development
15%	25%	15%	**45%**

Source The author based on the Evaluation Plan of the ATDC (MOC and MOA of the PRC 2012)

resides in that the aid-recipient countries lacked the financial, managerial and technical capability to keep the projects going on their own (Shi 1989; Cai 1992; Sun 1996; Zhou and Wang 1997). Against this background, the sustainability issue was brought to the fore in the designing process of the ATDCs (Xu and Qin 2011; Qin 2016). The emphasis on sustainability can be seen from the performance evaluation system of the ATDCs, in which the planning and realization of sustainable development occupies 45% of the total scores, more than any other indicators (Table 3.2). And the sustainability concern per se is also for the benefits of both a sustainable developmental effect for the recipient countries and 'value for money' for the Chinese side.

3.1.2 Actors: Government–Company Cooperation

In most cases, the ATDCs were run by Chinese agro-companies.[4] While it is not entirely new for the Chinese government to incorporate company actors into aid projects, which could be traced back to the 1980s, it is something new, however, to have private firms involved, such as in the ATDCs in Ethiopia, Liberia and Togo (Table 3.1). Considering the origin of this type of practice, the primary reasons for including company actors are for greater efficiency and sustainability of the projects (Sects. 2.2 and 2.3). To be qualified to operate and manage an ATDC, the companies, in principle, have to be national or provincial level leading agro-companies in China, which should have strong financial, managerial

---

[4] There are also several cases, for instance, in Congo, Rwanda, Zambia and Zimbabwe (see Table 4.2), that the ATDCs are run by Chinese universities or research institutes. They sometimes also register a company under their names to operate the Centre.

and technical capabilities (MOC and MOA of the PRC 2011). The companies need to go through a bidding process, though this is not fully open or competitive, given that the local and central Chinese governments have significant influence over the decision-making (Tang et al. 2014).

While the companies are the main role players in the daily management of the ATDCs, government actors especially those from the Chinese side still take a great responsibility in planning, supervising, and particularly in the first three years of the project, financing the operation of the ATDCs. The MOC and the MOA are the most involved central-level government actors on the Chinese side. They cooperatively macro-plan, facilitate and supervise the ATDC project. In most cases, each of the ATDC-hosting countries is twinned with one specific province (or provincial-level city) in China (Table 3.1), as designated by the central government. Apart from providing general support to the project-implementing company, the local Chinese governments are also expected to play a leading role in promoting agro-companies from their province to invest in the twinned African country (MOC and MOA of the PRC 2011). On the recipient side, various counterpart government agencies are also involved in the implementation of the ATDCs, but played only an assisting role.

Comparatively, the government–firm cooperative form as shown in the ATDCs bears certain similarity to the Public–Private Partnership (PPP) model that recently emerged in the Northern development cooperation field (Sect. 1.2). It is similar to the PPP model for its inclusion of partnership with a range of non-public actors, typically the private companies but also other sorts of corporate and/or non-for-profit entities (Table 3.1). It, however, could be regarded at best as a sort of quasi-PPP arrangement. That is firstly because business model—the defining feature of 'development PPP'—is only visible in the final 'Commercial Operation Stage' of the ATDCs (Sect. 3.1.3). And secondly, the non-public actors involved in the ATDCs play to a much lesser extent a role of 'resource partner' that is often highly emphasized in the Northern development PPP model; in the ATDC project, however, the non-public actors act largely as the 'implementers' of the government project, and it still remains to see whether and to what extent they would put in more resources, particularly in financial terms, in the 'Commercial Operation Stage'.

3.1.3 Modalities: A Mix of Technical Assistance and Business Model

Corresponding with the multi-dimensional motives and the diversity of actors involved in the ATDCs are the mixed modalities that combine both more traditional aid form of agro-technical assistance as well as an innovative element of commercial operation. Each ATDC has three operational stages: Project Construction Stage, Technical Cooperation Stage and Commercial Operation Stage. The Project Construction Stage normally takes about one year. While the host governments need to offer the required logistical support such as providing land, electricity and water, the Chinese side is in charge of the construction of infrastructure, as well as the provision of any needed agro-equipment and materials. In most cases, the construction is contracted to Chinese companies, but involves employment of local workers in the host countries. The majority of the fees incurred in this stage are paid by the Chinese government, averaged at about ¥40 million (approx. $660,000) for each of the ATDCs (MOC and MOA of the PRC 2011, the author's fieldwork).

Once the construction is completed, the ATDCs are transferred to the host governments and become the state assets of the latter. This also usually indicates the commencement of the three-year Technical Cooperation Stage. The main tasks for the ATDCs in this stage are to perform the four 'public-interest functions' as mentioned earlier, i.e. agro-technology research, demonstration and extension, training and display. A Chinese technical team is assigned to the ATDC to undertake these tasks. Moreover, in fulfilment of the 'business introduction' objective, the centre also acts as a platform for Chinese agro-companies, who are seeking agribusiness opportunities into the host country. This latter dimension is fundamental because through it the centre starts planning and setting the basis for the succeeding Commercial Operation Stage. To do that, many of the ATDCs set up small-scale agribusinesses based on the centres in preparation for the business-oriented operation in the future (MOC and MOA of the PRC 2011, the authors' fieldwork). In this stage, the implementing companies designated by the Chinese government take the lead in managing the centres on the daily basis. Financially, the Chinese government covers most of the centres' daily operations, including the funds needed to carry out the routine activities such as agro-research, demonstration and training, as well as the salary of the Chinese staff (MOC and MOA 2011, the author's fieldwork).

The host governments instead play a facilitation role in this stage, assisting, to varying degrees, with the technical and management issues and also sharing a small part of the financial responsibility (the author's fieldwork).

After the three-year technical cooperation ends, the ATDCs then enter the Commercial Operation Stage. In this stage, the ATDCs are expected to be able to establish a market-oriented, integrated agribusiness value chain. Meanwhile, the original 'public-interest functions' are supposed to remain and even to be expanded and diversified. As far as it was designed in the ATDC Guidance, the Chinese companies will continue taking full charge of the centres' management at the Commercial Operation Stage. Financially, it is hoped that the Chinese government only covers the operational fees of the ATDCs for the first three years of technical cooperation; afterwards, the centres should try to fund themselves through incomes from the commercial operation (Xu and Qin 2011). The specific roles and responsibilities of the local partners were not specified in the ATDC Guidance and thus need to be further negotiated on the ground on a case-specific basis (MOC and MOA of the PRC 2011).

While this stage is in line with the 'business introduction' objective, the purpose of having this prolonged cooperation period and adopting the business model is also, and perhaps more importantly, to ensure the sustainability of the ATDCs. As mentioned in Chapter 2, one of the important reform measures adopted in the 1980s that aimed to improve aid sustainability was to strengthen 'management cooperation' in the post-construction phase, which may take different forms such as: (1) sole management by the Chinese side on a entrustment or lease term (given that after transfer the project is part of the host country's assets), or (2) co-management through joint venture created by both sides (Shi 1989; State Council of the PRC 2011). Either a Chinese-led or joint venture way of management could be applied to the ATDC project. It could also be, in theory, an independent management by the recipient side as long as they are considered capable of operating the centre on their own. The specific cooperation model, particularly the unspecified responsibilities of the local partners, will be negotiated between the two sides as the Technical Cooperation Stage nears the end. The original plan as seen in the ATDC Guidance (MOC and MOA of the PRC 2011), however, seems to suggest a Chinese-led management model.

As mentioned in the beginning of the chapter, the ATDCs bear two key responsibilities—development-oriented *agro-technology transfer* and commercially oriented *business introduction*. Apart from that, *project sustainability* also stands as an important concern, which has both development and commercial implications. The following section, therefore, will be dedicated to examine how these three functions and concerns have been dealt with in the operation of the ATDCs in Mozambique and South Africa.

3.2 Case Studies: Chinese ATDCs in Mozambique and South Africa

3.2.1 ATDC in Mozambique: The Key Case

The Chinese ATDC in Mozambique ('Moz centre' or 'centre' hereinafter) was launched by the then Chinese president Hu Jintao during his state visit to Mozambique in 2007 and became one of the *earliest* ATDCs that were put into practice after the FOCAC pledges in 2006. It was further regarded and promoted as one of the *most successful* cases by the Chinese government in different occasions; for instance, according to an evaluation jointly conducted by Chinese MOC and MOA in 2013, the Moz centre was ranked the 1st among the 15 Chinese ATDCs in Africa that were under examination (Zhang and Zhang 2015). Considering also the fact that Mozambique is one of the *key agro-cooperation partners* with China in Africa as well as the centre's *close links with other Chinese agribusiness projects*, the Moz centre is thus justifiably chosen as the key case to examine the 'innovative agro-aid model' of China's agro-development cooperation with Africa.

Soon after the centre launch in 2007, a delegation was assigned by Chinese MOA to Mozambique to conduct a feasibility survey on the project. With the assistance of the Ministério de Agricultura (MINAG) and Ministério de Ciência e Tecnologia (MCT) of Mozambique, both sides finally chose a location for the centre in Boane, approx. 23 km southeast of Maputo, with an area of 50 hectares. The construction of the centre started in 2009 and finished in 2010. In July 2011, the centre was formally transferred to the Mozambican government (and thereby became national assets of the latter). From April 2012, the Moz centre entered into the Technical Cooperation Stage (TCS). According to the

Fig. 3.1 The ATDC in Mozambique, Boane, Maputo Province, 18 October 2013

initial design for the ATDCs, the Moz centre should in theory start its Commercial Operation Stage from 2015 (Fig. 3.1).[5]

Lianfeng Overseas Agricultural Development Company ('Lianfeng' hereinafter)—a Chinese state-owned farming enterprise (SFE, see Sect. 4.1.2) affiliated with the Bureau of State Farms and Land Reclamation (BSFLR) under the Hubei provincial government of China—was selected as the implementing agent to take full charge of the centre's construction and the succeeding management activities on the day-to-day basis. On the Mozambican side, MCT was the designated authority in charge of assisting in technical and managerial issues. In addition, the MINAG and the associated IIAM, Instituto de Investigação Agrária de Moçambique, also played an important facilitating role, particularly in the initial phase; for instance, the centre's land was actually provided by the IIAM and they were in reality neighbours to each other[6] (Interview 14 November 2013).

---

[5] The first-time fieldwork on the Moz centre was conducted during the period of September–December 2013, and the second-time during December 2014 and January 2015. After that I have maintained constant contacts with some of the key informants working in the centre through telephone, messages and meetings (in a third city) from 2015 until June 2017 to keep updated on the developments of the centre.

[6] For more details on the mechanisms and politics of the Mozambican government actors surrounding the ATDC issue, see Chichava et al. (2014).

Technology Transfer

The main areas of the Mozambican centre for agro-technology transfer concentrated on crop farming (e.g. rice, maize, vegetables) and animal husbandry (e.g. pig farming). These were largely decided according to the local conditions and based on negotiations between the Mozambican and Chinese sides. For instance, rice and maize were chosen because they form the main types of staple foods in Mozambique, though rice is more prevalent in urban areas; and the idea of developing pig farming came from the fact that standardized pig farms were still largely underdeveloped despite a growing demand for pork consumption in the country. Specifically, some of the key agro-technologies targeted include, for instance, rice direct-seeding, mechanical harvesting, chemical weed control, water-saving irrigation, fertilizing, plastic mulching, integrated pest prevention and control, and live pig keeping (Interviews 4 November 2013b and 8 November 2013) (Fig. 3.2).

The agro-technology transfer was conducted mostly through **demonstration and training**. The trainees were selected from the ten provinces across the country by the Mozambican government, specifically through the MCT and MINAG,[7] and largely fell into three major categories: farmers, technicians and officials. Among them, *ordinary smallholder farmers* were given the greatest emphasis because it was believed by the Chinese staff that, by training the actual front-line 'agricultural producers', the technology transfer could achieve the most direct and beneficial effects (for they could learn the agro-techniques and then use them immediately). Around 6–7 training sessions were arranged every year for the small farmers, with each session lasting for 10 days and focusing on one specific agro-technique (e.g. direct rice-seeding or chemical weed control, as listed above). They were taught some very basic and practical farming techniques in order for them to easily put what they learned at the centre into practice at home. The second group was *agricultural*

---

[7] In terms of selection of the smallholder farmers, the MCT partner said that they would choose (through the local branches of MCT and MINAG) from those who registered with agricultural associations, and there was no specific criteria for the selection expect for an acceptable health situation (Interview 14 November 2013). As will be mentioned later in the training model, the Chinese experts felt that maybe the Mozambican partner should select some relatively educated and experienced farmers, for they found a big knowledge gap when teaching the local farmers, which made the training process rather difficult, though they had later adjusted the course design to address the problem (Interview 18 November 2013). The Chinese experts, however, did not communicate this trainee selection issue with the Mozambican side.

Fig. 3.2 Vegetable fields and reservoir in the centre, Boane, 18 October 2013

technicians. There were 3 sessions for them per year and each of those lasted for one month. The training courses for technicians were designed at a higher level, covering agro-techniques such as rice breeding and pad management, among others. The centre also offered courses for *agricultural officials*. These courses were at a lower frequency compared to the others, only one 3-to-5-day session per year and revolving mostly around management matters such as introducing the experiences of running state farms in China. At times, the centre also provided study or internship opportunities to *college students* upon requests from the Mozambican side, which may last from several weeks up to 6 months (Interviews 18 October 2013, 4 November 2013a and 14 November 2013).

The training adopted a combined method of in-class teaching and fieldwork. Due to the fact that none of the Chinese agro-experts at the centre could speak English, Portuguese or any local language, the teaching process had to go through a translator; however, there was only one Chinese–English translator and none Chinese–Portuguese translator before 2016.[8] In practice, in order to counter the language barrier, what happened more often was a sort of 'collaborative teaching' conducted

---

[8] After 2016, the centre finally managed to hire some Chinese-Portuguese translator (first a Mozambican national who used to study in China and later a Chinese national), but according to the centre director, there were still communication problems particularly in daily work, both due to the mistrust between each other (for the former) and the less-qualified level of language (for the latter) (Interviews 19 October 2015 and 23 June 2017). Indeed, even for the Chinese-English translator (a Chinese national) before 2016, the Mozambican partner reflected that they found language a big barrier between the two sides and they could not always understand each other in day-to-day communications (Interview 14 November 2013).

by the Chinese experts together with their Mozambican colleagues. Specifically, the Chinese experts would first explain in English (through the Chinese–English translator) to the Mozambican staff from MCT or IIAM who usually had some agricultural background, and then let the latter take the lead in teaching the trainees in Portuguese or local languages. They also used bilingual (English/Portuguese) handouts and picture illustrations to make the contents easier for the trainees to understand. After that, the Chinese experts would demonstrate the agro-techniques just taught in the outdoor paddy fields and guide the trainees to apply the techniques by themselves. Given the smallholder farmers often had little agro-technology or even education background, the experts sometimes faced difficulties in explaining to the farmers some of the agro-technologies, especially when accompanied by theoretical contents. To counter this problem, the training was re-tailored to the actual abilities of the farmers by the Chinese experts, whereby theoretical contents were greatly reduced and correspondingly the time spent in the fields was much increased (Interviews 4 November 2013a and 14 November 2013).

The training was mostly funded by the Chinese government during the three-year TCS, while the Mozambican side shared some financial responsibility in covering some of the logistics fees, such as the transportation and accommodation costs of the trainees (Interview 14 November 2013). During the first two years of the TCS, in 2012 and 2013, more than 600 Mozambican smallholder farmers, technicians and officials received training at the centre (Interview 18 October 2013). There, however, was not yet any formal follow-up or feedback mechanism for the training results, mainly due to the lack of financial means (Interview 14 November 2013). However, basic feedback from the farmer trainees showed that they found the techniques that they learned at the centre useful for their production increase (e.g. the technique of plastic mulching). Some of the farmers reported a yield increase by 2–4 times through applying the Chinese technology to their farming practice; furthermore, these trained farmers were also able to play a demonstration role in their local areas (Interviews 4 November 2013a and 14 November 2013) (Fig. 3.3).

Apart from demonstration and training, the Moz centre also conducted some *research* activities, to a much lesser extent though,[9] which

---

[9] To recall the introduction of the main tasks of the ATDCs in Sect. 3.1.1, 'research' was designed as one of the key functions of the centres but not treated as important as 'demonstration' and 'training'. This is partly because the capital and human resources that

Fig. 3.3 The Mozambican workers hired by the centre to grow rice. They were trained by the Chinese experts first and were now being able to work independently in the rice paddies. Boane, 28 October 2013

was concentrated primarily on seed testing. The centre served as one of the experimental stations of the Chinese 'Green Super Rice' initiative[10] that was taking place in a number of Asian and African countries. By 2013, the centre had tested more than 100 different crop varieties, both Chinese and local types (e.g. rice and cotton mostly Chinese; maize and vegetables mostly Mozambican), and reported the results to both governments (Interview 8 November 2013).

pure agricultural research requires is far beyond what the centres could effectively offer (Interview 8 November 2013). Thus, 'research' is usually constrained to a few limited areas that closely links and contributes to the 'demonstration' and 'training' activities of the ATDCs.

[10] The initiative was a joint program by the Chinese Academy of Agricultural Sciences and the Bill Gates Foundation.

Unexpectedly, the seed testing conducted by the centre turned out to become a subject of disagreement and controversy between the two sides. The Mozambican side called for more tests of Mozambican varieties as they would probably be better suited to the local taste and were also more affordable to the local people (Interview 14 November 2013, Chichava and Fingermann 2015). The Chinese experts, on the other hand, believed that their main responsibility revolved around introducing higher-yield Chinese varieties into the host country in order to realize the 'technology transfer' objective; in light of this, the aim of seed testing was to examine whether certain Chinese varieties were suitable to be grown and extended in Mozambique (Interview 8 November 2013).[11] Also, they expressed the difficulty in procuring local varieties given that there were very few seed suppliers on the market. And they did not think that their Mozambican partners had committed adequately to providing the centre with, or at least facilitating its procurement of, the local varieties needed for testing (Interviews 4 November 2013a and 8 November 2013). Despite the disagreement around the seed testing issue, there did not seem to be adequate communication between the two sides; while the Mozambican requirement seemed to be somehow ignored, the Chinese did not express their concerns and difficulties to their counterparts either.

Business Introduction
In terms of the 'business introduction' dimension of the centre, the ATDC in Mozambique seemed to have quite successfully brought Chinese agribusiness into the host country. Their efforts could be seen from three aspects. First, Lianfeng, the project-implementing company, had started agribusiness based on the centre. Along with performing the centre's technology transfer functions, Lianfeng also developed *crop and animal production* by using the land of the centre (approx. 50 ha, see Table 3.3) and already distributed the output into the local market. The main products were rice, vegetables (particularly some Chinese varieties) and pork. Much of these products were sold to the Chinese community in Mozambique such as the Chinese supermarkets and Chinese

---

[11] There was also speculation that links the centre to a greater strategy of the Chinese government trying to distribute Chinese seeds in the global market for commercial benefits (Chichava et al. 2014).

Table 3.3 Initial plan of land use for the centre's future agribusiness (Unit: [ha])

Total	Rice	Vegetables	Animal and aquaculture	Cotton seed production
50	25	5	10	10

Source Interview 8 November 2013

companies based in Maputo (the author's fieldwork[12]). The products were also popular among Mozambicans due to the lower prices and different varieties (Interviews 18 October 2013, 4 November 2013a and 23 June 2017). *Seed production*, both Chinese and Mozambican varieties, was also deemed promising and regarded by the Chinese as another possible business option in the future (Interviews 18 October 2013 and 8 November 2013). The seed sector of Mozambique, as briefly mentioned earlier, was not well developed and there was inadequate seed supply on the local market. Lianfeng, along with its shareholder Hubei BSFLR, on the other hand, had special expertise in seed production. In addition, the company also was considering the possibility of providing paid *agro-technical extension services*, which was already common practice in China, once the three-year technical cooperation was due to end. However, for that to happen, support from the Mozambican government, for example, in the form of giving agro-subsidies to the farmers, was required—as it was envisaged by the Chinese experts that these services would be uneconomical to the majority of the local farmers (Interview 18 October 2013) (Fig. 3.4).

Second, Lianfeng had expanded its agro-investment in Mozambique. Apart from the business enterprises based on the centre, Lianfeng also participated in a couple of agribusiness projects in other provinces of Mozambique in collaboration with some private agro-companies from Hubei (the author's fieldwork). Third, the Moz centre had served as a platform to introduce and assist other Chinese agro-companies to invest in Mozambican agricultural sector. They had worked closely with several Chinese agro-companies and individuals, providing information and technical support that facilitates their investment. An individual

---

[12] Some of the information was gained through the author's site visits and general conversations with people on the sites, but not through formal interviews; these are referenced to as 'the author's fieldwork' in the present chapter and hereinafter.

Fig. 3.4 People queuing to buy the produce from the ATDC and to sell on the local markets. Boane, 18 October 2013

agro-investor from Shandong province of China, for instance, visited the centre regularly to seek technical guidance on his 300-ha rice field near Maputo (Interviews 29 December 2014 and 14 January 2015). Wanbao, as mentioned earlier, also gained plenty of assistance from the centre, particularly in its initial period of investment, including the selection of the project site and rice varieties; it has since maintained constant contacts with the centre (Interviews 4 November 2013b and 23 June 2017). The same happened also to Hefeng, another Hubei company producing rice in the central province of Sofala (23 June 2017). As commented by the manager of a state-owned agricultural enterprise, 'If we find our investment work a bit easier here, this should be attributed to the ATDC' (Interview 10 January 2015).[13]

[13] It was later (after the author's fieldwork) revealed by a research by FECC of Chinese MOA that, through the Moz centre, eight companies from China's Hubei province were introduced to Mozambique and invested six agro-projects across the country with a total farming area of about 18,000 hectares (Qin 2016).

Project Sustainability

The three-year TCS for the Moz centre was due to end in May 2015. Future development plans for the centre, once the technical cooperation phase ends, had yet to be finalized between the two governments by the time the second-time fieldwork was conducted in early 2015. The general feeling from the Chinese side, however, was that the Mozambican counterpart was not capable of operating the centre independently. A likely scenario by then seemed to be that the Moz centre would have an extension of the TCS for another three years, as already requested by the Mozambican government, and in that case, Lianfeng would continue to run the centre[14] (Interviews 18 October 2013, 4 November 2013a and 29 December 2014).

First, *financially*, although the centre had been able to earn economic profits on its own terms and had conceived a business expansion plan for the future, the profits that had been gained from the commercial operation were not sufficient to cover the running costs of the centre. Similarly, it was anticipated by the Chinese staff that future profits would not be adequate to run the centre either, which was primarily due to the limited resources the centre had—only around 50 hectares of land and a handful of staff (Interviews 8 November 2013 and 29 December 2014). From the *managerial* point of view, although the Mozambican side had contributed greatly to the centre's training activities, it had not fully participated in the management process. Although positions were opened and offices were made available to the Mozambican staff, they only engaged on a part-time basis (as they also worked for the MCT). Seemingly, they went to the centre only when they had specific problems that needed to be addressed. While the Mozambican partners sometimes complained that they did not know what was happening at the ATDC (Interviews 4 November 2013a and 14 November 2013), the Chinese felt helpless as they surely could not force their Mozambican colleagues to work with them on a daily basis—although to them, working together seemed to be the most effective way to keep the centre's operation transparent to their Mozambican counterparts (Interview 4 November 2013a).

---

[14]According to a more recent interview conducted by the author (23 June 2017), the Moz centre is currently under the Commercial Operation Stage, not receiving funding from Chinese government any more—though not without difficulty in making ends meet.

In fact, in response to the abovementioned 'lack of transparency' complaint, the Chinese negotiated with the Mozambican government several times and finally managed to persuade them to assign at least three staff to the centre. However, due to a number of bureaucratic reasons, there was in effect still no Mozambican staff working at the centre. For instance, the Mozambican staff considered Boane too far out, especially given that their government did not pay for the petrol; also, the lack of Internet at the centre was a deterrent (Interview 4 November 2013a).[15] The Chinese travelled to the MCT two to three times per week, but mainly to address administrative affairs, such as visa and invitation issuing, rather than management issues (Interviews 18 October 2013 and 4 November 2013a). This lack of participation raised doubts concerning the ability of the Mozambican side to operate the ATDC on its own. To the least, it is seemingly challenging for them to do so.

3.2.2 ATDC in South Africa: The Comparative Case

The China-South Africa Agriculture Technology Demonstration Centre ('SA centre' or 'centre' hereinafter) was also one of the first 14 ATDCs (Table 3.1). As a neighbouring country in Southern Africa but with distinctive dynamics in terms of domestic agriculture and agro-cooperation with China, South Africa (and its ATDC) is chosen here as a complementary case to Mozambique in order to provide a comparative perspective. A broader plan on economic and technological cooperation between China and South Africa was initiated in 2007; in the same year, a feasibility study for the SA centre was completed and the site was selected by the South African government at Gariep Dam in the central province of Free State. The preliminary exchange letter between the Chinese Ambassador in South Africa and the Minister of Agriculture and Land Affairs of South Africa was signed between 2008 and 2009. The construction of the centre commenced in 2009 and finished in 2011. In October 2013, the final exchange letter was signed between the two

---

[15] According to a more recent update, the situation has improved with a few Mozambican colleagues now working at the centre full time; that said, things remain the same in that the two groups of people (Chinese and Mozambican) worked in a rather independent way (e.g. separate offices), without too much interactions or 'collaboration' in the real sense (Interview 23 June 2017).

Fig. 3.5 The ATDC in South Africa, Gariep Dam, Free State, 29 January 2015

sides along with a proposed operational plan, which signified the official transfer of the ATDC to the South African government and the completion of all the necessary preparation work. From February 2014, the ATDC formally entered the Technical Cooperation Stage (TCS) (Fig. 3.5).

China National Agricultural Development Corporation (CNADC) was the implementing agent of the centre designated by the Chinese government. CNADC is one of the six central SAEs (state-owned agricultural enterprises, see Sect. 4.1.2) that are under direct control of the State-owned Assets Supervision and Administration Commission of Chinese State Council. More specifically, it is China Agriculture International Development Co Ltd. (CAIDC), one of CNADC's subsidiaries, that took the actual responsibility of running the centre. CAIDC also worked closely with China Freshwater Fish Research Centre (FFRC), with the latter dispatching aqua-experts and providing technical support to the centre. On the South African side, the most relevant actors were Free State Department of Agriculture and Rural Development (FSDARD) and South African National Department of Agriculture, Forestry and Fisheries (DAFF). A number of South African staff, including two full-time staff based in the centre, were working together with the Chinese in running the ATDC. According to the preliminary exchange letter, while the South African side—particularly the FSDARD—played more a supportive role in the TCS (2014–2016), it was supposed to run the centre independently once this stage ends.

Technology Transfer

The focus of the SA centre was on freshwater aquaculture, which was decided through bilateral negotiation between China and South Africa. Being fairly advanced in agro-technology in general, freshwater aquaculture was identified as a relatively weak area of the South African agriculture (Interview 29 January 2015). It was also in line with the sectorial development of South African agriculture given the fact that aquaculture is gaining more emphasis and support from the government.[16] From the Chinese experts' perspective, freshwater aquaculture was deemed meaningful in that it could help enrich the sources of protein intake and reduce poverty in the local area of the Free State. They also believed that South Africa had the economic, technical and social conditions required to develop this sector (Interview 30 January 2015b). Some of the key knowledge and technologies covered by the centre's demonstration and training activities included, for example, freshwater fish biological features, fish breeding and farming techniques, fish health, fish harvesting, hatchery management and so on. Apart from aqua-production per se, the courses also incorporated downstream stages, such as fish processing and marketing, from 2015 on. These two parts of the training targeted the same group of trainees to make sure they can grasp the entire value chain of freshwater fish farming (Interview 29 January 2015).

As for the trainees, it is the South African side, specifically the FSDARD, that determined who was eligible to receive the training (Harding 2014). The trainees included smallholder farmers, technicians/extension officers and government officials. During the first year of the technical cooperation stage, 9 training sessions were held, with 165 trainees attending the courses. The majority of the trainees, totalling 100, were smallholder farmers working for six government-backed fish farms in the Free State.[17] The extension officers and technicians, 65 in total—coming from different districts of the Free State—were trained prior to the farmers. These officers played an important role in assisting the Chinese experts with technology extension.

---

[16]This can be seen from a series of recently approved documents and initiatives by the South African Ministry of Agriculture, Forestry and Fisheries, such as the National Aquaculture Strategic Framework, the National Aquaculture Policy Framework, the Aquaculture Development and Enhancement Program, and the development of aquaculture zones.

[17]The government had funded six community fish ponds throughout the Free State. All equipment and inputs had been provided to the ponds by the government, while the community representatives run the ponds. Once there is a sufficient quantity and quality of output, the government finds willing buyers.

Fig. 3.6 One of the six government-backed fish farms in Free State (left: the author, middle: Chinese fish expert, right: local fish farmer), 29 January 2015

In addition, the centre had also formed a cooperation programme with the University of Free State, with the plan to give lectures and provide training courses to college students (Interview 29 January 2015) (Fig. 3.6).

The training courses in the SA centre combined both theory and practice. The Chinese agro-experts made use of the centre's facilities for training and demonstration purposes. In the case of the smallholder farmers, the experts also went to their fish farms to assist in solving practical issues experienced on the ground. In general, based on the feedback from the smallholder farmers, the training provided was positively evaluated. Recipients, in particular, came to realize the importance of water temperature and quality and how these factors affect the growth rate of the fish (Interview 30 January 2015c). However, several difficulties were experienced during the provision of the training. First, the farmers did not have the same technologies as the centre; thus, the advanced techniques learned at the centre cannot be implemented on their own fish farms. Second, there was a communication barrier between the Chinese aqua-experts and the local trainees. The experts did not speak English and had to depend on a translator throughout the training process, translating from Chinese to English. In addition, the experts had difficulties in explaining the technicalities of fish farming; this was specifically related to the selected trainees who were not previously fish farmers and thus had limited knowledge of fish farming (Interviews 30 January 2015a/b/c).

The centre also began with some preliminary research activities with the view of scaling up in 2015–2016. The plan was to incorporate local institutes, such as the University of Free State and the Agricultural Research Council of South Africa, into the research agenda, whereby they will have access to the facilities of the centre (Interview 30 January 2015a). It seemed that the primary aim of the research, in line with the ATDC mission, was to serve the centre's demonstration and training functions. For example, the Chinese technical team had initiated the collection of data on the differing aspects that affect the growth of the fish. This information would feed into determining which fish species was easiest to grow for the local smallholder farmers, particularly those who worked on the six fish farms (Interview 30 January 2015b) (Figs. 3.7 and 3.8).

Fig. 3.7 Fish hatchery of the centre, 29 January 2015

3 CHINA'S AGRO-DEVELOPMENT COOPERATION ...   91

Fig. 3.8 Fish pond of the centre, 29 January 2015

Business Introduction
Different from the general design for ATDCs by the Chinese government, the business operation was not one of the chief concerns for the centre in South Africa (Interview 8 March 2015); no business plans for the centre were developed in the exchange letters.[18] However, plans still needed to be worked out in order to deal with the output of the centre. A few options were proposed: for instance, the fish could be sold on the open markets, but mainly to the Chinese communities in Bloemfontein, Johannesburg and Pretoria, given that Chinese people have the dietary habit of eating freshwater fish (Interview 29 January 2015). Also, a

---

[18] This may have something to do with the plan of transferring the management to South Africa after the *Technical Cooperation Stage*; for if so, there was no urgent need for the centre to develop commercial activities with an aim to finance itself in the long run.

private South African company had plans to open a fish processing plant in the vicinity of the centre; the fish output from the ATDC and the government-backed fish farms could then feed into the processing plant. The output from the plant could also supply the hospitals, schools and police stations within the country while also being exported overseas, particularly to China (Harding 2014).

This lack of clarification might be related to the fact that the South African side had stated in the agreement that they would take over the management of the centre and fund it independently once the first three-year Technical Cooperation Stage ends. Considering the main purpose of the business operation is to maintain the financial and managerial sustainability of the centre, it then seems less meaningful or necessary for the Chinese to develop supportive agro-businesses if the host government was willing and able to run the centre on its own. Having that said, CAIDC, the project-implementing agent, was looking for external opportunities for agro-investment in South Africa. The Chinese staff had been collecting information on the local investment environment and keeping their Beijing-based headquarter updated on a regular basis (Interview 8 March 2015).

Project Sustainability
By the time the fieldwork was conducted in early 2015, the SA centre had five full-time positions for South Africans. At least two of these local staff, one research assistant and one freshwater scientist, lived in the centre and work closely with the Chinese concerning both administrative and technical issues (Table 3.4). The Chinese had also kept in contact with several other government officials from the FSAARD for the daily operation of the centre (Interview 30 January 2015a). This proves to help guarantee the sustainability of the management and technical aspects of the centre after the handover. However, the majority of the staff were yet to be employed permanently at the centre. Until early 2015, there had not yet been a final agreement as to the future development after the three-year technical cooperation phase. Yet, according to the preliminary exchange letter/operational plan in 2013, the centre should be handed over to the FSDARD in February 2017. The management team from the CNADC will be replaced by the South Africans, while the Chinese technical team may stay, if requested by the South

Table 3.4 Governance structure for the South African ATDC

Human resources	Nationality	Responsibilities
Project Manager	Chinese	Overall operation and management of the centre
Deputy Project Manager	South African	Manage and arrange the facility, strategic planning, assistance to project manager
Technology Officer	Chinese	Oversee hatchery-related issues: in charge of fry production, technology demonstration and personnel training
Deputy Technology Officer	South African	Assist with hatchery related activities
Financial Officer	Chinese	Financial planning and monitoring of expenses
Administrative Officer	South African	Ensure all administrative work is completed

Source Harding 2014

African side, until February 2020. Financially, the FSDARD will be responsible for all costs relating to the centre once the second phase of cooperation commences.[19]

3.2.3 Integrated Analysis: Results and Problems

Technology Transfer
Overall, the transfer of Chinese agricultural technology as conducted by the ATDC in Mozambique proved to be beneficial to the local communities. The training courses were designed by the Chinese agro-experts according to the specific needs of the different types of trainees and tailored to the actual abilities of the latter due to the knowledge gap between the trainers and trainees. Moreover, the participation of the local partners helped overcome the language barrier and improved the effects of the technology transfer. In addition, from the feedback perspective, the farmer trainees, for instance, confirmed that Chinese

---

[19] This is confirmed by the recent development of the SA centre—the management of the centre has been formally transferred to the South African government since September 2017; the CAIDC has withdrawn and the centre now is entirely run by South Africans (CNADC 2017; CCTV.com 2018).

agro-techniques were useful and could help increase the outputs, as seen both in Mozambique and in South Africa; in the case of Mozambique, the output was enhanced by 2–4 times, compared to their previous unit output not using Chinese techniques, according to both the Chinese and Mozambican sides (Interviews 4 November 2013a and 14 November 2013).

Nevertheless, the impacts of the technology transfer were also to some extent limited, mainly for three reasons. The first problem concerned the design of the *training model*. In both cases, the majority of the trainees are the *smallholder farmers*. This was surely sensible in that by transferring farming techniques to the actual agricultural producers, it would have the most direct results. However, the potential benefits were reduced both in quality and quantity terms as the technology transfer was largely not connected to the host country's agro-technology extension system. Indeed, by training more local *agro-extension officers*, they could better digest the Chinese techniques given their professional backgrounds and thus have a greater impact on disseminating the information to farmers due to the elimination of communication barriers (between the extension officers and local farmers) and the links to their broader extension networks, including follow-up extension and support services.

In the case of South Africa, there were a handful of local extension officers and technicians trained at the centre who turned out to have played a positive role in coordinating the technology transfer between the Chinese and local farmers (Interview 29 January 2015). In contrast, in Mozambique, where a long-standing national agricultural extension system does exist, the Chinese ATDC did not seem to be linked to it in any meaningful way: No extension officers had been involved in the training (Interview 14 November 2013), and even the 'agro-technicians' who received the training were mostly office staff without a mandate to work in the fields (Interview 18 October 2013). The detachment with the country's extension systems implies that the effects the centre has might be only moderate and less durable, despite the fact that hundreds of small farmers were being trained each year.

Another problem concerns the *post-training application*. Even if the technology transfer process per se could be successful, it may not necessarily change the livelihood of the farmers, unless they have an enabling environment whereby they can put the learned techniques into application. In Mozambique, unfortunately I did not manage to interview the farmer trainees of the ATDC as they were scattered all over the country, but a very useful reference example could be provided here given the very similar scenario: a Chinese agro-firm, Wanbao, who was engaged in agribusiness and transfer of Chinese rice-farming techniques to the locals in the Gaza Province of Mozambique (Sect. 4.2.1). In that case, despite the specially designed training sessions for the local farmers, the techniques taught by the Chinese experts could not be implemented on a daily basis simply due to a lack of tools and irrigation equipment on the farmers' own lands; thus, the training courses had no sustainable effects on the farmers' livelihood (Interview 18 November 2013). Indeed, this problem was not only seen in the Mozambican case. Similarly, in the ATDC of South Africa, the heating systems on the six government-backed fish farms, which were fundamental to apply the techniques that were taught at the centre, were left broken for months, causing stunted growth of the fish and thus reduced profits (Interview 30 January 2015c).

A potential challenge also lied in the *different farming cultures*. According to the Chinese experts involved in the training activities, it really took time for the African smallholder farmers to learn and get used to the Chinese way of intensive cultivation that emanated from, among others, the land constraints in China (Interview 18 October 2013). Similar problem was also observed in the Wanbao agribusiness project where the local trainee farmers showed little interest in learning the very laborious Chinese farming techniques (Sect. 4.2.1). Furthermore, it was even more difficult for the African farmers who were used to an extensive way of farming to *stick to* the much more technically demanding and time-consuming Chinese techniques *on their own* and especially *for a long time*—the dilapidation of the Chinese-aided farms in Sierra Leone during the 1970–1980s after the leaving of the Chinese aid workers provides a vivid illustration to this point (Bräutigam 2009, 238). Therefore, training only focusing on agro-technology transfer but without full consideration (and corresponding countermeasures, if any) of the farming culture differences, as showed in the case study, may inevitably reduce the potential, especially long-term effects of the technology transfer.

Although the 'research' aspect of the technology transfer is not treated as the main focus of the ATDCs, there are still some problems worth noting. Take the 'seed testing' issue for example, while the selected Chinese high-yielding seed varieties were able to upscale the outputs, the suitability of those varieties to the local taste seemed somehow to be neglected. This is the case in both ATDCs: in Mozambique where the seed testing was largely restricted to Chinese varieties due to the unavailability of local seeds, and in the South African case where the market for freshwater fish was relatively small and specialized.

Business Introduction
As seen in the cases of Mozambique and South Africa, apart from performing the core function of agro-technology transfer, both centres had started or planned to start market-oriented production activities. This can be seen as a form of business introduction although the primary purpose of the commercialized operation of the centre was to maintain project sustainability. More essentially, both Chinese companies, Lianfeng and CAIDC, had either already set up separate agribusinesses or been actively seeking for external agro-investment opportunities by using the ATDC project as a springboard.

Indeed, available data suggest that at least 9 out of the first batch of 14 Chinese-aided ATDCs in Africa, specifically in Tanzania, Uganda, Zambia, Sudan, Mozambique, Cameroon, Liberia, Malawi, Benin, have successfully established their independent agribusiness outside the ATDCs. Even for those which haven't formally started with agribusiness—that in South Africa, for instance—the Chinese staff have been collecting information on the local investment environment and keeping their Beijing-based headquarter regularly updated (Interview 8 March 2015), which may help smooth the way for their future investment in South Africa. Furthermore, the Mozambican case has demonstrated a greater role of the ATDC as a business platform through providing information and technical support to other Chinese companies and individuals, and thus facilitating their local investment.

Considering the difficulties of the first-time entry into a foreign market, the ATDC project did seem to make it easier for the companies to get into, and invest in, the host countries, with the assistance and facilitation from both the home (China) and local (host country) governments. It was also relatively easier for these companies to start separate agribusinesses due to their identity as the implementing agents for a government aid project, for instance, in terms of land lease or tax exemption. Moreover, it seemed that the participation or intervention of the Chinese government agency could make a big difference as to how much an ATDC can exert its influence. The provincial government of Hubei, for example, had definitely played an essential role in magnifying the platform function of the Mozambican ATDC by establishing contacts and forging cooperation between the centre and other companies from Hubei province.

Project sustainability
The project sustainability issue of the ATDCs concerns at least three aspects. First, *financial sustainability*—according to *guidelines* (Sect. 3.1.1), the Chinese government only fund operation of the centres for the first three years, after which the centres are required to find other ways to finance themselves (Sect. 3.1.3). Second, *managerial sustainability*—a capable managerial team needs to be in place in order to keep the centres running while making sure the key functions are performed. Last, *technical sustainability*—this requires qualified staff to work at the centres and conduct agro-technical activities. The prescriptions provided by the Chinese government to realize *sustainability* in the development of the ATDCs are to incorporate company actors and to run the centres as a business. Financially, by developing a market-oriented production, it is expected that the profits earned could be used for financing the daily operation of the centres, including the realization of the 'public-interest function'. Also, the presence of Chinese companies could help maintain the managerial and technical sustainability. From what we've seen from practice, however, this plan is not always achievable.

First of all, as shown in the Mozambican case, although some business attempts were made, the centre was still not able to fully achieve *financial independence* through selling self-produced agro-products. This was despite the fact that the production costs had been much lowered since the land, water and electricity were provided by the host country, for free, during the Technical Cooperation Stage (Interview 14 November 2013). In fact, most of the ATDCs were facing similar constraints: limited land, capital and human resources, among others. Therefore, it did not seem very likely that the ATDCs would be able to sustain themselves financially through commercial operations, or at best, they may just manage to make the ends meet but with very limited profit margins, particularly given the current production scale.[20] In order to achieve financial independence, an expansion of investment inputs, and thus production scale, is necessary. This can either be based on the centre or a separate business outside the centre. However, two main challenges emerge here.

[20] This has been confirmed at least by the case of Mozambican ATDC two years after the completion of the Technical Cooperation Stage since 2015; the centre has been just able to cover the day-to-day operation fees while always trying to save costs (e.g. through hiring even fewer working staff) (Interview 23 June 2017).

First, how likely is it that the bolt-on investment will be successful? The question then is translated into another issue: feasibility and profitability of conducting agribusiness in Africa. The thorniest problem affecting Chinese agro-investors seems to be the financing of investment, given their usually limited self-owned capital and difficulties to raise money in China (Sect. 4.2.3). No less importantly, it also depends on the motives of the implementing firm—*to what extent and even whether* they would like to invest self-owned capital at all into this sort of 'development cooperation' rather than a real 'agribusiness' project; the Mozambican case has so far shown limited signs of Lianfeng being interested in so doing (Interview 29 December 2014).[21] Even if they are truly interested and could manage to raise the required money, they would meet a range of practical problems in the agro-investment process in Africa, such as land ownership, labour regulation, market channels, government efficiency, and natural disasters, among others. According to the author's interviews with a number of existing and potential Chinese agro-investors in Mozambique, they have expressed without exception that the difficulties in operating in Africa were far beyond their expectations before they came to the continent. None of the existing investors has managed to make any profits to date after years of operation. This may cast some doubts on the prospect of the ATDCs' commercial development in the host countries.

Second, even if the company could make good profits, to what extent would the company financially support the 'public-interest functions' of the centre? Although it was, in essence, the application of the government–firm cooperation, or a quasi-PPP model in development aid, the Chinese government and the companies had not concretely entered into any formal agreement that would regulate each other's rights and obligations. It is unrealistic to expect the company actors to willingly fulfil, by default, the public-interest functions of the ATDCs, especially given the generally low-profit margins. This leaves the situation uncertain as to whether the public-interest functions of the ATDCs would be fully performed in the Commercial Operation Stage, as the designers had envisioned; or, it is also not unlikely that these aid-type functions

---

[21] This has been confirmed again two years later—Lianfeng has indeed not injected extra capital into the ATDC; the centre has been kept running only by its limited scale of market-oriented production (Interview 23 June 2017).

gradually diminish while the ATDCs transform into a pure commercial project.

In terms of *managerial and technical sustainability*, while the immediate danger of project failure does seem to be mitigated with the continuing stay of the Chinese team, potential problems are still visible. For instance, the lack of effective participation of the local partner in the daily management of the ATDCs, compounded by the typical Chinese-dominated structure of governance, run the risk of leaving the local partner incapable of operating the ATDCs independently if the Chinese team pulls out of the project. Technically, the overwhelmingly farmer-centred training model also makes it less likely for the local agro-technicians to conduct the extension of Chinese farming techniques on their own.

Alternatively, as mentioned before (Sect. 3.1.3), the ATDCs could also be operated through joint venture, or independently by the host government, instead of following the Chinese-led management model. As to the option of the *joint venture*, based on the common practice of this type of 'management cooperation' since the 1990s, it is quite likely that the joint venture would be formed between a Chinese company and the host government, with the latter holding a share as per its ownership of land or other assets, whereas the management responsibilities would still largely rely on the Chinese side.[22] In that case, the actual operation, as well as the challenges of the ATDCs for sustaining its development, would be similar to what has been discussed above. Or, *independent management* by the host government is also a possibility, as shown in the South African case. However, given the general financial constraints of African states, it remains questionable whether the ATDCs would become financially stable without external support. In addition, the lack of technical and managerial capability building for the local counterparts, during the Technical Cooperation Stage, increases the likelihood that the ATDCs will not be sustainable under independent operation. The South African ATDC, in these respects, can be seen as an exception given the country's middle-income status of development and relatively greater technical strengths particularly in agriculture.

---

[22] There have been very few cases till now of local private actors participating in an agricultural joint venture with the Chinese side.

Summary

While admitting some of the positive outcomes, the investigation of the ATDCs—mostly through the cases of Mozambique and South Africa but also combining some other cases—has revealed much gap between the expected objectives and the actual results, which is particularly evident in terms of technical transfer and project sustainability. The dimension of business introduction proved to be relatively successful, but it is worth noting that the introduction of Chinese firms is only the first step. As will be demonstrated in Chapter 4, there are a number of practical obstacles that greatly affected the survival and profitability of the Chinese agribusiness projects in Mozambique after being introduced to the country. The 'innovative agro-aid' model of development cooperation as embodied by the ATDC project, therefore, still needs much reflection and improvement before being able to realize the 'mutual-development' goals as designed.

INTERVIEWS

(Only formal interviews included here [see Methodology in Introduction]. All the informants are well informed of the identity and research purposes of the author; they are all kept anonymous to protect their privacy)

Interview with the Chinese director A of the ATDC in Mozambique. Interviewed by Lu Jiang. Boane, Maputo province, Mozambique. 18 October 2013.

Interview with a Chinese staff A working at the ATDC in Mozambique. Interviewed by Lu Jiang. Maputo, Mozambique. 4 November 2013a.

Interview with a Chinese staff B working at the ATDC in Mozambique. Interviewed by Lu Jiang. Boane, Maputo province, Mozambique. 4 November 2013b.

Interview with the Chinese director A of the ATDC in Mozambique. Interviewed by Lu Jiang. Boane, Maputo province, Mozambique. 8 November 2013a.

Interview with several Mozambican workers hired by the ATDC in Mozambique. Interviewed by Lu Jiang and Sérgio Chichava. Boane, Mozambique. 8 November 2013b.

Interview with a Mozambican staff working at the MCT. Interviewed by Lu Jiang and Sérgio Chichava. Maputo, Mozambique. 14 November 2013.

Interview with two of Wanbao's management team. Interviewed by Lu Jiang. Xaixai, Gaza province, Mozambique. 18 November 2013.

Interview with a Chinese working for a private Chinese agro-company in Mozambique. Interviewed by Lu Jiang. Maputo, Mozambique. 29 December 2014.

Interview with a Chinese staff working at the ATDC in Mozambique. Interviewed by Lu Jiang. Boane, Maputo province, Mozambique. 29 December 2014.
Interview with the Chinese manager of CAAIC's Mozambican project. Interviewed by Lu Jiang. Maputo, Mozambique. 10 January 2015.
Interview with a Chinese staff working for Hefeng. Interviewed by Lu Jiang. Buzi, Sofala province, Mozambique. 14 January 2015.
Interview with a Chinese staff working at the ATDC in South Africa. Interviewed by Lu Jiang and Angela Harding. Gariep Dam, Free State province, South Africa. 29 January 2015.
Interview with a Chinese staff A working at the ATDC in South Africa. Interviewed by Lu Jiang and Angela Harding. Gariep Dam, Free State province, South Africa. 30 January 2015a.
Interview with a Chinese staff B working at the ATDC in South Africa. Interviewed by Lu Jiang and Angela Harding. Gariep Dam, Free State province, South Africa. 30 January 2015b.
Interview with several South African farmers working at one of the six fish farms. Interviewed by Lu Jiang and Angela Harding. Gariep Dam, Free State province, South Africa. 30 January 2015c.
Interview with a Chinese staff working at the ATDC in South Africa. Interviewed by Lu Jiang. [By phone] London, UK. 8 March 2015.
Interview with the Chinese director B of the ATDC in Mozambique. Interviewed by Lu Jiang. [By phone] London, UK. 19 October 2015.
Interview with the Chinese director B of the ATDC in Mozambique. Interviewed by Lu Jiang. Shanghai, China. 23 June 2017.

REFERENCES

Bräutigam, Deborah. 2009. *The Dragon's Gift: The Real Story of China in Africa*. Oxford: Oxford University Press.
Cai, Lingming. 1992. 'Woguo Dui Feizhou de Nongye Yuanzhu (China's Agricultural Aid to Africa)'. *Guoji Jingji Hezuo* (International Economic Cooperation) 2: 43–44.
CCTV.com. 2018. 'Zhongfei Nongye Hezuo: "shouren Yiyu Buru Shouren yiyu" (China-South Africa Agricultural Cooperation: Teaching Others How to Fish Is Better Than Giving Them Fishes)', 26 July. http://sannong.cctv.com/2018/07/26/ARTIzbS3iLbcbeSRBwCHQnxL180726.shtml.
Chichava, Sérgio, Jimena Duran, and Lu Jiang. 2014. 'The Chinese Agricultural Technology Demonstration Centre in Mozambique: A Story of a Gift'. In *China and Mozambique: From Comrades to Capitalists* (Alden and Chichava Eds.).
Chichava, Sérgio, and Natalia Fingermann. 2015. 'Chinese and Brazilian Agricultural Models in Mozambique. The Case of the Chinese Agricultural

Technology Demonstration Centre and of the Brazilian ProALIMENTOS Programme'. China and Brazil in Africa Agriculture Project. Future Agricultures.

CNADC (China National Agricultural Development Group Co. Ltd.). 2017. 'Woguo Yuanzhu Nanfei Nongye Jishu Shifan Zhongxin Jishu Hezuoqi Xiangmu Shunli Yijiao (China-Aided South African ATDC Successfully Transferred to South Africa After the Technical Cooperation Stage)'. *Zhongguo Nongfa (CNADC)*, 22 September. http://zgnfb.com/jqckj/news/9/37/111-1.shtml.

FOCAC (Forum on China Africa Cooperation). 2006. 'The Forum on China-Africa Cooperation Beijing Action Plan (2007–2009)'. Ministry of Foreign Affairs of the People's Republic of China, Beijing. https://www.focac.org/eng/zywx_1/zywj/t280369.htm.

———. 2009. 'The Forum on China-Africa Cooperation Sharm El-Sheikh Action Plan (2010–2012)'. Ministry of Foreign Affairs of the People's Republic of China, Beijing. https://www.focac.org/eng/zywx_1/zywj/t626387.htm.

Harding, Angela. 2014. 'New and Interrelated Facets of Land Acquisition: The Case of the Chinese Investments in South Africa (Master's thesis, Unpublished)'. University of Pretoria.

Huang, Jikun. 2010. 'Liushinian Zhongguo Nongye de Fazhan He Sanshinian Gaige Qiji (Sixty Years of Chinese Agricultural Development and Thirty Years of the Reform Miracle)'. *Agro-Technology Economy* (Nongye Jishu Jingji) 1: 4–18.

MOC and MOA of the PRC (Ministry of Commerce and Ministry of Agriculture of the People's Republic of China). 2011. *Guanyu Cujin Yuanfei Nongye Jishu Shifan Zhongxin Xiangmu Kechixu Fazhan de Zhidaoyijian* (Guidance on Promoting the Sustainable Development of the Agriculture Technology Demonstration Centre Project in Africa).

———. 2012. *Yuanfei Nongye Jishu Shifanzhong Xinjiance Pingjia Banfa (Shixing)* (Supervision and Evaluation Measures of the Agriculture Technology Demonstration Centre in Africa [Under Trial]).

Qin, Lu. 2016. 'Yuanfei Nongye Jishu Shifan Zhongxin: Chengxiao, Wenti He Zhengce Jianyi (ATDC in Africa: Effectiveness, Problems and Policy Suggestions)'. *Guoji Jingji Hezuo* (International Economic Cooperation) 8. http://www.fecc.agri.cn/yjzx/yjzx_zxxx/201709/t20170901_295884.html.

Shi, Lin, ed. 1989. *Dangdai zhongguo de duiwai jingji hezuo* (Foreign Economic Cooperation of Contemporary China). Beijing: Zhongguo shehui kexue chubanshe (China Social Science Press).

State Council of the PRC (People's Republic of China). 2011. 'China's Foreign Aid'. State Council of the People's Republic of China. http://news.xinhuanet.com/english2010/china/2011-04/21/c_13839683.htm.

Sun, Yihou. 1996. 'Shilun yingxiang nongye yuanzhu xiangmu xiaoyi de zhuyao yinsu (Main Factors Affecting the Effectiveness of Agricultural Foreign Aid Projects)'. *Guoji jingji hezuo* (International Economic Cooperation) 7: 54–56.

Tang, Lixia, Xiaoyun Li, and Gubo Qi. 2014. 'Zhongguo Dui Feizhou Nongye Yuanzhu Guanli Moshi de Yanhua Yu Chengxiao (Evolution and Effectiveness of the Management Modalities of Chinese Agricultural Aid to Africa)'. *Guoji Wenti Yanjiu* (International Studies) 6: 29–40.

Xu, Jifeng, and Lu Qin. 2011. 'Zhongguo Yuanzhu Feizhou Nongye Jishu Shifan Zhongxin Kechixu Fazhan Jianyi (Suggestions on the Sustainable Development of Chinese Agriculture Technology Demonstration Centre in Africa)'. *Shijie Nongye* (World Agriculture) 12: 87–99.

Yun, Wenju. 2000. 'Cong guoji yuanzhu de fazhan kan zhongguo duifei nongye yuanzhu (The Development of International Aid and China's Agricultural Aid to Africa)'. *Xiya Feizhou* (West Asia and Africa) 2: 17–23.

Zhang, Xiaojun, and Xi Zhang. 2015. 'Hubei Nongken Chengdan Haiwai Yuanzhu Xiangmu Jihaiwai Nongye Hezuo Kaifa Xiangmu Jianjie (Foreign Aid and Overseas Agricultural Exploitation Projects Undertaken by Hubei Bureau of State Farm and Land Reclamation)'. http://www.hubeifarm.com/hwkf/gzjl/3876.htm.

Zhou, Jianjun, and Qiang Wang. 1997. 'Xin Xingshi Xia Dui Feizhou Nongye Yuanzhu de Tantao (Agricultural Aid to Africa Under the New Circumstances)'. *Guoji Jingji Hezuo* (International Economic Cooperation) 3: 9–11.

CHAPTER 4

China's Agro-Development Cooperation with Africa: The Agribusiness Model

As has been argued in the Introduction and repeatedly demonstrated in the previous chapters, one of the most outstanding features of China's contemporary development cooperation lies in its *flexibility* in terms of the cooperation modalities through the 'development package' model, and more essentially, the *pragmaticism* in terms of the underlying 'mutual-development' pursuits. It is because of this sort of mentality and guidelines that Chinese development cooperation can comfortably go beyond (the constraints of) the Northern ODA or its own 'pure aid' as practiced in the earlier years and choose from a much broader range of cooperation forms. In the area of agriculture, more specifically, we've already seen that, while more traditional aid forms such as technical assistance and infrastructure projects remain (Sect. 2.4), Chinese government has also started to try out some more innovative ways in conducting agricultural aid, typically the Agriculture Technology Demonstration Centre (ATDCs) (Chapter 3). The present chapter will continue to investigate another important modality of China's agricultural development cooperation with Africa, that is, the 'agribusiness model'.

By 'agribusiness model', it basically means the incorporation of Chinese agro-firms and their commercial operation models into the development cooperation field in order to enhance the performance of the agricultural sector (e.g. agro-productivity and value-added of agro-products) and the livelihood of the rural population in Africa. The developmental impact of the 'agribusiness model' could be understood at two

© The Author(s) 2020
L. Jiang, *Beyond Official Development Assistance*,
Governing China in the 21st Century,
https://doi.org/10.1007/978-981-32-9507-0_4

levels. In a narrower sense, similar to the PPP scheme that has been gaining increasing popularity in the Northern donor community (Sect. 1.1), agribusiness projects are often partially supported by government finance and thus expected to bear more developmental responsibilities, such as creating more jobs, providing free trainings and helping build schools, etc.—in other words, efforts are *intentionally* made to create more developmental impacts (i.e. 'additionality') on the local communities where the agribusiness is located. In a broader sense, however, especially in the case of those purely self-financed agro-firms, the developmental impacts are demonstrated more as a *natural spill-over* effect of agribusiness given the very nature of agricultural sector that feed and sustain the largest population in Africa, and especially those extremely poor.

Equally important, the agribusiness model also fully demonstrates the idea of 'mutual development'. The chapter, therefore, will discuss how China's agricultural cooperation with Africa has been enmeshed with its own agricultural development agenda, namely the 'Agriculture Going Out' strategy, and meanwhile with Chinese agro-firms' attempts of investing abroad. The chapter is composed of two main sections. Section one will first provide a brief introduction to the general developments of Chinese agribusiness investment in Africa in the recent decades. It will then introduce the 'agribusiness model' of development cooperation by exploring its motives, actors and modalities. The second section will further unpack the model by examining four in-depth case studies of Chinese agribusiness projects in Mozambique—one of the most significant partner countries of China's agro-development cooperation on the continent. A preliminary analysis as to the results, especially problems, of China's 'agribusiness model'—as has been implemented in Mozambique so far—will be provided at the end of the chapter.

4.1   Chinese Agribusiness Investment in Africa

The earliest practice of Chinese agribusiness investment in Africa started in the 1980s in a few West African countries such as Senegal and Guinea-Bissau in the fishery area (CNFC). With respect to crop farming, the early investment attempts started in the early 1990s, mostly carried out by Chinese state-owned agricultural enterprises (SAEs) (Sects. 2.2 and 2.3). The scale of investment, however, had remained at a very low level in terms of both the total value of investment and the number of participating companies. A few private individuals also invested, but at a much lower rate.

Table 4.1 Chinese agricultural FDI around the globe in/by 2016

	FDI flow ($ Billion)	FDI stock ($ Billion)	Number of newly established firms	Main FDI destination countries (by flow in 2016)
Total	3.29	15.76	863	
Asia	1.71	8.7	472	Singapore, Thailand
Oceania	0.81	2.29	63	Australia, New Zealand
Europe	0.33	2.75	136	The Netherlands, Russia
South America	0.23	0.55	30	Brazil, Peru
Africa	*0.18*	*1.27 (8.1%)*	*108 (12.5%)*	*Tanzania, Mauritania*
North America	0.03	0.2	54	United States, Canada

Source The author based on MOA of the PRC (2017, 1–10)

Entering the new millennium, particularly since the Beijing Summit of FOCAC in 2006, Chinese government began to formally encourage Chinese companies to invest in the agricultural sector of Africa (Sect. 1.2). This occurred roughly during the same period when China initiated its overseas agricultural investment policy, or, as termed as 'Agriculture Going Out' policy (Table 4.4) in alignment with the country's broader 'Going Out' strategy. In 2010, Chinese government convened a separate, high-profile 'Forum on Agricultural Cooperation with Africa (FOCAAC)' and invited official representatives from 18 African countries to Beijing to discuss the possibilities of deepening cooperation in the agricultural field. On this occasion, the Chinese government, again, placed special emphasis on the role of corporate actors in the 'new era' of agricultural cooperation and called for joint efforts from both Chinese and African sides to create a favourable environment that could facilitate agro-investment activities.

Chinese companies' agribusiness engagement in Africa has since stepped up. China's agro-FDI stock in Africa was about $289 million in 2009 (MOC of the PRC 2010), which has increased to $1.27 billion by the end of 2016 (Table 4.1). This is, however, not a significant figure in a comparative sense, representing around 8.1% of China's overall overseas agricultural FDI in the world and only 3.2% of China's total investment in Africa.[1] It is estimated that around 108 Chinese companies were involved in agro-investment in Africa by 2016, standing roughly as 12.5% of the total in the world (Tables 4.1, 4.2, 4.3).

---

[1] That is $39.8 billion by the end of 2016 according to the online database of National Bureau of Statistics of China (http://data.stats.gov.cn/english/easyquery.htm?cn=C01).

Table 4.2 Chinese overseas agricultural FDI by Sector in/by 2016 (Unit: $ Million)

	Crop farming	Husbandry	Forestry	Fishery	Agro-processing	Agro-services
Flow	1510	360	170	120	270	860
Stock	7340	880	740	460	710	5630

Source The author based on MOA of the PRC (2017, 2–4)

Table 4.3 Chinese overseas crop-farming FDI in 2016 (Unit: Thousand tons)

	Grain crops			Cash crops		
	Corn	Rice	Wheat	Rubber	Sugarcane	Soybeans
Overseas production	892	500	138	1483	981	548
Local sales	10	5	2	196	5.5	8.3
Exports	109	4	0.3	1.8	0.1	31

Source The author based on MOA of the PRC (2017, 38)

4.1.1 Motives: Mutual-Development Pursuits, Tripartite-Interest Balances

Chinese investment, particularly in financial terms, is very much needed for African agriculture. Despite with a great potential in boosting economic growth and poverty reduction, African agriculture has virtually been stuck in a lengthy stagnation in the decades following the continent's independence. While agricultural transformations have achieved great success in Asia and Latin America since the 1960s, Africa still suffers from severe backwardness in terms of agricultural production; the *per capita* output in sub-Saharan Africa fell by around 5% between 1980 and 2001 while in developing counties as a whole it increased by about 40% during the same period (EC 2005). It is reported to have less irrigation, less fertilizer use, less soil and seed research, less mechanization, less rural financing and poorer infrastructure than any other farming region in the world (Thurow 2008; Harsch 2004). Capital injection is thus of crucial importance to the improvement of agricultural production conditions and thus agro-productivity on the continent, which however is hampered by the often limited financial strengths of African governments.

Agriculture and agribusiness together account for nearly half of the GDP in Africa and is further projected to be an industry of one trillion USD in sub-Saharan Africa by 2030. In particular, the more market-oriented agribusiness (in contrast to the basic production agriculture) is believed to have an essential role to play in jump-starting economic transformation through the development of agriculture-based industries that creates jobs and incomes. Thus, it is suggested that the recently renewed interests and attention from governments and other actors in African agriculture should be extended to agribusiness (World Bank 2013, xiv–xvi). And foreign investments can be useful in upstream and downstream of agriculture to overcome the weaknesses of African industries, as well as in infrastructure to complement public funding (NEPAD 2013, 10). As a result, African governments are all very keen to introduce agro-FDI, including that from China, in order to boost the development of domestic agricultural sector. At the 2010 FOCAAC noted earlier, for instance, many African leaders expressed their interests in inviting Chinese investment to help with agro-infrastructure, research, and experience sharing, among others (Xinhua 2010).

Meanwhile, as a key feature of China's contemporary agro-development cooperation with Africa, such investment is expected to fulfil mutual-development objectives of both African countries as development cooperation recipients and China as the provider. In the 'agribusiness model' under discussion, although Chinese government does not explicitly link its self-interested motives to its agricultural development cooperation efforts, these motives are almost self-evident and fairly justifiable within the mutual-benefit framework. Different from the 'innovative agro-aid model' of the ATDC wherein company actors play more an implementing role, they are not only the 'front fighters' but also decision-makers as to the business plan, thus leaving much room for their own corporate interests. Therefore, to understand motives of the Chinese side under the 'agribusiness model', one has to distinguish that of the government and that from the companies' point of view.

In the first place, the 'agribusiness model' of development cooperation, characterized by its agro-FDI element, fits well into the internationalization strategy of Chinese domestic agricultural sector. The so-called Agriculture Going Out policy was formally launched by the government in 2006, with a strong mandate to promote and facilitate Chinese agro-companies to 'go out' and conduct agricultural investment

Table 4.4 China's 'Agriculture Going Out' policy

Policy objectives	• Guarantee the adequate supply of the major agricultural products by utilizing overseas agricultural resources • Explore and expand international markets for China's advantaged agricultural products and technology • Utilize advanced foreign agro-technology • Enhance the international competitiveness of Chinese agricultural enterprises (Song et al. 2012)
Investment destinations	*Principle: prioritize neighbouring countries, countries rich in agricultural resource, and countries with good investment environment* • Neighbouring countries (Russia, Central/Eastern Europe, Central/Southeast Asia) • Latin America • Africa • The West (Europe, America, Australia, etc.) (NDRC and MOC 2013; Song et al. 2012)

Investment fields	*Principle: prioritize cash crops of high import-dependency and develop grain crops in appropriate regions*
	• Crop farming
	• Southeast Asia: palm oil, rubber, rice, maize,
	  – Russia, Central Asia and Central/Eastern Europe: soybean, rape, cotton, wheat, barley, maize,
	  – Latin America: soybean, cotton, sugar products,
	  – Central/Southern/Eastern Africa: cotton, grain crops,
	  – Central/Western Africa: cotton, palm oil, rubber,
	  – South Asia, Australia, North America: soybean, cotton, rape, wheat, sugar products,
	• Animal husbandry
	• Fishery (NDRC and MOC 2013; Song et al. 2012; Ye 2007)

Investment value chain	*Principle: start from and focus mainly on storage and logistics, complementing by production, processing and international trade* • Production • Processing • Storage • Logistics • Trade (NDRC and MOC 2013; Wan 2012)
Investment modalities	• Greenfield investment: to start a new enterprise (farm and/or progressing factory) in the investment destination country • Equity investment: to participate in the corporate operation by the form of share purchase or M&A (Mergers and Acquisitions) with established agro-enterprises in the investment destination country (Wan 2012; Zhang 2009)
Investment entities	• To support some central enterprises and large-scale agricultural enterprises to become the main force of China's overseas agricultural investment • To encourage non-agricultural, private and medium-/small-sized firms to participate in the agricultural foreign investment process (NDRC and MOC 2013; Wan 2012)
Supporting measures	• Policy encouragement and investment guidance • Financial support • Insurance and tax measures • Diplomatic backup (NDRC and MOC 2013; Ma et al. 2014)

Source The author based on the documents as indicated above

abroad (Table 4.4). Despite other important considerations,[2] this state-led overseas agricultural strategy is largely resource-oriented (Zhai 2006; Ye 2007; Zhang 2009; Wan 2011, 2012). There has been high tension between the increasing demand for the major agricultural products, including both grain crops and cash crops, and the actual capability of the domestic supply. This is primarily attributed to the low people-to-land ratio in China, wherein the arable land area *per capita* is only about 0.08 hectares, less than half of the world average of 0.2 hectares (World Bank online database). Even with great efforts made by the Chinese government, including strengthening farmland protection and increasing unit yield, it still appears rather difficult for China to fulfil the needs for all the major agricultural products solely through domestic production. Filling this gap between demand and supply by utilizing external agricultural resources, through either imports or agricultural FDI, is almost an inevitable course of action for China.

That said, it is however worthwhile to clarify the target crops of China's agricultural imports and FDI, which seems particularly necessary in the face of the often emotionally fuelled debates that frequently assume that 'China is laying an expansive agricultural cooperation framework across Africa, tapping into the continent's immense potential, as a means of securing long-term domestic food security' (Freeman et al. 2008). In fact, for a series of strategic considerations (Jiang 2015), the Chinese government has made every effort to try to maintain a high-level self-sufficiency rate (SSR) for some of the key grain crops, especially those for human consumption and thus are considered essential in food security terms (Appendix A). As a result, the SSRs for rice, wheat and maize have stabilized at around 98–100% both in total and separate terms (Jiang 2015). Meanwhile, the Chinese government has also developed an integrated grain reserves system across the country in order to further strengthen the national food security.

Indeed, largely because of this policy priority given to grain crops farming at home, which has consequently occupied up to 80–90% of the country's total arable land, it is made an almost inevitable choice for China to resort to international trade and FDI in order to ensure effective supply of other important types of agricultural products, especially

---

[2] For instance, to optimize and upgrade the agro-industrial structure through growing crops of comparative advantages, e.g. labour-intensive vegetables and fruits, and accordingly, developing land-intensive crops in suitable foreign countries.

those land-intensive cash crops like soybeans, cotton and rubber. It is hoped by the Chinese government, for instance, that through agricultural FDI, China could have access to overseas equity holdings of soybeans, cotton, sugar crops, palm oil and rubber amounting to respectively 20, 40, 30, 15 and 20% of their total imports by the year of 2020 (NDRC and MOC of the PRC 2013). This trend is also widely seen in China's actual practice of overseas agricultural investment (Appendices B–E) and that in Africa as well (Table 4.7). According to the Ministry of Agriculture of China, Chinese companies produced about 105,000 tons of cash crop (mostly cotton and sugar) in Africa in 2016, while the output of food crops (with a majority of maize) was around 48,000 tons in the same year (MOA of the PRC 2017, 26). Therefore, instead of importing or growing grain crops that are of significant food security implications (FAO 2003), the main focus of Chinese agricultural imports and FDI is effectively different types of cash crops.

From a corporate point of view, furthermore, there is also an urgent need for many of Chinese agriculture-related companies[3] to start seriously considering their overseas strategies, particularly in the face of the mounting costs and unstable supply of agricultural raw materials which, among other things, have continually reduced the companies' profit margin.

To give some examples for this case: in the grain industry, for instance, the Chinese government has set minimum prices for agro-companies to purchase certain types of grains from farmers in order to protect the interests of the latter. These prices are usually much higher than that of those produced in some other countries, e.g. the Southeast Asian neighbours, due to China's increasing land constraints and growing costs of labour and agro-inputs. The rational choice, therefore, would be to buy raw materials from abroad. However, under the government's Grain and Cotton Import Quota System ('Import Quota System' hereinafter), agro-companies are not allowed to conduct imports of rice, wheat, maize and cotton unless they can obtain the quota required, which nevertheless is often awarded in favour of the SAEs. For the majority who cannot obtain the 'import quota', they would have to bear the high costs of raw agro-materials, which makes them less profitable and also less competitive compared to their foreign counterparts operating in China. Furthermore, despite the high prices, it is not guaranteed that companies

---

[3] For more details about Chinese 'agriculture-related companies', see Sect. 4.1.2.

can secure the raw materials they need. The large number of Chinese agro-processing companies, compounded by the massive intrusion of powerful transnational agro-firms after China's entry into World Trade Organization (WTO) since 2001, has created a rather grim scenario in every harvest season in which numerous agricultural companies—state or private, domestic or foreign—scramble for the relatively limited supply of agro-products from Chinese farmers. For those who are not able to obtain the raw materials, processing lines may have to be shut down.

Another example would be the soybean industry, where problems experienced are different but equally challenging. Because soybean is not under the Import Quota System, Chinese companies are free to purchase soybeans from foreign traders. However, it is precisely because of the absence of strict protective measures, and consequently the high dependency upon imports—nearly 80% of the soybeans consumed in China in recent years were imported from abroad—that Chinese soybean processing firms became increasingly subject to the price fluctuations on international markets. During the soybean price fluctuation in 2004, for instance, more than half of Chinese medium-/small-sized soybean processing firms shut down or went bankrupt, and 70% of those affected Chinese firms were purchased by transnational grain giants, whereby leading to a total of 60% of China's soybean processing volumes to be purchased and controlled by foreign enterprises (Comnews 2014).

Against this background, the primary and most direct motives for Chinese agricultural enterprises to 'go abroad' is to offset the disadvantageous business environment at home with a view to maintaining and maximizing their profitability; specifically, they need to secure cheaper and stable sources of agricultural raw materials through conducting agro-FDI. Meanwhile, the government's motive for promoting 'Agriculture Going Out' is to assure adequate supply of major agricultural products; and it is for that purpose that the government started to encourage Chinese agro-companies to gain access to overseas agricultural resources via investing abroad. Furthermore, on the African side, the underdeveloped agricultural sectors in many African countries are calling for FDI both as a capital catalyst and as a growth engine of agriculture and agribusiness industry, with a view to uplifting people from hunger and poverty to the greatest degree possible. There is, therefore, considerable compatibility among the tripartite interests of the Chinese government, Chinese agro-firms and African states; indeed, this potentially 'win-win-win' scenario could serve as an indispensible cornerstone for the 'agribusiness model' to truly fulfil its envisioned mutual-development pursuits. That said, the too many actors and interests co-existing will inevitably entail the problem of interests balancing and actions coordination, as will be shown in the forthcoming case studies (Sect. 4.2).

4.1.2   Actors: Company–Government Cooperation

Corporate Actors
In the 'agribusiness model' wherein FDI is utilized as a means of agro-development cooperation with partner countries, the different types of Chinese agriculture-related firms naturally take a leading role. Currently, there are four major types of companies that have been actively engaged with Chinese overseas agricultural investment, namely the central SAEs, local SAEs, private agro-companies and some non-agricultural but agriculture-related firms. As observed from the ground (Chapters 2, 3 and Sect. 4.2), these four kinds of companies have all been involved in Chinese agro-development cooperation with Africa, particularly under the 'agribusiness model'.

Specifically, *central SAEs* refer to those state-owned agricultural enterprises that operate at the central government level, and in most cases, under the direct governing of the State-owned Assets Supervision and Administration Commission of the State Council (SASAC).[4] Currently, there are around six central SAEs in China, three of which—respectively China National Agricultural Development Group Corporation (CNADC), China National Cereals, Oils and Foodstuffs Corporation (COFCO) and Chinatex Corporation (Chinatex)—have been more active in conducting agro-foreign investment (Appendices B and C), whereas the others tend to focus more on their domestic business. *Local SAEs*, on the other hand, indicate state-owned agricultural enterprises operating at the local, mostly provincial, government level and thus accountable to the local SASAC. Among them, the state-owned farming and reclamation enterprises ('state farming enterprises' hereinafter SFEs)

---

[4] This is a very important government agency in China. Authorized by the State Council, the SASAC is entrusted with investor's responsibilities on behalf of Chinese people and government, supervising and managing the state-owned assets of the enterprises under the supervision of the Central Government (excluding financial enterprises), thus enhancing the management of the state-owned assets.

as well as the local grain groups have played a pioneering role among the diverse types of local SAEs who are engaged in overseas investment. Particularly, with specialist expertise in land reclamation and cultivation, the SFEs have long taken an important part in the agro-development cooperation area between China and Africa, which could be dated back to the 1960s (Chapter 2). In the new era since the 2000s, the SFEs of Shanxi (shǎnxī) and Hubei provinces, for instance, are still presently undertaking Chinese government's flagship agro-aid projects of ATDC, in Cameroon and Mozambique, respectively (Chapter 3). Against the background of the country's 'Agriculture Going Out' policy, the SFEs also play a leading role in the process of overseas agricultural exploitation. By the end of 2013, the Chinese state farming enterprises had established 113 agro-investment projects in 42 countries across the Americas, Australia, Europe, Africa and Southeast Asia (Ding 2014). And the country's state farm system in total owned approximately 266,000 hectares (including 233,000 of grain crops and 20,000 of rubber) of farmland abroad and about one million tons of grain crops were produced overseas, for instance, in 2013 (Yu 2014, see also Appendix D).

Together, the central and local SAEs basically constitute the 'Chinese national team' that, allowing for their self-interested pursuits, assumes the main responsibility of implementing the government's FDI-centred 'Agriculture Going Out' policy. That said, *private agro-companies* also participate, and indeed may occupy a much larger proportion of the total engaged in agricultural foreign investment, partly due to the limited number of the SAEs in absolute terms (see Appendix E). One of the major differences between the two lies in the fact that the SAEs are often involved in those relatively more sizable projects given their company strength, ownership nature as well as the government support, whereas the project size of private agro-firms is usually more moderate. Also, unlike the SAEs whose foreign investments tend to be more strategic—in the sense of keeping strict alignment with the government priorities such as that of land-intensive cash crops—the fields that private agro-companies have set foot in are obviously much more diversified, ranging from major food crops like rice and wheat to relatively random types of cash crops such as coffee, sesame, Chinese medicine and anything that is considered profitable to them.

Apart from the majority of agro-companies, either state-owned or private as discussed above, a number of companies that are *not directly associated with agro-industry but agriculture-related* have also joined the team of 'Agriculture Going Out', which can be further grouped into three categories. The first group includes mostly manufacturing companies that are heavily dependent on agro-raw materials, such as textile/garment companies or chemical enterprises. The second group of non-agricultural companies are those closely linked to Chinese agricultural aid. Some of them can be traced back to China's earlier agro-aid during the 1960–1990s—for instance, SINOLIGHT and COMPLANT, who used to implement agro-aid projects in Africa and transformed them later on into commercial operation for the purpose of project sustainability (Sect. 2.3); some others are presently running separate agribusiness while implementing Chinese agro-aid projects, such as Shandong Foreign Economic and Technical Cooperation Corporation (Sect. 3.1.1). Lastly, there are also some who are investing or intend to invest in overseas agriculture either as a way to diversify their business or simply due to the profitability of certain specific projects, among other motives. They are, therefore, not particularly driven by agriculture-oriented, state or company strategies as most of the others are.

In Africa, more specifically, there were about one hundred Chinese companies involved in agribusiness by 2016, investing in a diversity of sectors (Tables 4.5 and 4.6). For the purpose of the book, this chapter concentrates only on the crop-farming companies; most of them were located in East and Central Africa, with Angola, Zimbabwe, Tanzania, Zambia and Mozambique hosting the largest number of Chinese companies (Table 4.6). There are thirty or so relatively sizable projects among all the Chinese crop-farming projects in Africa—that is, projects with at least 1000 hectares of land or $1 million of investment involved as collected by the author (Table 4.7). Insofar as these sizable projects are concerned, almost two-thirds of them are invested by Chinese state-owned enterprises (SOEs) or mixed-ownership companies with state element; and the majority of them are cash-crop projects (Table 4.7), which is largely in line with China's national strategy (Sect. 4.1.1).

Governmental Actors
Despite the leading role naturally taken by the different types of agriculture-related companies, Chinese government actors also play a part, particularly in terms of mobilizing, supporting and supervising the company actors in a range of ways, in the 'agribusiness model' of development cooperation with Africa.

Table 4.5 Chinese agricultural FDI in Africa in/by 2016

Sectors		FDI flow ($ million)	FDI stock ($ million)	Number of firms
Agro-production	Crop farming	29.6	454.3	51
	Fishery	60.9	112.2	18
	Husbandry	9	37.6	4
	Forestry	5.9	27.9	3
Agro-processing		17.2	61.54	5
Agro-services		58.1	578.4	27
Total		*180*	*1270*	*108*

Source The author based on MOA of the PRC (2017, 25–26)

Table 4.6 Top five SSA countries hosting Chinese agro-investment Firms

Countries	Crop-farming	Fishery	Husbandry	Forestry
1	Angola	Mauritania	Ethiopia	Mali
2	Zimbabwe	Mozambique	Uganda	Gabon
3	Tanzania	Tanzania	Angola	DRC
4	Zambia	Ghana	Cameroon	Cameroon
5	Mozambique	Guinea	Chad	Equatorial Guinea

Source The author based on the online database of Ministry of Commerce of China (http://femhzs.mofcom.gov.cn/fecpmvc/pages/fem/CorpJWList.html), updated by 30 September 2018

The Ministry of Agriculture (MOA) and Ministry of Commerce (MOC) at the central government level, along with the Department of Agriculture and Department of Commerce at the provincial government level, take the main responsibilities on behalf of the Chinese government to formulate and implement the country's agricultural foreign investment policy. At the central level, while the MOA, given its specialist expertise, is usually involved in formulating action plans, providing suggestions and coordinating matters that require specific agricultural background, the MOC facilitates the process in a more general commercial sense, such as approving and registering agro-investment projects and firms, providing country-specific investment guides to the investors. The two systems, agricultural and commercial, of both central and provincial governments closely work with each other in promoting and regulating China's agricultural foreign investment on a day-to-day basis.

More specifically, three entities under the MOA play important roles in agro-investment related matters. The Department of International

Table 4.7 Some of the sizable agribusiness projects invested by Chinese companies in Africa

Company types	Company names	Investment destinations	Investment fields	Total areas and production models (ha)[a]	Investment value (USD)	Financing methods	Others
Central SAEs and non-agro-SOEs	(CNADC-) CAAIC	Zambia (1994–present)	Crop farming and husbandry	3600 (plantation)		Concession loans of EXIM Bank + CADFund	
		Tanzania (1999–present)	Sisal farming and preliminary processing	6900 (plantation)			
	(CNADC-) CSFAC	Zambia (1999–present)	Grain and vegetable farming and husbandry	3000 (plantation)			In cooperation with Jiangsu SFE
	SINOLIGHT	Mali (1960s–present)	Sugarcane farming and sugar production	Approx. 30,000 (plantation)		Concession loans of EXIM Bank	*Deriving from earlier aid project
	(SDIC-) COMPLANT	Sierra Leone (1980s–present) Madagascar (1997–present) Benin (2003–present) Togo (1980–present)	Sugarcane farming and sugar production	Approx. 40,000 (plantation + contract)			*Deriving from earlier aid project
	(SDIC-) China SDIC International Trade	Central Africa Republic (2012–present)	Cotton farming and preliminary processing	[50,000 planned] (contract)			Not fully operational due to political turmoil
	(Hengtian-) SINOTEX	Zimbabwe (2012–present)	Cotton seed breeding, cotton farming and preliminary processing	20,000 (contract)	30 million		Not fully operational yet

Company types	Company names	Investment destinations	Investment fields	Total areas and production models (ha)[a]	Investment value (USD)	Financing methods	Others
Local SFEs and Other non-agro-SOEs	Jiangsu SFE	Zambia (1990s–present)	Grain and vegetable farming	2300 (plantation)			
	Hubei SFE	Mozambique (2007–present)	Rice (and sugarcane) farming	300 (plantation)			*Implementing ATDC in Malawi
		Zimbabwe (2010–present)	Tobacco and vegetable	3000 (plantation)			
	Anhui SFE	Zimbabwe (2010–present)	Wheat, corn, soybean and tobacco	10,000 [50,000 planned] (plantation)	240 million	EXIM Bank loans	
	Hainan SFE	Sierra Leone (2013–present)	Rice and rubber farming and preliminary processing	45,000 [135,000 planned] (plantation + contract)	45 million	Concession loans of EXIM Bank	
	Shanxi SFE	Cameroon (2006–present)	Rice and cassava farming, ostrich keeping	100 [10,000 planned] (plantation)		CDB loans	*Implementing ATDC in Cameroon
	Jinlin OAID Group	Zambia (2013–present)	Corn and soybean farming, poultry, mushroom breeding and processing	2000 [100,000 planned] (plantation)			*Implementing ATDC in Zambia
	Jiangsu haiqi	Tanzania (2014–present)	Jiangsu-xinyanaga Agro-industrial-trade Modern Industrial Park	45 (square meters)		Cotton farming, cotton seeds processing, textile manufacturing, agro-equipment extension, technical training, etc.	
	Jiangsu yueda	Zimbabwe (2014–present)	Cotton seed breeding, cotton farming and preliminary processing	20,000 (contract)	30 million		In cooperation with SINOTEX

(continued)

Table 4.7 (continued)

Company types	Company names	Investment destinations	Investment fields	Total areas and production models (ha)[a]	Investment value (USD)	Financing methods	Others
Agro- and non-agro- companies of mixed ownership	SDIETC Group (Shandong)	Sudan (2012–present)	Cotton farming and preliminary processing; Agro-industrial Park	6700 (contract)	53 million	CADFund + CAFIC	*Implementing ATDC in Sudan*
	Tianli Group (Shanxi)	Madagascar (2013–present)	Cotton farming and preliminary processing	60,000 [200,000 planned] (contract)	150 million	CDB loans + CADFund	
	COVEC	Ethiopia (2014–present) Nigeria (2005–present)	Husbandry and Processing Park Abuja Agro-industrial Park	2000			
Private agro- and non-agro-companies	Yunshi Seeds (Hunan)	Madagascar	Seed breeding and production; rice farming and preliminary processing	1200 (contract)	11 million	Rice farming and seed breeding Establishing R&D centres and seed breeding stations in Liberia, Angola, Ethiopia and Nigeria, etc	
	Ruichang (Shandong)	Zimbabwe, Mozambique, Zambia, Malawi, etc	Cotton farming and preliminary processing	Hundreds of thousand (contract)	60 million	CDB loans + CADFund	*Implementing ATDC in Malawi*
	Wanbao[b] (Hubei)	Mozambique (2011–present)	Rice farming and preliminary processing (*Wanbao Moz Agricultural Park*)	20,000 (plantation + contract)	200 million	CDB loans + CADFund	In cooperation with Hubei SFE
	Hefeng (Hubei)	Mozambique (2012–present)	Rice farming and preliminary processing	6000 (plantation + contract)	6.4 million		In cooperation with Hubei SFE
	Youhao hengyuan (Sichuan)	Uganda (2014–present)	Agro-industrial Park	400	220 million		*Technical training, farming demonstration, seeds extension, agro-processing, trade and services*

Company types	Company names	Investment destinations	Investment fields	Total areas and production models (ha)[a]	Investment value (USD)	Financing methods	Others
	Jinfengyu (Shanghai)	Tanzania	Rice farming, agro-produce trade and services	2600 (through purchasing local firms)			
	Xinjiang wuzheng (Shandong)	Uganda (2016–present)	*Agriculture Demonstration Park*	200			Technical extension, farming demonstration, seeds breeding, agro-processing, trade and services
	Jiangzhou nongye (Jiangsu)	Angola (2014–present)	Soybeans and corns farming and preliminary processing	10,000	60 million		
	Ganliang shiye (Jiangxi)	Equatorial Guinea (2014–present)	Cassava and rice farming and preliminary processing		540 million		

Note SAE—State-owned Agricultural Enterprise; SOE—State-owned Enterprise; SFE—State Farming Enterprise
Source The author based on Chinese media reports, company websites and the author's fieldwork; updated by September 2018
[a]'Plantation' here indicates 'plantation/farm production model', and 'contract' indicates 'contract farming model'. For more details about the production models, see Sect. 4.1.3
[b]The project has been transferred to CR20, a Chinese SOE, since 2017 (see Sect. 4.2.1)

Cooperation acts like the policy-making body, the Foreign Economic Cooperation Centre is largely in charge of policy implementation and the Research Centre for Rural Economy serves as a think tank that provides reports and drafts policies for the Ministry. On the MOC side, the most relevant entities include the Department of Outward Investment and Economic Cooperation who is the main implementing body of the government's 'Going Out' strategy, regional departments—in the case of Africa, for instance, the Department of West Asian and African Affairs—which are in charge of drafting and implementing regional economic cooperation policies, and very importantly, the Economic and Commercial Counsellor's Offices, the MOC's overseas branches (often located within Chinese embassies) that play an assisting role to help Chinese agro-companies with local issues such as boosting public relations and solving business-related conflicts of the companies.

Apart from these two systems, some other Chinese government agencies also to different degrees participate. The National Development and Reform Commission (NDRC),[5] for instance, played an important part in drafting the *Suggestions on Overseas Agricultural Investment and Cooperation* (*Suggestions* hereinafter, Table 4.8), one of the most important official documents on Chinese overseas agro-investment. To achieve a better coordination result, there are also two inter-ministry cooperation mechanisms in place, both of which are led prominently by the MOA and MOC. One is called 'Agriculture Going Out' Inter-ministry Coordinating Leading Group, made up of 10 different central ministries and established in 2006; the other is Inter-ministry Working Mechanism on Overseas Agricultural Resources Exploration formed by 14 different ministries and established in 2008 (Table 4.8). These two mechanisms, however, do not seem to have played an active or adequate role in real practice (Jiao 2013).

In addition, some policy-oriented national banks and insurance companies have worked closely with the government in facilitating Chinese agro-companies to invest abroad. The most relevant ones include the Export and Import Bank of China (EXIM Bank), the China Development Bank (CDB) and the China Export & Credit Insurance Corporation (SINOSURE).

---

[5] NDRC is the key ministry under the State Council that is responsible for monitoring and guiding the national macro-economy and social development.

Table 4.8 Policy and institutional developments of China's 'Agriculture Going Out' policy

2006	*Suggestions on Hastening the Implementation of the 'Agriculture Going Out' Strategy* by the Ministry of Commerce (MOC), the Ministry of Agriculture (MOA) and the Ministry of Finance *Development Plan of the 'Agriculture Going Out' Strategy* by the MOA *Founded the *'Agriculture Going Out' Inter-ministry Coordinating Leading Group* made up of 10 different central ministries and led by MOA and MOC
2007	*No. 1 Document* of the Chinese Communist Party (CCP) Hasten the implementation of the 'Agriculture Going Out' strategy (focusing more on the agricultural trade aspect)
2008	*Decisions on Several Key Issues of Promoting the Rural Reform* by the CCP Expand the 'Agricultural Opening Up': combine 'inviting in' and 'going out'; strengthen the capability to utilize the 'two markets' and 'two resources' both at home and abroad; develop the agricultural international cooperation; foster the development of transnational agricultural firms; gradually build up an international integrated system for agricultural production, processing, storage, logistics and trade *Medium/Long-term Plan of China's Grain Security (2008–2020)* by the State Council Strengthen the international cooperation in the grains and oils area; implement the 'Agriculture Going Out' strategy; encourage Chinese enterprises to invest abroad; establish stable and reliable guarantee system for grain imports; enhance the capability of ensuring grain security *Set up the *Inter-ministry Working Mechanism on Overseas Agricultural Resources Exploration* formed by 14 central ministries and led by MOC and MOA
2010	*No. 1 Document* of the CCP Enhance the level of the 'Agricultural Opening Up'; strengthen the international cooperation on agricultural technology and resources; formulate encouraging policies and promote qualified enterprises to invest abroad
2011	*The 12th Five-year Plan of the Food-processing Industry* by the National Development and Reform Commission (NDRC) and the Ministry of Industry and Information Technology (MIIT) Develop international grain cooperation, encourage Chinese enterprises to go abroad and establish processing firms for rice, cotton and soybean; encourage qualified enterprises to invest abroad in palm, soybean, sunflower seeds and other oil products, and establish overseas edible oil production and processing bases; build up the guarantee system for diverse types of oil products and editable vegetable oils *Development Plan of the Agricultural Investment and Cooperation* by the third conference of Inter-ministry Working Mechanism on Overseas Agricultural Resources Exploration
2013	*Suggestions on Overseas Agricultural Investment and Cooperation* by the NDRC and the MOC (for more, see Table 4.4)
2014	*No. 1 Document* of the CCP Utilize the international agricultural product market; hasten the implementation of the 'Agriculture Going Out' strategy; foster the development of large-scale, internationally competitive enterprises of grains, cotton, oils; support the agricultural production and export/import cooperation especially with the neighbouring countries; encourage the financial agencies to innovate in financing types and methods for agricultural international trade and 'Agriculture Going Out'; explore the feasibility of establishing special fund for international trade and overseas agricultural development

Source The author based on the relevant official documents during 2006–2014

These government and related agencies have made a joint effort—through a diversity of methods from policy encouragement, financial support, tax and insurance measures to diplomatic backup—to mobilize and support Chinese agro-companies' FDI activities. The Chinese government has, since the mid-2000s, issued a series of policy documents and statements that highlight the necessity of conducting overseas agro-investment and encourage Chinese enterprises to take an active role in this process (Table 4.8). These policies, although still relatively rough, do help bolster the confidence of domestic investors and also lay the foundations for relevant agencies to put forward more concrete measures. The abovementioned *Suggestions* made by the NDRC and MOC in 2013 set out for the first time the principles, destinations, fields and methods for the country's foreign agro-investment, which can meanwhile serve as a general guidance for Chinese companies (Table 4.4). Notwithstanding these developments, there is still urgent need for more detailed, country- or sector-specific agro-investment instructions that can better equip the companies and make successful investments more likely (Song et al. 2012).

In terms of financial support for agricultural foreign investment, the two national banks mentioned earlier have both established cooperation partnerships with the Ministry of Agriculture. The EXIM Bank, for instance, signed an agreement with the MOA in 2008, pledging to offer up to $8 billion credit to support agro-FDI projects by Chinese companies that involve overseas agro-resource exploitation, agro-processing, agro-technical exchange and agro-equipment exports, among others (MOA and EXIM Bank of the PRC 2008). By the end of 2017, the MOA had sponsored six batches of overseas agro-investment projects. The agreement was then renewed in 2014. The CDB also signed a MOU with the MOA in 2011 on supporting China's agricultural development, including overseas agro-investment. By 2018, the CDB had provided loans of $21.3 billion to support 488 overseas agro-projects (Guo 2018). Furthermore, the leading Communist Party of China also encouraged Chinese financial agencies to explore the possibility of establishing Overseas Agricultural Development Fund with a specific mandate to sponsor China's 'Agriculture Going Out' policy (CCP 2014).

Another source of financial support for overseas agro-investors is government subsidies. There are both direct subsidies and loan discounts under the so-called Special Fund for Foreign Economic and Technological Cooperation (SFFETC), a government preferential package sponsored by the state fiscal system and set up specifically for backing up Chinese enterprises in 'Going Out'. Agricultural overseas exploration is one of the most supported areas by the SFFETC.[6] To be eligible to apply for the fund as an agricultural project, the minimum investment value of the project should be no less than $1 million (MOF and MOC of the PRC 2012).

That said, in general, the financial support, either by policy-oriented banks (e.g. bank loans) or by state finances (e.g. government subsidies), is limited in type and scale. More importantly, such financial support tends to be biased towards a minority of agro-companies, particularly SAEs or large-sized private firms, due to the oft-closer link of their projects to the state strategy. The larger proportion of medium-/small-sized private agro-companies, on the other hand, is generally facing financial difficulties in the operation of their overseas agribusiness (Song et al. 2012; Jiang 2014).

Concerning insurance services, due to a number of constraints such as the high risks of foreign investment and the inadequate experience in insuring this kind of investment, there have not been many insurance providers or choices available for Chinese companies engaged in overseas investment. SINOSURE, the policy-oriented insurance company, seems to be the only agent so far with the ability of providing insurance services for Chinese companies' foreign investment including that in agriculture. In 2014, for instance, SINOSURE offered insurance to over 30 overseas agro-investment projects, with the total value amounting to $1 billion (Economic Information 2015). Yet, SINOSURE insures the investors against a very limited number of risks including only currency exchange ban, war or political turmoil, and requisition or breach of contract by the foreign government (SINOSURE). Natural disaster, for example, which stands as one of the biggest risks facing agricultural investors, is not covered.

In terms of tax measures,[7] Chinese agro-companies can benefit from general preferential policies, such as the export tax rebate, as all foreign investment-involved companies do. Also, the Chinese Ministry of Agriculture has signed bilateral agreements with a number of countries in

---

[6] Others also include general foreign investment, foreign engineering project contracting, and foreign labour cooperation.

[7] There are mainly three types of taxes applied in the overseas investment area, namely business income tax, goods and labour tax and import and export tariff.

order to prevent double taxation upon Chinese agro-companies. However, there have not been many special tax incentives for the agricultural enterprises. Particularly, under the current Grain and Cotton Import Quota System, only a limited number of agro-companies, mostly the SAEs, are able to gain the import quota; the others have to pay high tariff if they want to import their products to China from their overseas bases. This has actually become a big obstacle for many Chinese agro-investors. Notably, there have been a few exceptional cases wherein the government granted extra quotas to agro-companies. For instance, Jilin Overseas Agricultural Exploration Group Corporation (JOAEC), a provincial SAE, shipped back around 30,000 tons of rice from its overseas farms in Russia in 2013. The normal tariff standard for this type of rice import is 65%, but with the granted quota, JOAEC paid only 1% of the tariff (Observer 2013). This kind of quota allocation and tax advantage can potentially serve as a very useful economic incentive to Chinese overseas agro-investors, but it is nevertheless only an exceptional occurrence at the present stage.

Finally, the Chinese MOA has established bilateral working mechanisms with more than 50 countries in the world, signed a series of agreements on agricultural international cooperation and helped launch a number of agricultural investment projects (Yang 2012). According to the 'Suggestions' disclosed in 2013, the government will further strengthen cooperation with the most important agricultural partners in a wide range of areas, such as investment protection, avoidance of double taxation, inspection and quarantine, in order to better protect the overseas interests of Chinese enterprises (NDRC and MOC of the PRC 2013). However, this sort of diplomatic backup seems to have worked more effectively in the pre-implementation stage, i.e. establishing business partnership through diplomatic channels, while it is less visible after the projects are settled and put into actual operation (Sect. 5.2).

4.1.3 Modalities: Agro-Investment and Its Development Implications

The discussion about modalities of the 'agribusiness model' of Chinese agro-development cooperation in this section mostly revolves around some of the key aspects (i.e. financing, value chain investment, production models and market allocation) of Chinese companies' agro-investment in Africa, and accordingly, the (positive and negative) developmental implications of the investment activities.

Financing
Under the 'agribusiness model', financing for the agro-investment projects launched in different African countries largely comes from the Chinese side, which may to certain extent help alleviate the widely experienced financial bottleneck of the agricultural sector in Africa. In most cases, the investments are financed by Chinese companies' *self-owned capital* as well as *state supports* particularly from the two policy-oriented national banks, i.e. the EXIM Bank of China and China Development Bank. Apart from general financial facilities provided for overseas agro-investment (Sect. 4.1.2), the projects in Africa, specifically, can benefit also from some preferably or exclusively Africa-focused financial facilities such as the Government Medium/Long-term Concessional Loan and Preferential Buyer's Credit of the EXIM Bank (the often-called 'two concessional loans', see, e.g., Sects. 2.2 and 2.3) and the China-Africa Development Fund (CADFund)[8] provided by the CDB. It is, however, worth noting that, given the 'policy-oriented' nature of the two banks, they tend to offer financial support to state-owned enterprises (SOEs), or in the case of private ones, stronger firms (thus often larger-scaled projects) and especially those engaging with agro-products that are of strategic importance to China (Sect. 4.1.1 and Table 4.7).

Value Chain
There are different stages along the agribusiness value chain that foreign investors could engage with, from the upstream input supply and seed propagation, to the primary stage of agro-production, until the downstream trading and logistics, processing, and retailing. Chinese investors in Africa have so far focused mostly on the *production segment* of the value chain; and this is largely through 'greenfield' investment but

---

[8] The CADFund was established in 2007 as one of the practical measures pledged by Chinese government during the 2006 FOCAC with the view to boosting China-Africa economic relations. Specifically, it is aimed to support Chinese companies entering African markets and conducting foreign investment. As a sovereign fund, CADFund is provided by China Development Bank and adopts the PE (private equity) model in financing the targeted projects, which is different from the traditional free aid or loan model (CADFund website). The funding scale of CADFund reached $10 billion in 2018; and by the same year, the Fund had established 5 branches in Africa and financed more than 90 projects across 36 African countries, with pledged and realized investment value totaling at $4.6 billion and $3.3 billion, respectively (Zhou 2018). Agriculture is among the Fund's key areas of investment (others include, for instance, infrastructure, manufacturing and energy).

in some fewer cases also by mergers and acquisitions (M&A). Many Chinese agro-projects do involve some processing activities, but in most cases are limited to preliminary rather than deep processing, which is often attributed to the high costs involved. There have been a small (though growing) number of Chinese companies at the current stage who are investing in upstream or other downstream (from processing) agribusinesses in Africa—for instance, the emergence of seed-industry investment by a few Chinese firms and more recently, a new trend of establishing agro-industrial parks that often entail full agribusiness value chains (Table 4.7).

The idea of investing in agro-production abroad, or overseas plantation, used to be advocated by many from the academia and policy circles in China, especially during the early years after the 'Agriculture Going Out' policy was launched (for example, see Wan 2011). The argument was straightforward and reasonable: given China's domestic land constraints, Chinese companies should go abroad, buy or lease land, and establish overseas agro-production bases in relatively land-abundant countries. There have been some subtle shifts, however, in terms of the agro-investment value chain focus in recent years, as seen at both policy and practice levels. According to the *Suggestions* released in 2013 (NDRC and MOC of the PRC), Chinese companies are now more encouraged to invest in the downstream activities of foreign agribusiness, such as the storage and logistics, with other segments (including production) serving only as a supplement. While being in line with the common practice of transnational agro-companies for the consideration of higher economic returns (UNCTAD 2009, 2), this policy modification might also be related to China's own overseas agro-investment experience in the past and half decade—particularly that of a few setbacks caused by some land deals in Africa and Latin America.

Yet, the new policy rests on the precondition that host countries must have a mature and well-organized domestic agro-production system, which is however often lacking in the context of African countries. This means that even though this modified policy may be increasingly seen in Chinese overseas agricultural investment practice in the future, it would still be difficult to be massively applied in African environments. The land-involved, production-based type of agro-investment, therefore, is to some extent an inevitable choice for foreign investors, including the Chinese, who are operating on the continent. That said, despite the often-controversial land deals for the locals as well as the relatively lower profits for the investors, the upside of this sort of agro-investment is that it can make a direct contribution to productivity increase in the agricultural sector, and in the case of grain crops, enhancement of food supply and security of the recipient countries.

Production Models
There are primarily three production models currently being adopted by Chinese agro-investors (esp. greenfield-type investors) in Africa, respectively farm/plantation production, contract farming and a combination of both.[9] The main differences between the three largely revolve around the ownership or lease terms of land and accordingly, the different implications to landowners—particularly those more vulnerable smallholder farmers. That said, under all of the three production models, a large number of locals are hired to work on the projects and often offered with free training; this may to certain extent help boost employment, reduce poverty and build capability in the rural areas of investment-recipient countries.

The farm/plantation production model has been the most commonly seen model among Chinese agro-investment projects in Africa. Under this model, Chinese investors need to either buy or lease land from local governments or private owners to build their farms. These can be small farms of only several hectares or big plantations up to tens of thousands of hectares. The length of the lease also varies from 15, 20 years up to 99 years or more, on a country-specific basis. The farms/plantations are usually run by a small Chinese management team and employ local workers to crop on them. The number of local employees range from dozens to hundreds, depending on the size of the project. For instance, the sisal farm developed in Tanzania through CAAIC's investment— one of the Chinese central SAEs—operates on a 99-year lease of 6900 hectares of land obtained from a local Tanzanian in 1999 (Table 4.7). The farm is run by a small top-level management team of 6 Chinese people along with a larger middle-level management team of 100 local staff who are in charge of different areas such as production, administration, accounting, safeguarding, engineering and medical care. These local staffs are hired on a permanent basis—formal labour contracts are

---

[9] In less-common cases of agro-investment through M&As, Chinese companies may not be directly involved in the production process.

signed with the farm. In addition, the farm also employs hundreds of farm workers (700 long-term, 500 temporary in 2013) who are working on a seasonal basis. The output of this farm once amounted to one tenth of the entire sisal production in Tanzania, ranking the third in terms of company asset value among a total of 32 sisal farms in the country (Chen 2013; Yuan 2013).

Contract farming, on the other hand, normally features a contract agreement signed between farmers and companies that clearly specifies obligations of the former to produce agricultural commodities of certain quality and quantity, and that of the latter to off-take the goods and realize the payment as agreed beforehand. The companies also often provide embedded services such as agro-inputs, pre-financing and other non-financial services to the contracted farmers (Will 2013). Different from the farm/plantation model, contract farming usually depends on the lands of the contracted farmers and does not necessarily require investors to possess their own lands for production purposes. In the case of Chinese agro-investment in Africa, contract farming has not been widely adopted except for a number of cotton projects wherein the contract form has seemed to work quite effectively. A typical case is the private China-Africa Cotton Company (CACD) which has established affiliates in seven African countries, working with more than 200,000 contracted cotton farmers (Wang 2014; see also Sect. 4.2.2).

Under the combined form (of farm production and contract farming), Chinese companies source agricultural produce from both their own farms and the contracted local farmers. The main efforts are usually put into their own farms over which they have greater control and thus could ensure the basic production output (Interview 18 November 2013). They also work with the neighbouring local farmers primarily for the purpose of expanding production, but also at times as a way to benefit the local community (Interview 18 November 2013 and 14 January 2015). This combined production model can be seen, for example, in the cases of several rice farms run by Chinese private companies in Mozambique (Sects. 4.2.1 and 4.2.2), and the sugarcane and rubber plantations run by Chinese SAEs in Madagascar and Sierra Leone (Table 4.7).

Market
As mentioned earlier, the large majority of Chinese crop-farming projects are food crop projects focusing on different types of grains and vegetables (Sect. 4.1.2). In most cases, they are relatively small-scaled

except for the few bigger ones run by the SOEs (Table 4.7). Due to their limited scale, they mostly serve the local markets only and thus play a positive role in increasing food supplies of the recipient countries. In Zambia, for instance, the Chinese farms run by CSFAC, one of the central SAEs, since the 1990s supply all of their outputs to the locals, including Zambian government, local agro-processing firms and the open markets. One of these farms alone used to occupy 20% of Lusaka's agro-market share (Zhang, Zhe 2010; Mu 2013). The farms, in Angola, in which Xinjiang Production and Construction Corps invested, one of China's provincial state farming companies, have become the largest supplier of vegetables for Luanda (Chen et al. 2012, 83). Several rice projects in which Chinese private companies invested in Mozambique have also targeted mainly the local market, through different channels such as own outlets, small convenience stores or big local supermarkets (Interview 18 November 2013, 29 December 2014 and 14 January 2015).

Meanwhile, an often-neglected fact is that the ever-expanding Chinese community in Africa has also been a key selling audience for these Chinese farms. Chinese people are used to eating rice and Chinese varieties of vegetables, instead of other staple foods typical of Africa such as maize or cassava. Many of these farms, especially small-scaled farms, were actually initiated with the aim of supplying the large number of Chinese engineering and construction companies. Fenghui, a private firm in Sudan, for example, has become the largest food supplier for Chinese companies. Fenghui's chief executive officer used to work for CNPC when the oil giant began its oil exploration in Sudan between the late 1990s and early 2000s, and started his agribusiness in that period (Niu 2013). Some of these farms are even run by the construction companies themselves. For instance, the rice project by COVEC in Nigeria is an industrial diversification attempt by the company, after its long presence in the host country (Table 4.7). In Mozambique, Chinese agro-firms and some individual farmers supply their products to Chinese supermarkets and have direct and fixed selling channels to a large number of Chinese firms. Examples where this happens are the cities of Maputo and Beira (Interview 3 January 2015 and 14 January 2015).

Some larger food-crop projects do consider the possibility of exporting their products to the neighbouring countries in Africa. Yet, the plan does not seem to be feasible—at least in the short run—due to a series of practical constraints like the companies' limited production, the grain export and import control of the host countries, and the lack of selling channels abroad (Interview 18 November 2013 and 10 January 2015/14 January 2015). There is no solid evidence until now that the Chinese companies have grown food in Africa and have shipped it back to China.

For cash crops, the market channels of Chinese agro-investment have been more diversified. It may target local markets of the recipient countries and thus satisfy their domestic demand–supply gap, or international markets including that in China, thus contribute to the countries' foreign exchange earning. The local market is prioritized if there is demand from the host country. The three sugarcane plantations in which Chinese central SOE, SINOLIGHT, has invested in Mali, for instance, aim primarily to fulfil local needs. With the expected annual output of 140,000 tons of sugar by 2015, these three sugarcane plantations will be able to satisfy the total demand of the Malian domestic market (China.com.cn 2012). In many African countries where cash crops are mostly export-oriented, agricultural commodities are also sold directly on the international market. The sugar products produced by the central SOE, COMPLANT, supply both African countries, where its four subsidiaries are located, and increasingly EU markets, as well as other transnational sugar traders (People.cn 2012). In some other cases, the cash crops are shipped back to China. For instance, the sisal farm in Tanzania exports 80% of its production to China (Yu, Y.Y. 2014). China-Africa Cotton Company exports around 40,000 tons of raw cotton back to China every year (People's Daily 2013). Some other larger cotton projects—such as that run by SDIETC Group (a provincial SOE) and China SDIC International Trade Company (a central SOE) (Table 4.7)—have also expressed the intention to export cotton to China, though not fully realized yet, which is largely in line with Chinese government's policy objective to utilize overseas agro-resources (Sect. 4.1.1).

4.2 Case Studies: Chinese Agribusiness Investment Projects in Mozambique

Mozambique is one of the countries in Africa that hosts the largest number of Chinese agro-investors and the most sizable Chinese agribusiness projects (Tables 4.6 and 4.7). For this reason, it has been chosen as the country case study to investigate China's 'agribusiness model' of development cooperation with Africa. Specifically, four Chinese firms—Wanbao, Hefeng, CAAIC and CACD—and their respective investment projects in Mozambique are selected as the cases of the 'agribusiness model' to be examined. These four cases bring to light different types of corporate actors (e.g. private/state-owned/mixed), governmental relations (both with the Chinese and Mozambican), investment fields (e.g. rice/cotton) and modalities (in terms of financing, production and processing). At the same time, they also share certain similarities with each other and thus provide a good basis for a comparative integrated analysis. Among the four cases, that of Wanbao is treated as the key case given its representativeness and three others as complementary cases.

4.2.1 Wanbao: The Key Case

The agricultural project under discussion—originally called Hubei-Gaza Friendship Farm ('Friendship Farm' hereinafter)—was first set up in 2007 according to a local-government-level agreement on agricultural cooperation between the Hubei province of China and the Gaza Province of Mozambique. The link between the two provinces started in 2005 when Yu Zhengsheng, the then provincial Party secretary of Hubei, made his visit to Mozambique on behalf of the Chinese Communist Party (CCP).[10] In 2006, another senior official from Hubei followed it up and visited Mozambique again. On this occasion the Gaza province expressed its intent to invite the Chinese to help build a demonstration farm in Gaza with the aim of enhancing local agro-production and food security. To facilitate that, Gaza offered to provide 1000 hectares of land in Xaixai, a district under Gaza, where the farm could be built. A Memorandum of Understanding on agricultural cooperation was then signed between the two sides (FAOHB 2012) (Fig. 4.1).

As one of the tangible measures, Lianfeng Overseas Agricultural Development Company ('Lianfeng' hereinafter) was created by the Bureau of State Farms and Land Reclamation (BSFLR) of the Hubei provincial government, and entrusted to operate the prospective

---

[10] Mozambique is among a few African countries with which China also maintains good inter-party relations, which is surely a boost to inter-state relations of the two countries and helps pave the way for wider political and economic cooperation.

Fig. 4.1 One of the farms under Wanbao project, Xaixai, 20 November 2013

agro-project[11] (Zhang 2008). Soon after President Hu Jintao's state visit to Mozambique in earlier 2007, the Friendship Farm was formally started. The project, especially at its early stage, also had a close link with the Chinese Agriculture Technology Demonstration Centre (ATDC) in Mozambique, a Chinese agricultural aid project that was launched around the same period in the neighbouring province of Maputo (Sect. 3.2.1). Both projects were assigned to Lianfeng to operate and the Friendship Farm in Xaixai served partly as a test site for the ATDC in Boane. In 2008, Hubei and Gaza formally signed a five-year-long twinning agreement (Liu 2011; FAOHB 2012; Interview 4 November 2013) (Fig. 4.2).

The Gaza province initially provided 300 hectares of land for a pilot plantation and promised to give another 1000 hectares at a later stage.

[11] 19 farms were chosen from the 53 state-owned farms under the Hubei state farming system to form the Lianfeng company (Zhang 2008).

4 CHINA'S AGRO-DEVELOPMENT COOPERATION ...   135

Fig. 4.2 Wanbao project, Xaixai, 18 November 2013

Lianfeng tested the farming of rice, wheat, cotton, vegetables and others in the first year and the results proved to be very positive. Thanks to the perfect combination of Mozambican natural conditions and Chinese agricultural technology, the unit output of the rice production averaged above 9 tons/ha, significantly higher than local production standards, which vary between 1 and 2 tons/ha (Liu 2011, Interview 18 November 2013, FAO 2002; Kei Kajisa and Ellen Payongayong 2013). However, due to factors such as insufficient machinery and capital, Lianfeng's speed in expanding rice farming to the full land lot was quite slow, using only 150–180 hectares up to the year 2011/12. In 2011, Lianfeng had to go back to China to seek further support in order to fulfil its promise to the Mozambican government (Ganho 2013). Shortly after, Wanbao Grains & Oils Co., Ltd. ('Wanbao' hereinafter), a private agricultural company from the same province of Hubei, took over the whole project from Lianfeng. Different from Lianfeng, which is a typical state farming enterprise (SFE)[12] specialized in land reclamation and farming, Wanbao focuses more on downstream agribusiness including purchase,

[12]For more information about state farming enterprise, see Sect. 4.1.2.

processing, storage, sales and logistics. With annual revenue of around 2 billion RMB in 2011 (approx. 300 million USD) (Wanbao, n.d.), Wanbao can be considered a medium-/large-scale agricultural company in China[13] and one of the leading agro-firms in Hubei.

It is worth noting that the CDB played an important role in this project-transfer process. The Mozambican working group of the CDB, which is in charge of the Mozambique-related business and based within the bank's Hubei branch, contacted Wanbao's CEO in May 2011, introducing the Friendship Farm project and inviting him for a site visit. In early June, the CEO arrived in Gaza. He was impressed by the country's extraordinary natural conditions, regarding that as 'a combination of the climate in Hainan, the black soil in Dongbei, the typography of Hanjiang Plain, and the water resources of the Hanjiang River' (Min and Han 2012).[14] Based on this observation, he believed in the project's great potential and immediately signed an agreement with the Hubei BSFLR, taking over the project from Lianfeng. Only one month later, the first batch of machinery and equipment were shipped to Mozambique and the company even managed to catch the planting season in the same year. The process of land reclamation was significantly accelerated after Wanbao took over the project. The 300-ha pilot land was soon fully cultivated and ended up with a fairly good harvest in 2012, with a unit output reaching above 8 tons/ha (Min and Han 2012, Interview 19 November 2013c).

The Gaza government was surprised by Wanbao's speed and performance, and instantly expressed its willingness to provide larger tracts of land for further expanding the project. Wanbao then conceived an ambitious 20,000-ha development plan, and through the provincial governor of Gaza and the then ambassador of China, the proposal was handed directly to the then Mozambican president Guebuza (Min and Han 2012). Soon after, the proposal was approved and a new contract was signed between Wanbao and Regadio do Baixo Limpopo, EP ('RBL-EP' hereinafter). RBL-EP is a Mozambican state-owned irrigation company that is in charge of the management of the hydraulic infrastructure within the area of the lower Limpopo basin where the Wanbao project is located; the company

---

[13] This is by the Chinese standards: as set by the Chinese government, agro-companies with an annual revenue over 200 million RMB are considered 'large-scale', between 0.5 and 200 million RMB 'medium-scale' and under 0.5 million 'small-scale' (NBS of the PRC 2011).

[14] Hainan, Dongbei, Hanjiang are different regions in China that have good natural conditions for farming.

is directly accountable to the central government of Maputo. It is worth a mention though, that the key local partner of the project, when still under Lianfeng's operation, was the Direcção Provincial de Agricultura (DPA) under the local authority of Gaza (Ganho 2013). This shift of local partner, largely driven by domestic politics,[15] turned out to have direct impacts on Wanbao and its project, especially in terms of land issues (forthcoming).

According to the new contract, the investment volume totals at 250 million USD. The core content of the contract is the land concession offered by RBL-EP in exchange for infrastructure building and agro-technology transfer to be conducted by Wanbao.[16] Due to the nature of 'exchange', the land was provided to Wanbao for free. Not long after, Wanbao began to massively expand the project according to the new contract. However, the company was confronted with a severe setback in early 2013. A heavy flood, the worst in the past 50 years, hit Gaza and all the newly reclaimed farmland—about 3600 hectares of rice fields that were almost ready-to-harvest were inundated. The irrigation infrastructure that had been built since 2011 was also entirely destroyed. The direct economic loss was estimated to be $10 million (Interview 19 November 2013c). Despite the shock and financial loss, Wanbao decided to stay and started to rehabilitate the facilities and re-plant rice at once. By the time the fieldwork was conducted, in November 2013, Wanbao had finished the reclamation of 10,000 out of the 20,000 hectares awarded, and in total cultivated 7000 hectares (Interview 21 November 2013b). Apart from conducting agribusiness, Wanbao also built two schools for the children and transferred to the local chiefs (Interview 19 November 2013c, the author's site visits).[17]

[15] For more about the local politics between central and provincial Mozambican authorities around this issue, see Ganho (2013).

[16] More specifically, the main responsibility of RBL-EP is to grant Wanbao the concession of 20,000 hectares of land and ensure that the land will not be given or transferred to any third-party. The land lease expires in 50 years. Also, RBL-EP needs to help coordinate the entire process of the project development. In return, Wanbao takes the full responsibility to exploit the 20,000 hectares of land. In addition, the company is required to transfer Chinese farming technology and provide agricultural services to the local agro-producers and assist in the training of RBL in the area of irrigation, production and improvement of the market environment. According to the agreement, 10% of the cultivated and irrigated land within the project's perimeter should be allocated back to the local producers for the purpose of technology transfer.

[17] A most recent development of the Wanbao project is that, it's been transferred from the private Wanbao company to China Railway 20 Bureau Group Corporation (CR 20), a Chinese SOE, since September 2017 due to some management issue of Wanbao company.

Financing

A noteworthy feature of Wanbao's financing model is seen in its close partnership with the CDB. The Hubei branch of the CDB ('CDB Hubei' hereinafter) has long acted as an important financial partner to boost this private firm's agribusiness both at home and abroad. Years before the takeover of the Friendship Farm project in Mozambique, when Wanbao was still a newly transformed, medium-/small-sized agricultural company in Hubei, CDB Hubei had already begun to channel finances to support the company's domestic development. During the period 2009–2011, CDB Hubei provided bank loans of ¥41 million (approx. more than $6 million) to Wanbao (People.cn 2013). It is also through CDB Hubei, as mentioned earlier, that Wanbao was informed of the investment opportunity in Gaza and finally sent abroad to start the company's first overseas agribusiness project. In 2012, to help overcome the financial bottleneck confronted by Wanbao in the face of the new contract, CDB Hubei granted the company a bank loan of 20 million USD, effectively quenching the thirst of capital, in the initial phase of the project expansion (People.cn 2013).

As the project continued, particularly given the sheer size of the land areas (up to 20,000 hectares), the corresponding large amount of capital input still stood as a big challenge to Wanbao. This led it to seek further financial support from CADFund, one of the CDB's subsidiary investment funds with a specific aim to back Chinese companies' foreign investment in Africa (Sect. 4.1.2). In September 2013, CADFund signed an agreement with Wanbao, at the presence of the Mozambican ministers of agriculture and finance, to co-invest in the company's agro-project in Mozambique (Xiangyang Government 2013). According to this new agreement, the CDB would provide Wanbao with two types of financial support. With an estimate of 197 million USD for the total investment, the CDB would give the company a *loan* of 79 million USD while the remaining 118 million USD were to be *jointly invested by Wanbao and CADFund* (Xiangyang Government 2013). CADFund entrusted a third-party accountant firm to make an assessment of the money that Wanbao had already put into the project. CADFund would

---

The project is also renamed 'Wanbao Moz Agricultural Park' and has since operated well. The actual farming areas, however, remain at a similar level of around 3000 hectares (Sun 2019) with that in 2013 when the fieldwork was conducted (see above).

then rely on such assessment to provide the remainder (Interview 19 November 2013c). This injection of capital from the CDB significantly smoothed the way for the company's development in Mozambique; indeed, it is not common for Chinese policy-oriented bank, such as CDB, to provide such massive financial support to a private firm like Wanbao—the commitment of Chinese government to agricultural development in Africa as well as Wanbao's relatively larger company scale and its constant good relations with the bank may have played a role in here.

Production and Processing
Being well aware of the fundamental importance of the production aspect within the agribusiness value chain, which is particularly so in Africa given the continent's generally low agro-productivity, Wanbao made great efforts trying to establish an effective production system. There were, however, some practical difficulties for Wanbao itself, as mentioned earlier, is an agro-processing and trading company thereby lacking the expertise in farming. Also, unlike in China where it can largely depend on purchasing agro-products directly from Chinese farmers, in Mozambique the outputs of the local farmers are simply too low to satisfy the needs of Wanbao. To overcome this, Wanbao formed partnerships with a number of Chinese state-owned farms from China's domestic state farming system, namely Junken and Yunlianghu farms from Hubei state farming system,[18] and Shuangyashan and Jiangchuan farms from Heilongjiang state farming system. These four farms worked as Wanbao's subcontractors, hired only to take charge of the project's farming tasks. At the time of the author's fieldwork in late 2013, there were around 170 Chinese farmers from the four farms working for the Wanbao project (Interview 19 November 2013c, 20 November 2013a, and 20 November 2013b).

Specifically, Wanbao adopted two types of production models in their practice, namely plantation farming and cooperative farming (similar to contract farming). Plantation farming was applied mostly to the awarded 20,000 hectares of land, which was Wanbao's nucleus farm, considered the core business of the company. On this nucleus farm, apart from the abovementioned Chinese farmers, Wanbao also hired hundreds of local

---

[18] These two farms are also among the 19 Hubei farms that constitute the Lianfeng company.

farmers. Indeed, the medium/long-term plan was to gradually decrease the number of Chinese, keeping only a small number of very experienced Chinese farmers and agro-technicians in charge of technical training and support, while making use of more Mozambican farmers.[19] According to the calculation of Wanbao's farm manager, the ratio of Chinese-Mozambican labour in the future would be 1:5, more specifically, about one Chinese farmer/technician working with five local farmers on every 100 hectares of land (Interview 20 November 2013b). To facilitate this envisioned localized labour-usage strategy in the future, and also as required by the RBL-EP for the purpose of agro-technology transfer, Wanbao worked out a two-step action plan.

The first step is called Training Stage. The local Mozambican government was fully in charge of the trainee selection process while Wanbao would also suggest some selection criteria.[20] The selected trainees were usually organized in households, each of which would be allocated 1–2 ha of land within the training area of the Wanbao project, which amounts to around 180 hectares clearly demarcated within the 20,000 ha of total land. Wanbao hired an agro-expert from China who was specifically in charge of training local farmers. He taught and demonstrated Chinese rice-growing techniques (such as seed soaking, water management, weeding,

[19] There are several reasons for this. It is first and foremost required by the local regulations. There is a fixed quota for foreigners to be employed. In addition, it is also regarded by the Chinese managers as more costly and 'troublesome' to use Chinese farmers. Most of these Chinese farmers had never been abroad in their lives, not to say to places as far and tough as Africa. They tended to feel homesick, easy to get ill (malaria illness and even death) and violated local regulations or cultural rules unknowingly, which thus often caused troubles to the company. They were, therefore, regarded difficult to manage.

[20] Ganho (2013), for instance, casts doubt about the fairness of the trainee selection and suggests implicitly that Wanbao was involved in this unfair selection process. Indeed, as confirmed by a Mozambican scholar (Chichava 2013) who is well aware of the local situation, there were a lot of politics at play among *local* actors in this process in order to benefit from it. However, to what extent Wanbao was involved in it is not clear. First, Wanbao did not seem to know the local situations very well; for instance, they did not even clearly know the background and role of RBL-EP, their main partner. Second, the criteria they did propose to the Mozambican government were concerned mostly with agro-productivity; for example, they hoped the Mozambican government to choose trainees who have a family rather than being a bachelor so that, out of family responsibility, they would work harder and better. They would also prefer to have smallholders rather than people with other sorts of 'background' because the latter were often only half-hearted towards the training or even not present at all; this may have a direct impact on their performance and, accordingly, the productivity of Wanbao's project (Interview 18 November 2013).

fertilization) to the trainees. He was assisted by three Mozambican graduates in agriculture who helped translate between English and local dialects. It is, however, worth noting that, due to the language barrier and different farming cultures (between Chinese and Mozambican), the Chinese agro-technicians sometimes found it difficult, or at least quite slow, to get the Chinese way of rice-farming understood and well applied by local farmers. The training normally took one year; by the time I conducted fieldwork in late 2013, there had been around 100 households involved in this training scheme, 25 in 2012 and 70 in 2013. The training was free of charge[21] (Interviews 18 November 2013 and 19 November 2013b, the author's site visits) (Figs. 4.3 and 4.4).

Farmers who had finished all training sessions would then enter into what Wanbao called the Demonstration Stage. At this stage, the land area allocated to each household was increased to 4–5 ha and the farmers needed to work more independently in the field. In order to strengthen their economic responsibility, farmers, in this phase, would be asked to pre-pay 50% of the basic fees, around 23 thousand MZN (approx. $740), for using the seeds, fertilizers as well as the equipment provided by Wanbao. The other half of the fees would be deducted from the final payment Wanbao would make to the farmers for purchasing rice. Considering the fact that most of the farmers were too poor to afford the pre-payment, Wanbao negotiated and made a deal with a local bank CAPI that the bank would grant loans to the farmers upon the provision of a contract signed between the farmers and Wanbao. Wanbao would be responsible for paying back the money directly to the bank at an agreed time. Two female smallholders, who were among the first batch of farmers receiving the training in 2012 and entering the Demonstration Stage in 2013, reported that they did secure, without much difficulty, bank loans from CAPI by providing them with the contract signed with Wanbao (Interview 18 November 2013 and 20 December 2013a).

Apart from the plantation farming on its nucleus of 20,000 hectares, Wanbao also conducted cooperative farming with neighbouring local

---

[21] Ganho (2013), for instance, notes in her research that the farmers had to pay for the training, which was not true according to the author's interviews. She confused it with the fees the farmers were required to pre-pay for agro-materials and equipment in the Demonstration Stage. The training was free as per the 'exchange' agreement between Wanbao and EP-RBL in 2012.

Fig. 4.3 One of the lands allocated for training under Wanbao project, Xaixai, 21 November 2013

farmers.[22] There were two major differences between cooperative farming and plantation farming. First, the former is similar to contract farming whereby the farmers farm on their own lands and sell their products to Wanbao on a contract basis, while the latter consists of local farmers being employed to work on the land of Wanbao. Second, the farmers involved in the former are usually 'big' farmers (in relation to those smallholder framers) who owned relatively large lots of lands, while those engaged in the latter are mostly subsistence smallholders. However, by the time

---

[22] Having witnessed the performance of Wanbao, many Mozambican farm owners who had long suffered financial loss due to the low agricultural productivity expressed the interest of cooperation with Wanbao. Wanbao also found it feasible and thus started to cooperate with some of them since 2008. Specifically, the cooperative farming model is very much similar with that of the Demonstration Stage: While the farm owners would have to pre-pay 50% of the basic fees for the agro-materials, equipment and services that Wanbao provided, the other half of the fees would be deducted in the end.

Fig. 4.4 The Chinese farm director (on the left) explained to the translator (in pink) and the three young Mozambican graduates (the three from the right) who were going to assist the Chinese agro-expert in training the local farmers. Xaixai, 21 November 2013

fieldwork was conducted, this cooperative model had not developed into larger scale, due to the fact that there were not many such farm owners in the proximity of the Xaixai District where the Wanbao project was located. With the awarding of another 300 ha of land in the neighbouring District of Chókwè, Wanbao planned to massively expand this sort of cooperative farming model. In the long run, the ambition of Wanbao is to expand the area of local cooperative/contract farming to 80,000 hectares, which is 4 times the size of its own 20,000-ha nucleus farm[23] (Interview 18 November 2013 and 20 November 2013b) (Fig. 4.5).

---

[23] According to the most updated data from news report (Sun 2019), the households participating in Wanbao's cooperative/contracting farming has reached 491 with a total farming area up to 500 hectares, increasing significantly from 12 households and 60 hectares at the time when the fieldwork was conducted (Interview 30 November 2013b).

Fig. 4.5 The storage facilities under construction, Xaixai, 19 November 2013

In the meanwhile, Wanbao invested a large amount of money in building agro-processing facilities. By late 2013, three facilities for rice processing and another two for maize and flour processing were under construction. In addition, three high-standard grain granaries had already been completed, each of which having storage capability of 8000–10,000 tons (Interview 19 November 2013a; the author's site visits).

Market and Profit
By the time fieldwork was conducted in late 2013, the rice produced on Wanbao's farms had served Mozambique's domestic market only. There are two main markets: one in Xaixai, the capital town of Gaza province, to which Wanbao's farms sold the rice to the local Mozambicans through their own shops based on the farms; the other in capital city of Maputo, through a couple of Chinese supermarkets which served mostly the Chinese communities but also the Mozambicans (Figs. 4.6 and 4.7).

Apart from that, Wanbao also held an optimistic view as to the huge market potential existing in the neighbouring countries. As told by the farm manager:

> Zambia, Zimbabwe, Malawi and South Africa – these are not typical rice-producing countries, but they do consume rice; the neighbouring market therefore is large. We have no plan for now to ship our produced rice back to China due to the simple fact that even if there were ten more

Fig. 4.6 Local people queuing to buy rice directly from one of Wanbao's farms, Xaixai, 30 March 2013 (Taken by one of the accountants sent by CADFund to Wanbao)

Wanbaos growing rice here, they would still not be able to satisfy local demands from Mozambique and its neighbours. Many Indian, Pakistani and also Chinese grain merchants have come to us and tried to be our sale agent, which clearly shows that they do see the market advantages. But we wouldn't do that; we'd like to do the selling ourselves of course. (Interview 20 November 2013b)

Therefore, while it is usually assumed that the rice produced in Africa would be shipped back to China, in the case of Wanbao, for instance, that plan did not seem feasible, or at least it had not been put on the agenda for the near future.[24] In the long run, however, it is possible, and it could be highly profitable, to sell the rice produced in Mozambique back to China. Indeed, there had already been some Chinese grain merchants expressing their interest to become sale agents of Wanbao's Mozambican rice in China. As reported by one of the informants:

If the rice could be shipped back to China in the future, the return could be really high. The most valuable part of the rice produced here is that it is pollution-free. The quality of water in Limpopo is seven times higher than the top-quality water in China, and here we see no industrial pollution to

---

[24] Professor Bräutigam has come to the same conclusion based on her and her team's fieldwork in different African countries (Bräutigam 2016)

Fig. 4.7 Wanbao rice sold in the Chinese supermarkets, Maputo, January 2015

water or soil at all. Given the acceptable shipping costs, the Mozambique-produced rice would be able to occupy a large share of the market in China, especially if we target better-off cities like Beijing, Shanghai and Guangzhou. (Interview 20 November 2013a)

In terms of profits, according to the calculations made by the Wanbao management, the unit price of processed rice sold in local market is considerably higher than that in China; and if everything went smoothly, it would take about 6–7 years before the company can recover its investment costs in the project (Interview 19 November 2013c and 20 November 2013a).

Land Issue

The large amount of land involved in the project put Wanbao into a difficult unforeseen situation. As mentioned earlier, Wanbao was granted land concessions of 20,000 hectares in 2012 by the RBL-EP. The company then started to massively reclaim the awarded land since June 2013. This, however, immediately triggered huge controversy within the local community. It is worth noting that the vast majority of the 20,000 ha of lands, before Wanbao took over, were not really used for farming purposes. Rather, they had been largely left idle, for decades, mostly due to the dilapidation of the irrigation infrastructure as well as the mass exodus of the rural population since the country's civil war in the 1980s (Ganho 2013; Interview 20 November 2013b).

Yet, a number of local people were indeed affected by the project in different ways. The most prominent problem was that many smallholders—the exact figure varies significantly from one source to another[25]—who had used to live and farm on areas scattered within the project site were now deprived of these lands as a consequence of the massive reclamation work by Wanbao. Also, due to the disruption caused by the project, some cattle herders had to change their usual routes, or travel much farther, to access suitable lands to graze their animals. Some cemeteries located within the 20,000 ha were either despoiled, or had to be moved elsewhere, in order to make way for the project development (Interview 21 November 2013a, Ottaviani et al. 2013).

The main complaints concerned the fact that these changes mostly occurred without proper pre-consultation with the local people. The latter were thus largely left ignorant about the situation, only to find their own farmland being suddenly run over by Chinese tractors and bulldozers. Some of these affected people were also not happy with the relocation or compensation arrangement implemented by Wanbao. Great resentments aroused, and at least two large protests took place during 2013–2014, organized by local NGOs (Justiça Ambiental 2013; Ottaviani et al. 2013; MMO Notícias 2014).

Wanbao had not anticipated such situations. As put by one of the management,

> When we first came to Gaza with all the capital and equipment, they [the local government] thought we were serious investors and thus provided so readily the land we needed. They just laid out the map, demarcated areas for the project, without informing us of any possible scenarios like the ones we then experienced. (Interview 19 November 2013c)

Wanbao's most natural response, in the face of the confrontation, was to seek help from the local Mozambican government. They tried to persuade the affected people to talk directly to their government rather than protesting against Wanbao; for Wanbao believed that it acted entirely with the local authorities' approval by strictly following the contract

---

[25] As to the number of the population affected by the Wanbao project, the author interviewed people from RBL-EP, Wanbao, DPA and FONGA; they provided significantly different figures about that, varying from hundreds to tens of thousands of people (Interview 21 November 2013a, 21 November 2013b, 22 November 2013, and 20 December 2013).

signed between Wanbao and the RBL-EP, and that the responsibility had to rest with the Mozambican government in terms of addressing issues such as people relocation and cemetery moving. The company also went to talk with the local government many times in order to seek a solution for the problems. The negotiation, however, to their disappointment, did not turn out to be very fruitful.

> When the project really started and all the problems suddenly came up, it was so difficult trying to get some real help from the local government. We hoped that the government could be able to play an intermediary role between Wanbao and the local people, explaining the situation to them and coordinating the relations between us. But they don't really do that. They basically just leave all the problems to Wanbao to solve: for the relocation compensation, they don't want to spend one penny; for the cemetery moving, they asked us to negotiate with the local chiefs ourselves, despite the language barrier. The reason they provided to us for their passivity is that they have to take care of the interests of their people and do not want to get themselves into trouble. But do they really care about their people's interests? I really doubt. (Interview 19 November 2013c)

Having said that, in-depth interviews revealed that the Wanbao management had actually worked out rather concrete action plans; the problem, however, was that (as repeatedly emphasized by the managers during the interviews) they did not know who exactly—for instance, the RBL-EP, DPA, or provincial government—they should talk with about their plan. And even if they managed to introduce their plans, they seemed really doubtful about the executive capability of the local government.

> We have set aside a sum of money to build at least 500 houses for the displaced people. We know that they do not only need a place to live but also land to farm. So our suggestions would be to exchange land with them. More specifically, we can build houses along our farms within the project site. The displaced people would then move and live in these houses where they can have access to all the facilities of our farms like water, electricity, and proper roads that would not be available for them in their previous homes. During the day, they can simply work on our farms as our contracted farmers, taking advantage of the well-built irrigation systems. They could sell the products to Wanbao and we will pay them.

They must understand that we do not care about the land. What we really care are the final products. So it doesn't make any difference for us to exchange the land with the farmers and it could well solve the problems... And for the cattle farmers, we really don't see that the locals are doing the pasture in an efficient way. They are doing it in a very extensive way that is actually a waste of grass. What we would suggest is to call upon all sides – we can invite the experts of the Bureau of Animal Husbandry from China – and discuss the arrangement plan together. For instance, we can demarcate specific and suitable areas nearby for the cattle herders to graze their animals. It is just a matter of planning. (Interview 20 November 2013c)

The local-government actors themselves, particularly the RBL-EP and DAP Gaza, both believed that they had done their parts (Interview 22 November 2013c and 20 December 2013b). Interestingly, FONGA, one of the most active local NGOs that engaged with this issue and helped organize the smallholders' protests against Wanbao, told the author that they did not really mean to target Wanbao, but rather their own government. What they tried to achieve through organizing the protests was largely to pressure and push the government to act—there was a constant tension between FONGA and the Mozambican government. FONGA, for instance, even expressed their interest to talk and co-operate with Wanbao in order to work out some plans to solve the problems. Wanbao, however, did not particularly welcome the idea[26] (Interview 21 November 2013a and 21 November 2013b) (Figs. 4.8, 4.9, 4.10).

---

[26]This is actually also an interesting point, for Wanbao, and indeed including many other Chinese companies operating in Africa, normally feel hesitant to cooperate or engage too closely with local NGOs; instead, they tend to work more closely with the local governments. Many observers tend to criticize the Chinese companies for this and accuse them of nurturing corruption, which is in some cases true and fair, but not always. Many Chinese companies do not bribe local governments or officials but still tend to work closely and always in line with the local governments while keeping themselves at a safe distance from those civil society actors such as NGOs. A less mentioned point concerning this phenomenon is that these companies, to some extent, have got used to this sort of behavioral pattern that is very much shaped by the domestic environment in China. It is more effective, given the power of the Chinese government, and also much safer.

Fig. 4.8 One of the 20 houses (among the 500 planned) Wanhao already built for the Mozambican workers working on their farm (exterior). Xaixai, 19 November 2013

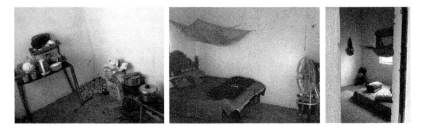

Fig. 4.9 One of the 20 houses Wanhao already built for the Mozambican workers working on their farm (interior). Xaixai, 19 November 2013

Fig. 4.10 FONGA, Xaixai, 21 November 2013

4.2.2 Hefeng, CAAIC and CACD: The Comparative Cases

Hefeng Oil & Grain Co., Ltd. (Hefeng)

Hefeng Oil & Grains Co., Ltd. ('Hefeng' hereinafter) is another private agribusiness firm that also came from the province of Hubei. With reported annual revenue of about ¥3 billion in 2013, Hefeng could be ranked among medium-/large-scale agro-companies in China. Its project in Mozambique was located in the Buzi district of the central province of Sofala. Through the local government of Buzi, Hefeng was provided with 4000 hectares of land, of which 3000 was uncultivated virgin land that required a large amount of investment and time to reclaim and prepare the land. For a cheaper and quicker project kick-off, the company decided to start with the 1000 hectares that had once been irrigated by the Portuguese during the colonial period. In spite of this, it still took an entire year—since the project started in late 2012—for Hefeng to reclaim the land and rehabilitate the irrigation system. They began with rice plantation on the prepared land in 2014 and cultivated a total of 300 hectares that year. The plan was to achieve full usage of 1000 hectares by the end of 2015 (Interview 14 January 2015) (Fig. 4.11).

Similar to the case of Wanbao, Hefeng was also introduced into Mozambique through the Hubei provincial government of China, specifically the BSFLR. Partially to avoid competition with Wanbao but also following the recommendation by some Mozambican officials, Hefeng finally chose to settle in Sofala. Initially, Hefeng's CEO was attracted by a potential investment opportunity in the sugarcane business, mostly for its high profitability. But the local government of Buzi expressed its preference for Hefeng to set up a rice project due to the food-shortage situation in the local area. Hefeng agreed. The idea was that they could start with a rice project first, which, according to the company staff, was treated as a semi-aid project given its rather limited margin of profit,

Fig. 4.11 The base of Hefeng Company, Buzi, 15 January 2015

Fig. 4.12 The canteen used by the Chinese and Mozambican workers (left: exterior, right: interior), Buzi, 15 January 2015

and launch the sugarcane business at a later stage (Interview 14 January 2015). Indeed, the real focus of the investment plan is definitely on the latter: in total, the company had intended to lease 50,000 hectares in three northern provinces along the Zambezi River and develop sugarcane production and processing during 2014–16 (Ning 2012). However, the plan was apparently postponed since nothing had been finalized by the time of the interview in early 2015 (Interview 14 January 2015).

Hefeng had also negotiated with the provincial government of Maputo and signed an initial land lease agreement for an 8000-hectare cotton project in the Marracuene district in 2012–2013 (Ning 2012). This project had not been initiated either at the time of research in early 2015 (Interview 14 January 2015). It is worth noting that, according to the Hubei BSFLR, all the projects mentioned above, i.e. the operating rice project and the prospective sugarcane and cotton projects, are under the name of Lianhe, a joint venture by Lianfeng[27] and Hefeng, although in effect, Lianfeng had not seemed to play a very noticeable role and Hefeng had operated quite independently (Fig. 4.12).

Financing
For the 1000-ha rice project in Buzi, Hefeng had invested more than ¥20 million (approx. $3 million) by early 2015, which was entirely financed by the company's *self-owned capital* (Interview 14 January

---

[27] For more information about Lianfeng, see Sect. 4.2.1.

2015).[28] The total investment value, including the cotton project in the Maputo province and sugarcane project in Sofala, was estimated at ¥1 billion (approx. $152 million) (Ning 2012), but a specific financing model for that had yet to be finalized. Considering the company's scale and profitability, it doesn't seem very likely that Hefeng could be able to finance the whole project entirely by itself.

Production and Processing
The production model adopted by Hefeng is also a combination of plantation and contract farming. However, at the time fieldwork was conducted, the bulk of the output had come from the 1000-ha self-owned nucleus farm. Similar to the sub-contracting scheme used by Wanbao, though much smaller in size, Hefeng divided the 1000 hectares into 20 lots of land and contracted them to 20 experienced Chinese farmers hired from Hubei. Each of the farmers is in charge of 50 hectares and required to employ at least 10 local workers to work with them in order to fulfil the production obligation. In total, at the time fieldwork was conducted, there were more than 200 Mozambican locals employed to work on Hefeng's farm, with a monthly income of around 3000 MZN (approx. $75)—slightly higher than the stipulated minimum wage standard in the agricultural sector in Mozambique. The company prepaid the Chinese farmers for the seeds, fertilizers, equipment and the salaries of the local workers. These costs would be deducted from the payment the company made for purchasing the final produce from the Chinese farmers. The unit output of Hefeng's nucleus farm amounted to 5–6 ton/ha during 2014–2015, whereas the local unit output averaged only about 800 kg/ha (Interview 14 January 2015) (Fig. 4.13).

Moreover, Hefeng also conducted contract farming in its neighbouring areas, providing agro-inputs and services to, and purchasing the rice from, the contracted local farmers. This, however, was at a very limited scale by the time of the fieldwork in early 2015, not making any significant contribution to the company's entire output.[29] Furthermore, the

---

[28] A more updated figure, as provided by Hefeng's CEO, is that by the end of 2015 the company's investment in Buzi had amounted to $6.4 million, including the reclaiming and infrastructure building of 5000-hectare land in total (Sohu News 2018).

[29] A recent news report on the project reveals that the current contract-farming area of Hefeng in the neighbourhoods had increased to 5000 hectares by 2018 (Cheng and Bai 2018).

Fig. 4.13 Land under Hefeng project, Buzi, 15 January 2013

company would have to differentiate the rice bought from local farmers—which are of lower quality due to technical disadvantage—from that produced on Hefeng's own farm and sell the former separately at lower prices. The limited availability of human resources made it difficult for Hefeng at the time to provide guidance and conduct extensive training in local farmers' paddies to assure the rice standard would be the same as that in the nucleus farm. That said, the operation of Hefeng still played a positive role in increasing rice production and grain supply locally—many smallholder farmers nearby started or converted to grow rice with the view to selling the produce to the Chinese company and earning incomes. The purchasing price in 2014, for instance, was about 30,000 MZN/ha (approx. $750/ha) (Interview 14 January 2015) (Fig. 4.14).

Hefeng had a small set of semi-automatic rice processing facilities in its production base at Buzi, with a processing capability of about 30 tons/day. These facilities were then adequate to process the rice produced on the nucleus farm and that purchased from local farmers.

Fig. 4.14 The simple processing facilities in the Hefeng base, Buzi, 15 January 2015

However, the facilities would surely need to be expanded in order to match the production potential. All the farming and processing equipment as well as agro-materials such as seeds and fertilizers were imported from China, which could enjoy tariff preference in Mozambique due to the country's agro-FDI promotion policies (Interview 14 January 2015).

Market and Profit

By the time fieldwork was conducted in early 2015, the processed rice had all been sold in the domestic Mozambican market, mainly in several central and northern provinces including Sofala, Manica, Tete, Nampula and Inhambane. It was quite challenging though for Hefeng, as a newcomer, to break into the local market. Unlike the case of Wanbao, a series of practical factors such as the less demand of the Buzi town, the isolation of the production base and the poor conditions of roads leading to other big cities, as well as the weaker financial capability of the company itself, made direct selling an unaffordable option to Hefeng. Instead, Hefeng had been heavily dependent on local, mostly Indian/Pakistani-run, sales distributers. In the beginning, local agencies were not sure about the quality and market response of Hefeng's rice and thus felt hesitant to buy them. Hefeng had to agree to leave its rice in the stores for free, without taking any deposit, as a trial sale until the rice was sold. Hefeng's rice could neither be sold to big chain supermarkets, like Shoprite, due to the lack of smaller-sized package bags[30] and its own barcodes (Interview 14 January 2015) (Fig. 4.15).

[30] At least in Sofala where Hefeng was based, there were not factories producing such-sized package bags.

Fig. 4.15 The AAA rice produced by Hefeng, Buzi, 15 January 2015

The only positive aspect for Hefeng to sell its rice through traditional sales agencies (rather than supermarkets) was that it may have more competitive advantages. Targeting mostly middle-/lower-class consumers, the Indian/Pakistani-run stores were dominated by cheap but relatively poor-quality, often long-stocked, rice imported from South and Southeast Asia. Comparatively, Hefeng's rice was newly produced and sold at very reasonable prices—around 24 MZN/kilo, which is among the lowest price range on the local market. Unsurprisingly, Hefeng's rice received quite positive feedback from local consumers, and after several months' trial sales, the agencies started to order rice from Hefeng's farm. This could be seen as a successful attempt in breaking into the local market, but the low price casts doubt on its profitability. Indeed, Hefeng hadn't managed to make any profit from the rice selling at the time when the fieldwork was conducted. It was expected to take at least 4–5 years before the company could possibly be able to recoup its initial investment (Interview 14 January 2015).

China-Africa Agricultural Investment Co., Ltd. (CAAIC)
A joint venture by CNADC[31] and CADFund, China-Africa Agricultural Investment Co., Ltd. ('CAAIC' hereinafter) was established under the FOCAC framework in 2010 and focuses on agribusiness specifically on

---
[31] CNADC is one of the six Chinese central-level SAEs (see Sect. 4.1.2).

the African continent (Table 4.7). The company had been in touch, since 2009, with the local government of Gaza province for a potential agribusiness project, which eventually led to a general agreement in early 2015 (not yet finalized) on a 6000-ha rice production/processing project in Chókwè district. The land will be provided free of charge, on the condition that CAAIC conducts technology transfer on the same amount of 6000-ha of land in its neighbouring areas (Interview 10 January 2015).

The reason for this long negotiation mainly lies with the Chinese side. The strict internal inspection procedure within the state-owned enterprise was identified as an important factor for the delay. Also, CAAIC was very cautious about all the clauses in the contract. For instance, whether the local partner would be able to fulfil the promise and provide the amount of land, which might be linked to the land controversy around the Wanbao project in Xaixai that is very close to Chókwè (Interview 10 January 2015). The local partner, on the other hand, appeared to be eager to see the deal finalized. There was also competition between different local governments of Xaixai and Chókwè, both trying to attract the Chinese investor into their own region (Interview 7 January 2014).

The project was estimated to cost around ¥500 million (approx. $80 million), of which a larger part, around ¥180 million, would be destined to building infrastructure such as irrigation systems. Self-owned capital, here mainly indicating that from the CNADC, is a main source of the finances, making up about one-third of the total investment. CADFund, as a major shareholder of CAAIC, will also provide a certain amount of money to the project. In addition, CAAIC may also try to gain support from SDIC (State Development & Investment Co.), a Chinese state-owned investment corporation that was established in the 1990s with a stated purpose to bolster a few key areas of the country,[32] and thus could be fairly regarded as an entity of state wealth funds. CAAIC doesn't intend to borrow money from banks in order to avoid the pressure of debts as much as possible (Interview 10 January 2015).

---

[32] The four key areas that SDIC has traditionally focused on are respectively infrastructure industry, burgeoning industries of strategic importance, financial service and other services, and international business.

CAAIC has planned to adopt a combination model of plantation and contract farming. On their 6000-ha nucleus farm, the company will employ both Chinese and local farm workers. Similar to Wanbao, the plan was to first use Chinese people, for their familiarity to the Chinese way of rice farming, and through training, gradually increase local labour usage. Outside the nucleus farm, CAAIC was required to demonstrate rice farming techniques to locals on the same amount of 6000 hectares' land surrounding CAAIC's farm with a view to help boost the local production. Apart from agro-extension, the company will also conduct contract farming with the neighbouring areas, providing agro-inputs to farm workers—mostly imported from China due to the lower costs—and purchase the final produce from local farmers at a previously agreed price. Processing was also deemed essential given the low-profit margin of production per se, but CAAIC may likely not build its own processing lines. Instead, the company was considering the possibility of utilizing two existing rice-processing factories nearby: one donated, years before, by the Chinese government, the other established by a British company. Both of them had been largely standing idle since being built due to the lack of agricultural output in the local area (Interview 10 January 2015).

Concerning its future business plan, CAAIC has mainly aimed at Mozambique's domestic and neighbouring markets. Different from Wanbao, CAAIC found it almost impossible to avoid using local sales agencies, particularly in the initial stage, given the fact that as a newcomer it does not have any of its own established selling channels in Mozambique. Although having yet to work out a specific marketing strategy, CAAIC is well aware of the potential fierce competition, especially with the Indian and Pakistani traders who massively import cheap rice from South and Southeast Asia. 'We'll probably be forced to lower our prices in order to compete with that imported rice, which accordingly would mean reduction of our profits' (Interview 10 January 2015). They also pointed out the lack of qualified Chinese staff in the company who can work effectively in the marketing area. Similar to the views of Wanbao, CAAIC also admitted the significantly greater profit margin for doing rice agribusiness in Mozambique than in China—as long as they could successfully fit into the local market. But even in that case, it was expected to take at least 14 years for the company to recoup its initial investment (Interview 10 January 2015).

China-Africa Cotton Development Co., Ltd. (CACD)[33]
China-Africa Cotton Development Co., Ltd. ('CACD' hereinafter) was established in 2009 as a joint venture by Ruichang, a private cotton company from Shandong province of China,[34] Huifu, a private textile company also from Shandong, and the CDB-owned CADFund which acts as a main stakeholder of CACD. CACD's investment in Malawi (in 2009) was the first agricultural project funded by CADFund, and back then the largest Chinese agro-investment project in Africa. By 2014, CACD had established subsidiaries in seven African countries, including Zambia, Tanzania, Mauritius, Malawi, Mali, Mozambique and Zimbabwe (Wang 2014); besides, it is also the implementer of Chinese ATDC in Malawi (Sect. 3.1). CACD entered Mozambique in 2011. The Mozambican affiliate, mainly the company office and its processing lines, is located in Beira, the capital city of the Sofala province; apart from that, CACD Mozambique has an exclusive access to approx. 700,000 hectares of land across three provinces of the country on a contract-farming basis. It also purchased the French-owned company, CDA, which helped further expand its local influence. It is now among the largest cotton production and processing firms in Mozambique, and the biggest one in the Sofala province (CACD, n.d.; Ren 2014).

The financing model adopted by CACD is quite similar to that of Wanbao—namely self-owned capital plus supports from the CDB (loans & CADFund)—particularly through facilitation of CDB's local branch in Qingdao, Shandong (Xu 2013). CACD has invested more than $60 million in its cotton business in Africa (CACD); and in Mozambique, the investment value had amounted to above $10 million (Ren 2014). Despite the support from the CDB, funding still stands as a major problem to CACD, especially as the company expands its cotton business across the continent (Wang 2014).

In terms of organizing production, what CADC adopts is the typical contract-farming model. They do not have their own nucleus farm, except for small lots of land for seed breeding; instead, they work with over 30,000 local cotton smallholders who farm on their own lands. The company provided seeds and upfront capital to the contracted farmers,

---

[33] The author tried a number of times through different channels but still did not manage to get interview and site-visit opportunities with CACD. Given the representativeness of CACD, I did not drop the case but had to base largely on secondary sources.

[34] Ruichang started to enter the African market, first through Zambia, since 2003.

and assigned Chinese agro-technicians to help with the plantation process. During the harvest season, they set up hundreds of purchasing stations in the small villages to collect the crops from the farmers and transported the cotton to the ginning factory based in the port city of Beira. The purchasing price in 2014, for instance, was about 9–12 MZN/kilo, slightly higher than the unitary price set by the Mozambican government (Ren 2014). The contract-farming model was believed by the CACD management to benefit the local community by helping enhance their incomes, while at the same time reduce the risk of land loss for the company in circumstances of policy changes (Wang 2014). The operation of CADC also helped to increase the local cotton production. As confirmed by a Mozambican official, the cotton output in the province of Sofala had been enhanced from 2000 to 5000 tons since the company arrived (Ren 2014).

Although CACD did establish processing facilities in Mozambique, only a small portion of the purchased cotton was locally processed. The majority of the raw cotton was shipped back to China (People's Daily 2013; Wang 2014; Pang 2015). The processing activities were also constrained at very primary levels; for example, the facilities they built in Beira were largely only cotton-ginning factories and oil mills (for the cotton seeds). They did consider developing deep processing (e.g. yarn, textile and cloth manufacturing) and thus extending the value chain (Pang 2015; Shen 2017), which, however, seemed too costly in the African environment. As put by CACD Mozambique's manager, 'We'll have to import everything from China, even for the screws, and it'll take months to arrive, which greatly increases the costs' (Ren 2014; Wang 2014; Pang 2015).

As mentioned earlier (Sect. 4.1.3), the main market of CACD's produced cotton is China. This is also the case for its affiliate in Mozambique wherein the local cotton industry itself is largely export-oriented. However, in terms of shipping the cotton back to China, CACD expressed their difficulty in not having adequate import quotas from the Chinese government (Sect. 4.1.1). Without quotas, CACD would not enjoy any price advantages and have to compete face-to-face with other transnational cotton traders on the international market, for which the company found itself still in a very disadvantaged position (Wang 2014).

As to profits, similar to the rice projects in Mozambique, there is large potential for profit earning in terms of growing cotton in Africa; the unit cost of locally produced cotton is about 4–5 times lower than that in China (Wang 2014). After more than one-decade's operation in Africa,

CACD has now managed to make profit from its business. Indeed, it's been one of the most profitable agro-projects funded by CADFund; by 2013, the CACD's pure profits had increased to about $6.5 million from merely $71 thousand in its earlier phase (Xu 2013). That said, the company's managers also expressed the difficulty in staying profitable given a number of practical challenges including, for instance, financial bottleneck, technical difficulties, lack of human resources, cultural differences, and limited experience in terms of operating in Africa (esp. compared to agro-MNCs of advanced countries), among others (Wang 2014; Liu and Liu 2016).

4.2.3 Integrated Analysis: Results and Problems

The 'agribusiness model' that features the incorporation of Chinese agro-firms and investment into China's agro-development cooperation with Africa has aimed to help invigorate the stagnant agricultural sector of Africa through both intentional efforts and the natural spillover effects of agribusiness, while in the meanwhile to facilitate Chinese agro-firms to go abroad and serve the development goals of China's own agricultural industry. As seen in the case studies in the previous section, this model has shown some positive prospects in terms of developmental impacts, for instance, through providing capital, creating jobs, supplying local markets with cheap foodstuff as well as cash crops and so on. That said, a number of challenges and problems have also been observed of this model, which have already affected and will likely to continue affecting the realization of the expected 'mutual-development' goals. Some of the key challenges are to be analysed and summarized in the section that follows.

Financing

While the capital infusion may potentially help fill the gap and development of agricultural sector on the African continent, the fact is that the Chinese agriculture-based firms themselves also face considerable difficulty both given their own limited financial strengths as well as relatively limited supports from the government. This may not only constrain their own business development in Africa but also the spill-over developmental impacts of their investment projects on the locals.

Difficulty in financing was frequently singled out by Chinese investors as a key obstacle for them to conduct agribusiness in Africa. First of all, it was by no means a cheap investment as some might naturally imagine, or at least not so for the medium-/small-sized agro-companies that made up the bulk of those engaged in Chinese agricultural foreign investment, including in Africa. There were indeed a number of pull factors in terms of the costs of doing agribusiness in Africa. For instance, land was more often than not provided at nominal costs, labour wages were also generally much cheaper than elsewhere (including China), and even inputs such as equipment, seeds and fertilizers that were generally expensive to local African farmers did not form a particular financial burden to the Chinese investors for most of these machinery and materials could be imported from China at relatively low prices. Having said that, a large amount of investment was nevertheless required for infrastructure building. This did not only concern infrastructure that was directly demanded by agro-projects such as irrigation systems, but also, quite often, roads, bridges and electricity, needed in order to facilitate basic transport and processing activities. For the entirely uncultivated virgin lands or those that used to be cultivated but had been left idle for long, which was quite a common situation facing Chinese agro-investors—like in the cases of Wanbao and Hefeng—the costs for infrastructure building or rehabilitation were even higher. It was estimated that almost half, or even more, of the total investment needed to be put into infrastructure building (Interview 10 January 2015).

Altogether, based on the data obtained in Mozambique, the investment for agribusiness on the African continent varied from ¥60,000 to 90,000 per hectare. For a relatively large-scale project, say beyond 1000 hectares, it then needed at least ¥60–90 million (approx. $9–14 million) as an initial capital input. While this was not a particularly large amount for a non-agricultural project or a big enterprise, it was not an easy job for the medium-/small-sized Chinese agricultural companies who earned only about ¥0.5–200 million of revenue (approx. $76 thousand to 30 million) per year at home (NBS of the PRC 2011) to finance such a project through self-owned capital.

Second, the financing channels for these medium-/small-sized, and mostly private, agricultural companies were limited and often 'biased'. It is true that, due to the underdevelopment of the domestic financing market and the high risks of overseas investment, fund-raising is generally difficult in China not only for agricultural but other types of investors too. That said, a series of factors such as the greater dependence on the climate, the relatively lower profits and longer period for capital returns, as well as the normally weak power of Chinese agricultural companies, have made it even harder for those agricultural foreign investors to raise the capital they need. By now, company self-owned capital and state supports were the two main sources of finances for Chinese overseas agro-investors (Sect. 4.1.3). This has been confirmed by the case studies in the present chapter. What is also confirmed, however, is the tendency of the state to support those state-owned enterprises or private companies whose mission aligns with the government's intentions. In the case of state-owned CAAIC, the three sources of finances—the self-owned capital from CNADC, the capital injection from CADFund, as well as the potential funds from SDIC—were, in essence, all using state capital. In the cases of Wanbao and CACD, both engaging with large-scale projects in significant crop types (rice and cotton), they both gained support from CADFund. Hefeng and other small-sized agro-firms in Mozambique—which actually represent the large majority of the Chinese agro-investors in Africa—were largely self-financed, and because of this, often face tremendous difficulty to survive or further expand.

Interestingly, even within the seemingly benign cooperation between the state and the private actors, in-depth examination has revealed certain tensions between the two sides. Take Wanbao as example. Mistrust started to emerge since the early stage of the agreement negotiation. The CADFund had once made an attempt to gain the majority holding of the project, but eventually gave up due to lack of expertise in agriculture.[35] Despite the abortion of the attempt, Wanbao had since been cautious towards its partner in order to maintain a leading role in the company's operations (Interview 19 November 2013c). Furthermore, as reported by a number of informants from different sources, Wanbao had, since 2014—or even earlier—encountered severe financial and managerial problems. These were considered to mainly revolve around internal problems, but

---

[35] What they proposed then was to let Wanbao be the majority shareholder (51% by Wanbao and 49% by CADFund) and take the full responsibility of the project operation and management, while the CADFund itself, apart from assigning a staff of their own to monitor the Wanbao's financial issue, will only regularly gain its deserved part of revenue from the company's yearly profits (Interviews 19 November 2013c and Interview 20 November 2013a).

perhaps more importantly, around their unwise investment strategies.[36] In addition, the accountants assigned by CADFund to Wanbao were not fully satisfied with the company's financial records in the recent years. As commented by one informant, 'While they (private companies) are always complaining about not getting enough support from the state, they themselves also do not do things up to the expected standards' (Interview 10 January 2015). This 'unhappy' experience, particularly given the high profile of the Wanbao project in both China and Mozambique, is very likely to have some impacts on the future choice of the CADFund in terms of private partners and may make it even harder for private investors to seek financial support or form financial partnerships with state actors.

Production and Processing
The four cases above have confirmed the general observation in Sect. 4.1 that the Chinese investors had primarily invested in the production aspect of the agribusiness value chain in Africa. This was almost an unavoidable choice, given the generally low agro-productivity on the continent. In terms of production models, similar to the general situation of Chinese agro-investment in Africa (Sect. 4.1), the Chinese agro-investors in Mozambique also adopted plantation farming, contract farming and sometimes a combination of both.

The productivity demonstrated through the different projects under investigation proved to be rather encouraging, usually much higher than the previous outputs without applying Chinese technology among other inputs. This is a positive sign that, leaving aside all other consideration and merely from the production point of view, the Chinese agribusiness model does bear the great potential to enhance the agricultural productivity and accordingly contribute to the food security or in terms of cash

---

[36]The 20,000-ha proposal is indeed a really ambitious business plan compared to many of those even relatively sizable agro-projects in which Chinese companies invested in Africa, especially for a private agro-firm like Wanbao. What seems to be more problematic is that the company started to put a large amount of capital into the downstream value chain, such as building large-scale processing lines and high-standard storage systems, even before reclaiming all the land allocated and thus without any corresponding productivity guaranteed. The downstream investment was so much that they later found not adequate capital to be put into the fundamental production activities, including paying salaries to the workers, and therefore faced both financial and managerial problems.

crops the export capability. And from Chinese company point of view, this high productivity lay the foundation for their downstream business and prospects for greater economic returns. Furthermore, some more nuanced details revealed by the case studies suggested that agro-inputs in terms of seeds, fertilizers and equipment were usually imported from China; this may benefit either the investors or a broader group of Chinese agriculture-related firms.

While a large number of local Mozambican workers were employed—indeed a localized labour strategy was preferred by the investors *in the long run*, as revealed in the case studies—Chinese farmers currently made up the majority of working force. One of the challenges in the stage of production is the agro-technology transfer, as seen in the transfer of Chinese rice farming techniques to locals in the case of Wanbao (Sect. 4.2.1) and cross-confirmed by the case of the Chinese ATDC in Mozambique (Sect. 3.2.1). The language barrier as well as the different farming cultures, among other aspects of the relations, had slowed down the technology transfer process and thus casted doubt upon whether a localized labour-usage strategy could satisfy the production demand of the Chinese farms, and if so, how long it would take.

Investment in processing (and other downstream agribusiness), on the other hand, had remained at a very preliminary stage. According to the fieldwork, developing local processing lines still did not seem to be a very welcome option by Chinese investors, despite its potentially higher value added that may bring greater benefits to both to the investors and the host country in the long run. This is mostly due to the high costs it will entail: a large amount of investment was required, not only for importing the equipment from abroad but also for sorting out the infrastructure bottleneck such as the lack of electricity (and transmission) and roads. Particularly, for companies producing export-oriented commodities, as seen in the CACD case, they may prefer selling the raw or preliminarily processed cotton directly to the international markets or shipping them back to China.

Markets and Profits
For all the Chinese agro-companies interviewed by the author, finding markets for their products was repeatedly mentioned as one of the biggest challenges. Take the rice value chain in Mozambique as an example. While it is true that there was a gap between domestic rice production and consumption, the gap had, however, already

been well fulfilled by rice imports from a diversity of foreign producers, particularly Southeast Asia (e.g. Thailand), South Asia (e.g. India) and South America (e.g. Brazil). Over time, this imported rice (of different types and grades) had also occupied different segments of the local market, from middle/upper-class to the relatively poor. In light of this, the Chinese agribusiness firms did not seem to have carried out adequate surveys so as to develop a comprehensive marketing strategy concerning, for instance, which consumer group they were targeting, how to fit into the local market by integrating with the established sales channels and how to distinguish themselves—especially newcomers—from other similar competitors. As of now, the main efforts, in terms of capital and human inputs, from Chinese agro-firms had been put into the production stage; no specified marketing department was in place, and very few professional staff familiar with agribusiness marketing, not to say the local environment and language, were involved.

Instead, the way they had been engaging with marketing, or simply sales, was quite random. The companies that had the potential markets in their immediate vicinity, or at least within cost-efficient distance from their production bases, tended to choose direct selling, without using any local sales agencies. They may open an outlet nearby their farms and sell rice directly to the locals as Wanbao did in Xaixai, or conduct door-to-door sales with the customers as Lianfeng did in Maputo and Hefeng in Beira. In some other cases, when they found direct selling impossible or too costly, they chose to depend on local sales agencies such as small retailing stores or big supermarkets. Examples were Hefeng's selling through local retailing agencies and Wanbao's selling through Chinese supermarkets in Maputo. Moreover, Wanbao, for instance, had expressed its hesitation in terms of conducting sales through agencies, mostly for the fear of losing control (e.g. over prices, profits) to the latter. However, they had yet to work out any effective alternatives.

Also, by the time fieldwork was conducted, the rice sales of all these Chinese agro-firms had been heavily dependent on Chinese communities in Mozambique. Wanbao's sales through Chinese supermarkets in Maputo was a typical case. Others who are not able, or cannot afford, to sell rice through Chinese supermarkets tended to establish informal but constant links with Chinese buyers, particularly different Chinese companies. This had been the case for Hefeng (and other small-sized private agro-firms). Given the increasing number of Chinese people as well as the language convenience, it was definitely the easiest way for agribusiness companies to market their rice among Chinese communities. However, this strategy would surely not be sustainable: only considering the farms discussed in this paper, the total area amounted to at least 27,000 hectares. All productivity released, it would produce 135,000 tons/year, whereas Chinese people may consume only a frictional part of this. Indeed, fierce and even unfair competition among Chinese agribusiness companies has already taken place. Due to the difficulty in expanding to other markets, some bigger companies started to sell the rice at very cheap prices. As a consequence, those smaller companies who were unable to decrease the price would be squeezed out of the Chinese community market. This 'new' problem emerging in the agribusiness area, unfortunately, reminds people of the 'old' story of vicious internal competition among Chinese companies operating in a range of sectors on the continent.

In terms of expanding to external markets, it may well be outside the agenda of many medium-/small-sized Chinese agro-firms. For some bigger players like Wanbao and CAAIC, they did consider the possibility of selling their rice abroad, which, however, also faced a number of challenges. First, there was policy restriction on grains export (including rice), given the food-insufficiency situation in Mozambique. Even if rice export was allowed, the poor transport infrastructure tends to increase the costs of inter-regional grain trade. Unless the Mozambique-produced rice was really successfully branded and can thus be sold at fairly high prices, on a large scale in the long run, it would be economically unviable to sell it in China considering the freight and tax costs, among other aspects. In addition, in terms of shipping the agro-products back to China, problems also lied in the Grain and Cotton Quota System, according to which Chinese agro-firms operating abroad either gain the quota from the Chinese government or have to pay a higher tariff, similarly to any foreign importers. As mentioned before (Sect. 4.1.2), at the current stage, it is still quite difficult, especially for private agro-firms, to gain quota from the government. The CACD case discussed earlier has also confirmed this.

Furthermore, none of the agro-companies being examined in this chapter have been able to earn profits from their projects in Mozambique. This was indeed not only the case in Mozambique, but it was a common situation for Chinese agro-investors in Africa (according to the author's broader survey and interviews). Given the general financial constraints facing Chinese investors, as mentioned earlier, successful sales seems to be even more important because revenues from the sales could be re-invested into the next round of production and thus reduce the pressure for the company to seek funds. The difficulty in sales, either in terms of finding markets or earning profits, as seen in the case studies, however, has further worsened their financial problem and made it even harder to make a successful agribusiness.

The difficulty in terms of finding markets as well as the economic unviability so far, caused by a variety of reasons as mentioned before, could become a serious impediment to the Chinese investors— dampening their enthusiasm in investing in African agriculture and thus diverting their capital and expertise elsewhere. Since the company actors and their commercial operation act as the cornerstone of the 'agribusiness model' of development cooperation, this may potentially have a major impact on the success or failure of the model, with implications to both the Chinese and African stakeholders.

Land Issue

To recap the 'motive analysis' earlier in this chapter, from the self-interest point of view, the current wave of Chinese agricultural investment in Africa, either for the government or private actors, is eventually resource-oriented—largely driven by the domestic land constraints in China. In this vein, the size of land obtained in overseas agribusiness activities does matter. Small lots of land would hold little significance in fulfilling the demand–supply gap from a government point of view, nor would that satisfy profit demand of the private investors, even admitting the relatively lesser effect of the economies of scale in agribusiness. Furthermore, it is widely believed by the Chinese officials, scholars and businessmen that Africa, blessed by its land endowments, is an ideal destination for Chinese resource-oriented overseas agro-investment.

It is true that, comparatively, the African continent is abundant with land resources and still with great potential of arable land. According to an estimate of the World Bank, almost half of the world's uncultivated but arable land, amounting to 450 million hectares, is located in Africa (World Bank 2013). However, as has been gradually recognized, the often seemingly less intensive use of land on the continent does not mean that the land is idle. Indeed, as pointed out by some scholars, virtually all valuable land is being used or at least claimed by local people

(Anseeuw et al. 2011; Wily 2011). Given the fact that investors would naturally be more interested in land that is fertile in quality, relatively well-infrastructured, easily accessed by transport systems, close to habitation and markets, among others, this sort of lands, understandably, have quite often already been intensively used by the locals for different purposes (Anseeuw et al. 2011).

Adding to the complexity, there are dualistic, both formal and customary, land tenure systems co-existing in the African environment and thus sometimes overlapping, if not conflicting, claims to the rural land rights. As a common practice prevailing in rural Africa, lands are often governed through traditional leaders/chiefs, by a set of customary rules deriving from, and sustained within, specific local communities, which determine how lands are owned, used and transferred. This is known as customary land tenure (Wily 2012). While customary land tenure is effectively operating as an overriding principle in the rural areas, the land rights of customary landholders are not always recognized or protected by their governments in the form of statutory law (Anseeuw et al. 2011; Wily 2011). In fact, the customarily held lands are more often than not overlaid with definition such as public, state, national or government lands. Both systems, the customary and state regimes, claim legitimacy over rural lands (Wily 2012; FAO 2013).

Foreign investors, in most times, obtain land through formal government channels. Given the capital needs and the inexplicitly biased policies against smallholders, African governments generally adopt a welcoming, albeit increasingly discreet, attitude towards the commercial use of rural lands. They, therefore, tend to make lands available for foreign investors and often at very low or only nominal costs. Due to the relatively weak presence of democratic governance in Africa, however, local communities are not always fully consulted and thus their land rights, particularly those of the majority of poor smallholders, are easily jeopardized in favour of more powerful government authorities or rural elites. This sometimes leads to involuntary dispossession of land and water resources, deprivation of livelihood, inadequate compensation, among others, and thus forms the basis of the 'land grabbing' discourse (Anseeuw et al. 2011; Wily 2011; FAO 2013; World Bank 2013).

Having said that, although foreign investors appear to be in a better bargaining position as fund-providers, the complex land situations on the continent also impose challenges to them. In cases where companies behave with responsibility, they have to accept the long time for negotiation and the high costs for compensation. In cases where they tend to cut the corner, risks are that they may provoke local resentments and conflicts, which may then cause financial and image losses, and even project failures (FAO 2013). The dual land tenure systems also make the land contract signed with the governments not entirely stable or secure.

Linked to the empirical evidence obtained from the field, the case studies of Chinese agro-investment in Mozambique seemed to largely confirm the abovementioned dynamics and challenges around the land issue. All the four Chinese agro-investors accessed land through government channels, and despite the awareness of the increasingly rigid conditions for foreign agro-investors,[37] they did not, in effect, encounter much difficulty obtaining the land areas they required. The local governments—in different regions and at different administrative levels—involved in the investment deals were generally very welcoming towards the investors, happy and quick in providing lands and facilitation, particularly in the initial period. They tended to have the investors secured and deals finalized as soon as possible. Arrangements such as the EIA (Environmental Impact Assessment) or RAP (Resettlement Action Plan) were not compulsorily required, nor the investors were informed about the local situations and potential problems (Sect. 4.2).

Conflicts with the local communities occurred, as seen in the Wanbao case. Neither adequate prior consultation nor appropriate compensation was in place (Sect. 4.2.1). This echoes the dualistic land tenure systems mentioned above. Indeed, Mozambique is one among several cases in Africa where customary land rights enjoy the greatest legal recognition and protection. In reality, however, as shown in the case study and also observed by other scholars, while investors seeking lands must consult with local communities, the procedure is ill-structured and undemocratic: it does not require organized participation and consent of the majority of the community, but only that of a handful of potentially self-selected representatives. Investors, therefore, enter into situations where local communities are unorganized and hence unable to negotiate on an equal footing with the investor (Wily 2011), which was also confirmed by the case of Wanbao. As a result, different groups of locals were negatively affected by the operation of the project (Sect. 4.2.1).

For Wanbao, the production was disrupted by local protests. The company had to spend a large amount of time negotiating the

[37] This is mostly due to the increasing number of foreign investors.

compensation with locals. Equally importantly, albeit not seeming to be really recognized by the Wanbao management itself, the land issue had triggered considerable controversy and imposed negative effects upon the company (Sect. 4.2.1). Also, partly due to the case of Wanbao, other Chinese companies, such as CAAIC, seemed to behave more cautiously in negotiating contracts with the local government. They felt insecure about their contract, particularly whether the local government would be able to deliver its promise to provide the agreed amount of land, and also, about the modalities under which the resettlement would be solved and financed at the later phase. This led to years of negotiation and has significantly postponed the project progress (Sect. 4.2.2).

The opposite example would be the case of CACD. By adopting a different production model and thus land use strategy, the company had largely avoided land-related controversy (Sect. 4.2.2). This is also in line with the suggestions proposed by the World Bank that investors should focus on enhancing the productivity of existing land users (World Bank 2013). However, it is worth noting that the Sofala province has the tradition of cotton cultivation, which makes the contract-farming model feasible. By contrast, in the case of Wanbao, it may take years before locals are able to well master the Chinese rice-farming techniques, and hence the company has to first establish from scratch its own nucleus farm, which, somehow, makes the conflicts between a first-time, inexperienced foreign investor on the one hand, and complex local conditions on the other, almost unavoidable. In short, despite all the potential benefits that could be possibly brought to the locals through the 'agribusiness model' of development cooperation, if the basic rights of residence and livelihood of the local people were deprived of, the claimed benefits are to be nullified or at least largely offset. There are hence many lessons to be learned both from China's own experience such as those seen in the case studies, as well as a broader range of experiences from other foreign investors (Cotula et al. 2009; FAO 2013, 2014).

Summary
As revealed by the four cases in this chapter, the 'agribusiness model' of Chinese development cooperation in Africa—while demonstrating certain positive developmental impacts in terms of, for instance, food security, job creation and poverty reduction—is also facing considerable practical challenges. These challenges not only constrain the profit margin and business prospect of the Chinese investors, but also limit the

'developmental' potential of these projects. Like what we've observed in the 'innovative agro-aid model' before (Sect. 3.2), implementation gap also exits in the 'agribusiness model'. The distinctive 'package' model of Chinese development cooperation with Africa—as far as the agricultural sector is concerned—seems yet to fully achieve the 'win-win' expectation envisaged and still needs much reflection and adjustment in this experimental phase before it can exert greater effects.

INTERVIEWS

(Only formal interviews included here (see Methodology in Introduction). All the informants are well informed of the identity and research purposes of the author; they are all kept anonymous to protect their privacy.)

Interview with the farm director of Hefeng. Buzi, Sofala province, Mozambique. 15 January 2015

Interview with two of Wanbao's management team. Interviewed by Lu Jiang. Xaixai, Gaza province, Mozambique. 18 November 2013.

Interview with a Chinese staff working for Wanbao. Interviewed by Lu Jiang. Xaixai, Gaza province, Mozambique. 19 November 2013a.

Interview with two Mozambican agro-technicians working for Wanbao. Interviewed by Lu Jiang. Xaixai, Gaza province, Mozambique. 19 November 2013b.

Interview with one of Wanbao's management team. Interviewed by Lu Jiang. Xaixai, Gaza province, Mozambique. 19 November 2013c.

Interview with a Chinese accountant assigned by CADFund to Wanbao. Interviewed by Lu Jiang. Xaixai, Gaza province, Mozambique. 20 November 2013a.

Interview with two of Wanbao's management team. Interviewed by Lu Jiang. Xaixai, Gaza province, Mozambique. 20 November 2013b.

Interview with the director of FONGA. Interviewed by Lu Jiang. Xaixai, Gaza province, Mozambique. 21 November 2013a.

Interview with two of Wanbao's management team. Interviewed by Lu Jiang. Xaixai, Gaza province, Mozambique. 21 November 2013b.

Interview with the chairman of the DPA Gaza. Interview by Lu Jiang and Idalêncio Sitoe. Xaixai, Gaza province, Mozambique. 22 November 2013.

Interview with two female Mozambican farmers. Interview by Lu Jiang and Sérgio Chichava. Xaixai, Gaza province, Mozambique. 20 December 2013a.

Interview with the chairman of RBL-EP. Interview by Lu Jiang and Sérgio Chichava Xaixai, Gaza province, Mozambique. 20 December 2013b.

Interview with a staff working for CAAIC. Interviewed by Lu Jiang. Maputo, Mozambique, 7 January 2014.

Interview with a Chinese working for a private Chinese agro-company in Mozambique. Interviewed by Lu Jiang. Maputo, Mozambique. 29 December 2014.

Interview with the Chinese manager of CAAIC's Mozambican project. Interviewed by Lu Jiang. Maputo, Mozambique. 10 January 2015.
Interview with a Chinese staff working for Hefeng. Interviewed by Lu Jiang. Buzi, Sofala province, Mozambique. 14 January 2015.
Interview with a Chinese staff B working at the ATDC in Mozambique. Interviewed by Lu Jiang. Boane, Maputo province, Mozambique. 4 November 2013.

REFERENCES

Anseeuw, Ward et al. 2011. 'Land Rights and the Rush for Land: Findings of the Global Commercial Pressures on Land Research Project'. http://www.landcoalition.org/sites/default/files/documents/resources/ILC%20GSR%20report_ENG.pdf.

Bräutigam, Deborah. 2016. *Will Africa Feed China?* Oxford: Oxford University Press.

CACD (China-Africa Cotton Development Ltd.). n.d. 'China-Africa Cotton Mozambique Limited'. Accessed 31 May 2019a. http://www.ca-cotton.com/en/company/c/.

———. n.d. 'Introduction'. Accessed 31 May 2019b. http://www.ca-cotton.com/en/aboutus/a/.

CCP (China's Communist Party). 2014. 'Guanyu Quanmian Shenhua Nongcun Gaige Jiakuai Tuijin Nongye Xiandaihua de Ruogan Yijian ("No. 1 Document of the CCP")'. http://www.gov.cn/jrzg/2014-01/19/content_2570454.htm.

Chen, Xiaochen. 2013. 'Gengyun Feizhou: Tansangniya Zhongguo Jianma Nongchang de Zhenshi Gushi (Farming in Africa: The Real Story of Chinese Sisal Farm in Tanzania)'. http://finance.sina.com.cn/roll/20130521/012715526584.shtml.

Chen, Yanjuan, Lu Qin, and Yan Deng. 2012. 'Zhongguo Dui Angela Nongye Touzi de Xianzhuang, Wenti Yu Duice (China's Agricultural Investment in Angola: Current Situations, Problems and Countermeasures)'. *Duiwai Jingji Shiwu* (Economic Relations and Trade) 12.

Cheng, Rongdong, and Xuelei Bai. 2018. 'Yangguang Xinwen Jujiao Hubei Hefeng Feizhou Zhongtian (CNR News Foduses on Hubei Hefeng's Farming in Africa)', 15 August. http://www.cnr.cn/hubei/yaowen/20180815/t20180815_524332005.shtml.

Chichava, Sérgio. 2013. 'Xai-Xai Chinese Rice Farm and Mozambican Internal Political Dynamics: A Complex Relation'. LSE IDEAS Africa Programme Occational Paper 2. http://s3.amazonaws.com/china_resources/17484/2013-07-24_09_26_57_-0400_Sergio-Chichava---Occasional-Paper-2.pdf.

China.com.cn. 2012. 'Mali Tanglian youdian "tian" (The Malian Association Is a Bit Sweet)'. http://finance.china.com.cn/roll/20120618/810592.shtml.

4 CHINA'S AGRO-DEVELOPMENT COOPERATION … 175

Comnews (Run by China's Ministry of Commerce). 2014. 'Guoji Liangcang Bicang, Dadou Hangye Ruhe Yingdui Weiji? (How Can Soybean Companies Cope with "Market Corner" Crisis Imposed by International Traders)', 16 April 2014. http://www.chinadaily.com.cn/hqcj/gjcj/2014-06-16/content_11840743.html.
Cotula, Lorenzo, Sonja Vermeulen, Rebeca Leonard, and James Keeley. 2009. 'Land Grab or Development Opportunity? Agricultural Investment and International Land Deals in Africa'. https://www.google.com.hk/url?sa=t&rct=j&q=&esrc=s&source=web&cd=1&ved=0ahUKEwj6v9iSnpfVAhUFwBQKHaZUBuQQFggkMAA&url=http%3a%2f%2fwww%2efao%2eorg%2f3%2fa-ak241e%2epdf&usg=AFQjCNHkljuMWiuA7EQjCKqNez-HSfdMDw.
Ding, Dong. 2014. 'Zhongguo Nongken Dazao Guoji Da Liangshang (China's State Farming System Aims to Develop into International Food Trader)'. http://www.chinanews.com/cj/2014-04-10/6046032.shtml.
EC (European Commission). 2005. 'The Crisis in African Agriculture: A More Effective Role for EC Aid?' http://practicalaction.org/docs/advocacy/the_crisis_in_african_agriculture.pdf.
Economic Information. 2015. 'Luoshi Zhongyao Yihao Wenjian, Zhengcexing Xinyong Baoxian Zhichi nongye "zouchuqu" (Realizing CCP's No. 1 Document: Policy-Oriented Insurance Supports Agricultural "Going Out")'. *Jingji Cankao Bao* (Economic Information), 20 March. http://news.xinhuanet.com/fortune/2015-03/20/c_127601043.htm.
FAO (Food and Agriculture Organization of the United Nations). 2002. 'FAO Rice Information: Mozambique'. http://www.fao.org/docrep/005/y4347e/y4347e17.htm#TopOfPage.
———. 2003. 'Food Security: Concepts and Measurement'. Trade Reforms and Food Security: Conceptualizing the Linkages. http://www.fao.org/docrep/005/y4671e/y4671e06.htm#fnB21.
———. 2013. 'Trends and Impacts of Foreign Investment in Developing Country Agriculture: Evidence from Case Studies'. http://www.fao.org/fileadmin/user_upload/newsroom/docs/Trends%20publication%202012%20November%202012.pdf.
———. 2014. 'Responsible Agricultural Investments in Developing Countries: How to Make Principles and Guidelines Effective'. https://www.google.com.hk/url?sa=t&rct=j&q=&esrc=s&source=web&cd=1&ved=0ahUKEwjo-MznnJfVAhUI7xQKHZH2AnMQFggpMAA&url=http%3a%2f%2fwww%2eregeringen%2ese%2f49bb90%2fcontentassets%2f5edb15744f844f-c590e478ef4f42bdea%2fresponsible-agricultural-investments-in-developing-countries&usg=AFQjCNF1hCe-r3yHYiDCUWFAQWHv3G4udw.
FAO of Hubei (Foreign Affairs Office of Hubei Provincial People's Government). 2012. 'Hubeisheng Yu Waiguo Dijie Youhao Chengshi Xiangqing (Twinned Foreign Cities with Hubei Province)'. http://www.fohb.gov.cn/swzx/show/648.aspx.

Freeman, Duncan, Jonathan Holslag, and Steffi Weil. 2008. 'China's Foreign Farming Policy: Can Land Provide Security?' Asia Papers. Brussels Institute of Contemporary China Studies. http://www.farmlandgrab.org/wp-content/uploads/2008/11/freeman-holslag-and-weil-2008-chinas-foreign-farmong-policy-biccs-asia-paper-vol-3-9.pdf.

Ganho, Ana Sofia. 2013. '"Friendship" Rice, Business, or "Land-Grabbing"? The Hubei-Gaza Rice Project in Xaixai'. LDPI (The Land Deal Politics Initiative) Working Paper 32. http://www.iss.nl/fileadmin/ASSETS/iss/Research_and_projects/Research_networks/LDPI/LDPI_WP_32.pdf.

Guo, Kaixuan. 2018. 'Guokaihang Zhaokai Zhichi Nongye "Zouchuqu" Yinqi Hezuo Tuidonghui (CDB Holds Bank-Company-Cooperation Meeting to Support Agricultural "Going Out")'. *Xinhua News*, 30 September. http://www.xinhuanet.com/money/2018-09/30/c_129964279.htm.

Harsch, Earnest. 2004. 'Agriculture: Africa's "Engine for Growth"'. *Africa Recovery*. http://www.un.org/en/africarenewal/vol17no4/174ag.htm.

Jiang, Lu. 2015. 'Chinese Agricultural Investment in Africa: Motives, Actors and Modalities'. Occasional Paper 223. Foreign Policy Programme. SAIIA (South African Institute of International Affairs).

Jiang, Yunzhang. 2014. 'Guangfang Baogao Dingdiao Nongye Haiwai Touzi (Official Report Set Tones for Agricultural Overseas Investment)'. http://www.eeo.com.cn/2014/0507/260161.shtml.

Jiao, Jian. 2013. 'Zhongguo Liangshi Anquan Baogao (Chinese Food Security Report)'. *Caijing Zazhi* (Financial Magazine). http://news.ifeng.com/shendu/cj/detail_2013_12/09/31912251_0.shtml.

Justiça Ambiental. 2013. '"Wambao Agriculture" os recentes e reais impactos de mais uma bolada dos dragões em nome do desenvolvimento ("Wambao Agriculture" Recent and Actual Impacts of Another Hefty Dragons in the Name of Development)'. Justiça Ambiental. http://www.verdade.co.mz/ambiente/39110--wambao-agriculture-os-recentes-e-reais-impactos-de-mais-uma-bolada-dos-dragoes-em-nome-do-desenvolvimento.

Kajisa, Kei, and Ellen Payongayong. 2013. 'Extensification and Intensification Process of Rainfed Lowland Rice Farming in Mozambique'. JICA Research Institute Working Papers 61. https://jica-ri.jica.go.jp/publication/assets/JICA-RI_WP_No.61_2013.pdf.

Liu, Dalong. 2011. 'Zongshu: Zhongguo Yu Mosangbike Kaizhan Nongye Hezuo Qianjing Guangkuo (Overview: China-Mozambique Agricultural Cooperation Has Great Prospects)'. Xinhua News Agency. http://news.xinhuanet.com/world/2011-09/19/c_131147121.htm.

Liu, Yanbo, and Min Liu. 2016. 'Six Experiences of Qingdao Ruichang in Investing African Agriculture (Qingdao Ruichang Touzi Feizhou Nongye Liuda Jingyan)'. 6 September. https://www.imsilkroad.com/news/p/6348.html.

Ma, Zhigang, Qi Wang, Zhihong Tian, and Xueling Zhai. 2014. 'Zhichi Nongye Duiwai Touzi Shouduan Fangshi de Tantao (Supporting Measures of China's Agricultural Foreign Investment)'. *Shijie Nongye* (World Agriculture) 2.
Min, Baohua, and Jie Han. 2012. 'Goujian Mosangbike de Guojia Liangcang: Wanbao Liangyou Youxian Gongsi Shishi "zouchuqu" zhanlue Jishi (Building Mozambique's National Grain Storage: Wanbao implementing "Going Out" Strategy)'. *Xiangyang Ribao* (Xiangyang Daily), 18 December.
MMO Notícias. 2014. 'Polícia Acusada de Impedir Marcha de Camponeses Em Xai-Xai (Police Accused of Preventing March of Peasants in Xai-Xai)'. *MMO Notícias*, 21 March. http://noticias.mmo.co.mz/2014/05/policia-acusada-de-impedir-marcha-de-camponeses-em-xai-xai.html.
MOA and EXIM Bank of the PRC (Ministry of Agriculture and the Export and Import Bank of the People's Republic of China). 2008. 'Agreement on Co-supporting Agricultural "Going Out"'.
MOA of the PRC (Ministry of Agriculture of the People's Republic of China). 2017. 'Report on Chinese Overseas Agricultural Investment and Cooperation'. Ministry of Agriculture, Beijing.
MOC of the PRC (Ministry of Commerce of the People's Republic of China). 2010. 'Zhongguo Yu Feizhou Jingmao Guanxi Baogao (China-Africa Economic and Trade Relations Report)'.
MOF and MOC of the PRC (Ministry of Finance and Ministry of Commerce of the People's Republic of China). 2012. *Guanyu Zuohao 2012nian Duiwai Jingji Jishu Hezuo Zhuanxiang Zijin Shenbao Gongzuo de Tongzhi* (On Applying for the Special Fund for Foreign Economic and Technological Cooperation in 2012). http://www.mofcom.gov.cn/article/cwgongzuo/huiyjl/201207/20120708225224.shtml.
Mu, Dong. 2013. 'Ji Zanbiya Zhongken Nongchang Nvchangzhang Lili (Documenting Lili, the Owner of Zhongken Farm)'. Xinhua News, 12 September. http://news.xinhuanet.com/overseas/2013-09/12/c_117340064.htm.
NBS of the PRC (National Bureau of Statistics of the People's Republic of China). 2011. 'Tongji Dazhongxiaowei Xing Qiye Huafen Fangfa (Classifications of Large/Medium/Small/Micro-Sized Enterprises)'. http://www.stats.gov.cn/statsinfo/auto2073/201310/t20131031_450691.html.
NDRC and MOC of the PRC (National Development and Reform Committee and Ministry of Commerce of People's Republic of China). 2013. *Guanyu Yinfa Guli Kaizhan Jingwai Nongye Touzi Hezuo Zhidao Yijian de Tongzhi* (Suggestions on Overseas Agricultural Investment and Cooperation).
NEPAD (New Partnership for Africa's Development). 2013. 'Agriculture in Africa: Transformation and Outlook'. http://www.nepad.org/resource/agriculture-africa-transformation-and-outlook.

Ning, Bo. 2012. 'Hubei Hefeng Touzi 10yi Mosangbike Kaifa Nongye (Hefeng from Hubei Province Invests 1 Billion RMB in Mozambican Agriculture)'. *Xiaogan Ribao* (Xiaogan Daily), 5 June. http://szb.xgrb.cn:9999/epaper/xgrb/html/2012/06/05/01/01_102.htm.

Niu, Qichang. 2013. 'Haiwai Nongchang de Zhongguo Shenying (The Chinese in Overseas Farms)'. *Jingji Daobao* (Economic Herald), 25 September. http://paper.dzwww.com/jjdb/data/20130925/html/2/content_2.html.

Observer. 2013. 'Woguo Haiwai Liangshi Jidi Shoudi Shuidao Yunhui (The First Batch of Rice Grown Overseas Were Shipped Back to China)'. http://www.guancha.cn/Industry/2013_12_15_192762.shtml.

Ottaviani, Jacopo, Andrea Fama, Isacco Chiaf, and Cecilia Anesi. 2013. 'China Accused of Stealth Land Grab over Mozambique's Great Rice Project'. http://www.theecologist.org/News/news_analysis/2177709/china_accused_of_stealth_land_grab_over_mozambiques_great_rice_project.html.

Pang, Lijing. 2015. 'Shiye Haiwai Touzi Chaoyong (A Wave of Foreign Investment)'. 13 July. http://www.eeo.com.cn/2015/0205/272190.shtml.

People.cn. 2012. 'Zhongcheng Jituan: Rang Tianmi de Shiye Zaofu Yu Feizhou Renmin (The COMPLANT: Sweet Career Benefits African People)'. People.cn, 12 November. http://finance.people.com.cn/n/2012/1112/c351563-19555158.html.

———. 2013. 'Guokaihang Hubei Fenhang Zhichi Nongye "zouchuqu" xingcheng "wanbao moshi" (CDB Hubei Supports "Agricultural Going Out" and Forms "Wanbao" Model)'. People.cn, 14 March. http://finance.people.com.cn/bank/n/2013/0314/c202331-20786349.html.

People's Daily. 2013. 'Gengyun Mengxiang de Haiwai Youzi (The Overseas Chinese Seeking for Dreams)'. *People's Daily (Overseas Edition)*, 21 September. http://paper.people.com.cn/rmrbhwb/html/2013-09/21/content_1301448.htm.

Ren, Jie. 2014. 'Zhongfei Mianye Daidong Mosangbike Miannong Zengshou (China Africa Cotton Company Promotes Income Increase of Mozambican Farmers)'. http://gb.cri.cn/42071/2014/06/18/7551s4581935.htm.

Shen, Junlin. 2017. 'Ruichang Mianye: Rang 100wan Feizhouren Shouyi (Ruichang Cotton Company: Benefiting 1 Million African People)'. *Qingdao Ribao* (Qingdao Daily), 9 June. http://www.qdbofcom.gov.cn/n32208327/n32208334/n32208552/n32208553/170609160637403446.html.

Sohu News. 2018. 'Zhongguo Nongye Zoujin Feizhou (China's Agriculture Expands to Africa)'. *Sohu News.* 4 September. https://www.sohu.com/a/251848387_782515.

Song, Hongyuan, Xiao Xu, Xueling Zhai, Xuegao Xu, Li Wang, and Hailong Xia. 2012. 'Kuoda Nongye Duiwai Touzi, Jiakuai "zouchuqu" zhanlue (Expand Agricultural Foreign Investment and Hasten the Implementation of "Going Out" Strategy)'. *Jingji Yanjiu Cankao* (Economic Research Review) 2444 (28).

Sun, Lihua. 2019. 'Mosangbike: Wanbo Mosang Nongyeyuan Shuidao Xiying Fengshou (Mozambique: Wanbao Agricultural Park Has a Rice Harvest)'. *Sohu News*. 3 April. http://www.sohu.com/a/305718995_201960.

Thurow, Roger. 2008. 'Agriculture's Last Frontier: African Farmers, U.S. Companies Try to Create Another Breadbasket With Hybrids'. *The Wall Street Journal*. http://www.wsj.com/articles/SB121185343060221769.

UNCTAD (United Nations Conference on Trade and Development). 2009. 'World Investment Report 2009: Transnational Corporations, Agricultural Production and Development'. http://unctad.org/en/Docs/wir2009_en.pdf.

Wan, Baorui. 2011. 'Guanyu Nongye "zouchuqu" wenti (On the Issue of "Agricultural Going Out")'. *Jingji Yanjiu Cankao* (Economic Research Review) 2380 (36): 19.

———. 2012. 'Jiakuai Shishi Nongye "zouchuqu" zhanlue (Quickening the Implementation of Agricultural Going Out Policy)'. *Renmin Ribao* (People's Daily), 5 June. http://paper.people.com.cn/rmrb//html/2012-06/05/nw.D110000renmrb_20120605_1-07.htm.

Wanbao. n.d. 'Gongsi Jieshao (Company Profile)'. Accessed 8 February 2016. http://en.wblyjt.com/?comContentId=8f102a02-541d-4fff-bf4d-c116189003ff.

Wang, Chao. 2014. 'Firm That Cottoned on to a Good Deal'. China Daily Africa. http://africa.chinadaily.com.cn/weekly/2014-06/13/content_17584808.htm.

Will, Magret. 2013. *Contract Farming Handbook: A Practical Guide for Linking Small-Scale Producers and Buyers Through Business Model Innovation*. Bonn and Eschborn: GIZ. http://www.unidroit.org/english/documents/2013/study80a/bibliogr-references/s-80a-will-contract.pdf.

Wily, Liz. 2011. 'The Tragedy of Public Lands: The Fate of the Commons under Global Commercial Pressure'. http://www.landcoalition.org/sites/default/files/documents/resources/WILY_Commons_web_11.03.11.pdf.

———. 2012. 'Rights to Resources in Crisis: Reviewing the Fate of Customary Tenure in Africa'. http://www.rightsandresources.org/documents/files/doc_4699.pdf.

World Bank. 2013. 'Growing Africa: Unlocking the Potential of Agribusiness'. The World Bank. http://siteresources.worldbank.org/INTAFRICA/Resources/africa-agribusiness-report-2013.pdf.

Xiangyang Government. 2013. 'Wanbao Liangyou Yu Zhongfei Fazhan Jijin Qianyue, Hezuo Touzi Kaifa Wanbao Feizhou Mosangbike Nongye Xiangmu (Wanbao and CADFund Signed Agreement to Co-operate in Agricultural Project in Mozambique)'. http://www.xiangyang.gov.cn/news/xyxw/xyyw/201309/t20130916_438735.shtml.

Xinhua News Agency. 2010. 'Hui Liangyu Zai Zhongfei Nongye Hezuo Luntan Bimushi Shang de Jianghua (Hui Liangyu's Speech on the Closing Ceremony of Forum on China-Africa Agricultural Cooperation)'. http://news.xinhuanet.com/2010-08/12/c_12440117.htm.

Xu, Juan. 2013. 'Guojia Kaifa Yinhang Qingdao Fenhang Zhuli qiye "zouchuqu" (CDB Qingdao Supports Enterprises to "Go Out")'. People.cn, 30 July. http://society.people.com.cn/n/2013/0730/c1008-22379126.html.

Yang, Shaopin. 2012. 'Zhongguo Nongye Jiakuai shishi "zouchuqu" (Hasten the Implementation of China's "Agricultural Going Out" Strategy)'. http://money.163.com/12/0822/12/89GTIALO00254S3A.html.

Ye, Xingqing. 2007. 'Zhongguo Nongye yiying "zouchuqu" (Chinese Agriculture Should Also "Go Out")'. *Liaowang (Outlook)*, no. 20: 50.

Yu, Wenjing. 2014. 'Nongken "zouchuqu" bufa Jiakuai (The State Farming System Has Hastened Its Pace to "Go Out")'. http://finance.china.com.cn/roll/20140410/2323715.shtml.

Yu, Yuanyuan. 2014. 'Tansang Jianma Xiangmu Qishilu (Learning from Tanzanian Sisal Farm)'. *CNADC (China National Agricultural Development Group Co. Ltd) News*, 10 October. http://www.zgnfb.com/news-5461.html.

Yuan, Jirong. 2013. 'Zhongguo Jianma Nongchang Zaofu Tansangniya (Chinese Sisal Farm Benefits Tanzania)'. http://world.people.com.cn/n/2013/0206/c1002-20444180.html.

Zhai, Xueling. 2006. 'Woguo Nongye "zouchuqu" de Wenti Ji Duice (Problems and Countermeasures of China's Agricultural "Going Out")'. *Guoji Jingji Hezuo* (International Economic Cooperation) 7: 7–10.

Zhang, Qingmin. 2009. 'Liushinian Lai Xinzhongguo Waijiao Buju de Fazhan (Development of the Overall Diplomatic Arrangement of the New China in the Past Six Decades)'. *Waijiao Pinglun* (Foreign Affairs Review) 4: 32–42.

Zhang, Yu. 2008. 'Zhongguo Nongken Haiwai Tuohuang (Chinese State-Farming Companies Explore Overseas)'. http://zzwz.qikan.com/ArticleView.aspx?titleid=zzwz20080816.

Zhang, Zhe. 2010. 'Zhongken Nongchang Chanpin Zhan Dangdi 20% (Products of Zhongken Farm Occupies 20% of Local Market)'. http://news.sina.com.cn/c/sd/2010-04-08/144520032529_3.shtml.

Zhou, Cui. 2018. 'CDB: Strengthening China-Africa Cooperation through Channelling Financial and Intellectual Resources (Guokaihang: Rongzi Rongzhi Zhutui Zhongfei Shenhua Hezuo)'. 21 September 2018. http://www.financialnews.com.cn/yh/sd/201809/t20180921_146550.html.

CHAPTER 5

Practical Challenges of Chinese 'Package' Model of Development Cooperation: A Public Policy Implementation Approach

Despite the innovation in cooperation modalities—as embodied in the 'innovative agro-aid' and 'agribusiness' models of Chinese 'development package' in Africa—there has been so far a lack of evaluation of the actual results of these new models of development cooperation. This chapter, therefore, aims to make an initial effort in *examining* and *explaining* the actual outcomes based on the in-depth, fieldwork-based case studies (Chapters 3 and 4). That said, given the limited number of cases entailed by the qualitative nature of research methods adopted, and the still short time of practice of these new modalities (starting only from the past decade or so), it is impossible (and also too early) to provide a comprehensive review evaluation of the effectiveness of Chinese 'package' model of development cooperation. What it can offer, instead, is only a qualitative (esp. ethnographic) evaluation of these models' progress until recent years.

Insofar as this modest aim is concerned, I have found a number of practical challenges in the actual implementation of China's current development cooperation models. The identified problems (as detailed in Sects. 3.2 and 4.2) do not only make the projects fail to meet the proposed policy objectives, but even have caused certain counterproductive effects. For instance, some ATDC projects, while not seeming able to achieve the expected sustainability, also experienced mutual mistrust and discontentment with local partners, mainly due to unsuccessful interactions. Similar cases can be seen in the agribusiness projects as well,

© The Author(s) 2020
L. Jiang, *Beyond Official Development Assistance*,
Governing China in the 21st Century,
https://doi.org/10.1007/978-981-32-9507-0_5

particularly considering the small level of commercial success and some controversies around land issues, among others. Such problems may cast doubts on to what extent the expected 'mutual-development' objectives have been or will be realized.

There are, therefore, certain *gaps* between the expectation and realities in terms of what Chinese agro-development cooperation policy in Africa can possibly bring about. In order to give a more systematic summary, I will adopt the public policy implementation (PPI) approach and analyse the observed problems, or implementation gaps, at three levels of policy, implementer and environment,, respectively.[1] While the three sets of factors—those on the development cooperation *policy* itself, the policy *implementers*, as well as the implementation *environment* of the policy— all play an indispensible role, the 'implementer' set of factors appears to act prominently in explaining the policy results (and especially the 'gaps') in the case of Chinese agro-cooperation with Africa. This is mostly due to the proactive role, or agency, that the implementers could potentially exert to remedy imperfect policies and counter unfavourable environments in this particular PPI situation.

5.1 Policy

Policy refers to a purposive course of action proposed and adopted by government authorities aiming to deal with specific public issues; and against the specific context, it here indicates China's development cooperation policy that aims to help address the issues of agricultural development in Africa. Before going to examine the 'problems' at the policy level, it should be noted that China's contemporary development cooperation policy, featuring its 'mutual-development' objectives and the 'package' models, is still largely a policy *in the making*. It came into being with the deepening of the country's aid reforms and economic interactions with Africa particularly during the recent two decades. Also, although having been publicly proclaimed in different official occasions, China's development cooperation policy is something that's kept being practiced on the ground more than that being carefully compiled by the

---

[1] For more about the PPI approach as well as the 'policy-implementer-environment' analytical framework adopted here, see Lu Jiang, 2016, *Beyond ODA: Chinese Way of Development Cooperation with Africa, the Case of Agriculture*. PhD thesis of London School of Economics, March, Sect. 1.5.

decision-makers. It thus can be seen at best as at a set of loosely defined arrangements that include the basic ends and means, but also entail much trial and error and accordingly an incremental process of policy testing and learning. For this sort of policies, it is easier or just normal to find problems compared to those delicately designed policies; constant reflection and quick learning, therefore, are more needed.

Two types of policy challenges—concerning policy design and policy control respectively—are observed in China's agro-development cooperation policy in Africa. In terms of *policy design* that involves the devising of key policy components particularly the objectives and action plans of a given policy, I find there are at least three notable issues existing in the area of China-Africa agro-cooperation. The first one is the *multi-objectives* involved in Chinese agro-development cooperation policy in Africa. This is shown not only in the co-existence of both Africa- and self-oriented objectives as informed by the 'mutual-development' mentality, but also demonstrated at more specific project levels—most typically, the ATDCs that combine the pursuits of developmental impact, business promotion and project sustainability all together in one project. This is not to blame multi-objectives for some of the implementation gaps; multi-goals are just more demanding but by themselves do not necessarily create a problem for implementation, as long as there are detailed and specifically designed action plans and no less importantly, competent and cooperative implementers in place to make sure that the disparate aims are able to be fulfilled simultaneously. For example, in the case of the ATDCs, adequate control over the company implementers, setting up of a capable marketing team, close collaboration and communication with local partners, among other factors, are naturally required by the multi-objectives to be included as parts of the action plan. As revealed in the case studies (Sect. 3.2), however, none of these—at least for the time being—are effectively in place, thereby leaving the implementation of that multi-objective ambition rather difficult.

In addition, the multi-objective design also easily causes confusion to 'outsiders', that is, the local African partners. The ATDCs, for example, are in most cases presented by Chinese government as a regular aid project with the primary aim to help enhance the continent's agricultural productivity through transferring China's most advanced agro-technology. The African partners, however, do not seem to have been well and adequately informed, consulted or negotiated with beforehand about the commercial objectives and mechanisms involved in the projects. What compounds the situation is the often Chinese-dominated management model of the projects, with quite limited local staff effectively involved. The actual outcome, then, is that the African partners see the Chinese aid-workers making business on the aid projects, with themselves, the supposed aid beneficiaries, to varying degrees being excluded from that process (Sect. 3.2.1). This, together with other reasons that will be discussed later on, contributes to the mistrust and discontentment of the local partners in certain circumstances.

The second issue surrounding policy design is the *lack of specificity*, particularly in terms of the policy action plans. Although some general guidelines of China-Africa agro-cooperation were proposed on different official occasions, very few concrete action plans have so far been put forward, in either formal or informal forms. In the case of the ATDCs, there was only a guideline document from the Chinese government, that is the 'ATDC Guidance' (Sect. 3.2.1). While it does outline some key elements of the projects such as the objectives, actors and tasks, the content in general is rather simple. It is especially so concerning the final phase of Commercial Operation, which—given its dual objectives of seeking agribusiness opportunities and achieving project sustainability— is supposed to be the most innovative and essential part of the ATDCs. The design for the Commercial Operation as presented in the 'ATDC Guidance' is very basic and ambiguous, giving few concrete directions or suggestions as to how the implementing agencies could possibly and successfully run the centres on a business basis. If this ambiguity is understandable given the early point at which the document was issued when the ATDCs were still largely in their Technical Cooperation phase, there have nevertheless been no follow-up documents or informal communications between the government and implementers [2] that further specifies the implementation plan even during the Commercial Operation phase.

Similarly, in terms of the 'agribusiness model', after more than a decade of discussion, there still have been few comprehensive official documents or practical action plans in place; some more detailed, country-specific agro-investment guidance in different African states, furthermore, is even more lacking. The state support system is still in an immature phase, which has been confirmed by the case studies (Sect. 4.2). For instance, while few new supportive policies (e.g. financial

---

[2] This is according to the author's personal confirmation with several front-line directors of the ATDCs in different African countries at different times in 2016 and 2017.

support and insurance/tax measures) are set up to facilitate Chinese companies' agribusiness investment in Africa, some long-standing constraints such as the Import Quota System haven't really been modified either. No real measures are taken to facilitate or benefit private investors who normally face more difficulties in conducting overseas agro-investment compared to state-owned enterprises. Therefore, although there is plenty of policy encouragement as to the great potential and necessity of bilateral agricultural cooperation, when it comes to concrete measures of translating all that into practice, there sometimes seems to be an awkward vacuum.

The third issue in respect of policy design is the *inadequate consideration of local environment*. A typical example is the active encouragement of agro-investment by Chinese government, particularly the enthusiasm for land investment as seen in the earlier years of this wave of agricultural engagement (Sect. 4.1.1), without adequate warning to the agro-firms about the complexity and difficulties of land issues and deals in Africa. This has seemed to, at least partially, contribute to the stalemate of many Chinese firms now operating agribusinesses in Africa. A similar case can be seen in the problem of economic unviability of the Commercial Operation phase of the ATDCs. It now proves to be rather difficult, as some of the cases have shown, for the ATDCs to be able to finance themselves through conducting agribusiness as expected by the Chinese government. In addition, the inadequate consideration of local environment is also reflected through the lack of incorporation of local personnel, in terms of either including them into the management team or consulting and collaborating with them whenever necessary. This is a common problem as seen both in the ATDCs and in different investment projects.

Secondly, problems revolving around **policy control** are also observed in China's agro-development cooperation with Africa. Even though a policy per se is well designed, it is not complete unless effective control is present. This is because a policy is rarely self-implemented; it depends on the cooperation of both policy implementers and the target groups whose behaviours, however, are seldom naturally obedient. In addition, control is needed also as a way of macro-coordination given the often messy and inefficient state of multi-organizational implementation. In the case of Chinese agro-development cooperation with Africa, the problem of (lack of) control is seen in almost all of the scenarios mentioned above.

In terms of *implementers*, the control problem appears to be particularly relevant because the main policy implementers either in the ATDCs or in investment projects are corporate actors who instinctively, and quite understandably, have less inclination to faithfully follow through government initiatives compared to government actors. Taking the ATDCs for example, with the aim of improving project sustainability, the Chinese government incorporates company actors into the government aid projects and makes them the key implementers on a daily operational basis. This is supposed to be a win-win scenario in the sense that, while the Chinese government provides a platform for the companies to seek business opportunities in Africa, the companies should in return take the responsibility for managing the government's overseas development projects in a more efficient and sustainable way. There is, however, no stipulation as to the obligations of the company actors, for example, what profit level should be attained in order to prepare for the ATDCs' Commercial Operation Stage, and how the profits should be distributed in the Commercial Operation Stage in order to sustain the 'public-interest' function of technology transfer. As a result, the implementing companies don't seem to be confronted with any serious pressure as to the performance of their agribusiness operation in the Technical Cooperation Stage. Even if the ATDCs could possibly sustain themselves in the Commercial Operation Stage financially—this, nevertheless, might be even more problematic given the potential conflicts, in the absence of any effective control measures, between the profit-seeking motives of the companies and the developmental nature of the ATDCs.

Policy *control over target groups* in the context of external policy implementation indicates often not coercive regulations or restrictions, but influence or direction of their behaviours towards the policy objectives; and the measures also tend to be softer due to their lack of governing legitimacy over foreign citizens. The target groups against the context of Chinese agro-development policy in Africa involve a diversity of local actors such as the African government counterparts, local farmers, businessmen, and NGOs. To pursue 'influence or direction' on the local actors, it requires, at the lowest level, adequate negotiation with them in the process of policy implementation. However, as will be analysed in more detail in the section that follows, while the Chinese government itself tends to take a hands-off position after the projects enter the implementation phase, the company actors lack both capabilities and motives to actively engage with the local actors.

Therefore, the Chinese side (in terms of both government and corporate actors) seems to have very little leverage over the local target groups through either direct (policymaker) or indirect (implementer) influences. This affects the implementation result in different ways. For example, for those locals who act as co-implementers such as the African government counterparts, lack of influence on them leads to the inefficiency of implementation; for those locals who are largely the recipients or objects of implementation such as the farmers, lack of influence on them sometimes increases mistrust and resentment.

In addition, there are also *no formal coordination mechanisms among different implementers.* As introduced before (Sect. 4.1), the Chinese government did establish a mechanism called 'Inter-ministry Working Mechanism on Overseas Agricultural Resources Exploration' which is comprised of 14 central-level ministries and led by the MOC and MOA of China. It is however more a mechanism for policy formulation rather than implementation; and even for the former purpose, it is indeed quite an empty one, existing largely only on paper. Furthermore, what is more urgently needed is the coordination between the Chinese governmental and the corporate actors, given that in this specific policy case it is the companies who are working on the front lines and playing the most important roles. The notion of 'governments setting up a platform, enterprises staging a show' (zhengfu datai, qiye changxi), which is a common model for public–private cooperation in China, seems also at work in the current case of the country's agro-cooperation policy in Africa. There is, however, no intentionally formed cooperation framework that aims to stick the government and companies together for a unitary policy goal.

5.2 Implementer

Implementers are the actors who put the centrally formulated policy into actual practice. In the case of Chinese agro-development cooperation with Africa, and particularly under the 'innovative agro-aid' and 'agribusiness' models, we have seen two main groups of implementers. The most important implementers who take the direct executive role and work at the very front lines are the *Chinese corporate actors.* There are a wide diversity of them: mostly agro-firms but also companies from other sectors; companies of different ownership—state-owned, private and sometimes mixed; and companies operating at different levels—both central and provincial. Among them, some are officially designated as policy implementers, as in the ATDC project; some are 'unintentional policy implementers', as in agribusiness projects, for although the companies largely follow their own agenda and would not consider themselves carrying out government policies, they nevertheless unintentionally contribute to the realization of the government policy objectives (Sect. 4.1.1). The second group and also secondary level of implementers are the *Chinese governmental actors*. They are also from different sectors, mostly the commercial and agricultural systems, and operating at different administrative levels—central or provincial. Although being official actors, they play a subordinate role as 'implementers', for they are not the ones directly involved with policy execution, either under the 'innovative agro-aid' or 'agribusiness' model. Instead, they are more in charge of facilitation and support. This actor mapping indicates not only the complexity of the implementation structure, but also imposes significant practical difficulties on the collaboration among different parties.

As noted in the beginning, despite the synergy of the three sets of variables (policy, implementer and environment), problems concerning implementers may have explained more about the observed 'policy gap' given the implementers' agency they could have potentially exerted. However, a number of constraints—respectively capabilities, motivations, discretion and multi-organizational cooperation—have made them unable to play such a proactive role. The first constraint—a very commonly seen one in Chinese agro-development cooperation in Africa—is the inadequate *capabilities* of the key front-line implementers, i.e. the Chinese agro-firms. The lack of capability of the Chinese agro-firms operating in Africa is demonstrated not so much in agricultural technical/professional terms; most of them are after all quite established agro-firms back in China, with fairly advanced agro-technology and equipment, well-trained technicians and long experience in conducting farm activities and agribusiness. Therefore, they find little difficulty, for instance, in building and managing farms, organizing production and processing, as well as conducting agro-technology extension in Africa as seen in different ATDC or investment projects. The limited capability, instead, is shown more evidently in their limited foreign language skills, lack of knowledge about local conditions, inexperience and sometimes hesitance in interacting with local actors, and accordingly, *difficulty in integrating into the local environment*. This seemingly indirect constraint, however, has become a repeated theme all through the case studies of the book and formed an important obstacle to satisfactory results.

The Mozambican ATDC, for instance, while having little difficulty in the process of conducting agro-technology transfer (e.g. training, demonstration, and experiments), has been increasingly confronted with challenges due to their inadequate and ineffective communication with the local partners. Most of the time, the ATDC operated in a rather separate way. Communication was constrained only on administrative issues such as visa issuing, but seldom upon the management of the centre. This not only partially led to the limitation of the agro technology transfer, but also caused some dissatisfaction on the Mozambican side as to the transparency of the ATDC's operation, including areas such as decision-making and finances. When the centre encountered problems, the Chinese staff tried to seek help from the Mozambican side, but often found the results frustrating due to what they believed to be 'low efficiency' of the Mozambican partners, among other bureaucratic reasons. However, interviews with the Mozambican side revealed that they found the communication very difficult, and a larger part of the reason was attributed to the language barrier. As a result, mistrust and even resentment arose and accumulated over time.

In the case of agribusiness projects, while the Chinese firms can normally copy the Chinese agricultural production model and achieve high yield very soon after they launch the project, they don't seem to be competent enough in solving problems related to the local context and don't seem to be able to create a successful business by transferring the production advantage into profits. For instance, as seen in the case of Wanbao, the company had very limited knowledge about the local social-political conditions. After years of operation, they still hadn't managed to figure out the role of RBL-EP in the Mozambican system, which was the most direct and important local partner of the company. They also did not understand why the local farmers protested against them, given that they had gained the land through formal government channels and secured legal contracts. They felt hesitant to talk with the local NGO—the main organizer of the protest; instead, they spent most of their time talking with and trying to seek help from the Mozambican government, but turned out to be extremely frustrated by what they believed as the 'low efficiency and inaction' of the government. At the same time, the company didn't seem to have any clear marketing plan as to where to sell their agro-products, how to compete with the existing transnational traders; the same problem was also observed, to a lesser extent though, in other companies such like Hefeng. As a result of this, there used to be internal and vicious competition among the Chinese firms for they tend to, as a natural easier option, all target the Chinese community in Mozambique as their main market.

The reasons for the lack of capabilities are multiple; one common problem that is shared among all these different projects, however, is the human resource constraint of the Chinese agro-firms. There is no lack of qualified professionals who are well equipped with agro-technical know-how and are often very experienced. But most of these technicians have very limited foreign language skills and little overseas working experience. Furthermore, there are very few people who are skilled in international business, or at least have some basic knowledge on the local environments (e.g. local political, social-economic, cultural conditions), acceptable language and negotiation skills. Indeed, language barrier and cultural ignorance of the Chinese staff were raised as the biggest difficulties by the management of Chinese projects (both for ATDC and investment) during the interviews (Interviews 19 November 2013 and 23 June 2017). In addition, these Chinese agro-firms seldom have a mature marketing team that endeavours to investigate local markets and formulate corresponding marketing strategies.

An ATDC, for example, has only a small number of staff, averaging a dozen or so, who are mostly Chinese; and the personnel structure is rather simple as well—normally a director, a technical team comprising several agro-technicians, a translator (optional, mostly in non-English speaking countries), an accountant and some other logistics staff (e.g. chefs and cleaners). This structure, while evidently showing an effort to meet the requirements for agro-technology transfer, demonstrates little attempt at fulfilling the centre's agribusiness function that was designed to serve both the commercial aim and the sustainability concern of the ATDC. Further, there is often not a particularly assigned person to take charge of the ATDC's external relations. Even the companies that are directly engaged with agribusiness do not often have a professional marketing team, nor any public relations department within the company structure.

Apart from the incapability in terms of integrating into the local environment, another important constraint on the company implementers' capability is their *limited financial strength*. The majority of

Chinese investment entities involved in the African agricultural sector are medium–small-sized agro-firms with limited financial power. Furthermore, under the current conditions, it is difficult for those companies to raise capital from the domestic financial market; their main support comes from the several policy-oriented national banks which, however, have a preference towards state-owned enterprises. Therefore, the companies often face great difficulties expanding the investment scale, as seen both in the performance of the ATDC commercial development and in other general investment projects. The human resource constraint, as mentioned earlier, also has much to do with this; these agro-firms often cannot offer good salaries to attract qualified personnel and even try to reduce costs by employing as few staff as possible.

Even if the implementing agencies are largely competent, it doesn't necessarily mean that they are going to exert their capability at full strength. At least two factors can be seen at work in this regard: the implementer's own motivation and the control from policymakers. We have seen in the previous section that policy control in the context of Chinese agro-development cooperation is not particularly strong, which therefore gives more weight to the implementers' *motivation*—and more pertinently, their independent aims and the extent of congruity of that with the officially set policy objectives. As analysed before (Sect. 4.1.1), there *is* certain congruity between Chinese agro-firms' own aims and the government policy objectives, especially in terms of commercial considerations and the need for 'going out'. Indeed, fieldwork interviews reveal that some of the agro-firms involved in the ATDC and investment projects do have true intentions of developing agribusiness in Africa. Having that said, doing agribusiness is neither the only nor the most prioritized concern to many companies. In-depth investigation tends to reveal a more complex picture.

For some ATDC-implementing companies, for example, developing agribusiness in Africa, particularly given all sorts of practical difficulties, is only an option rather than a must. It would be great if there were some good investment opportunities appearing, but it wouldn't be regarded (by themselves) as a defeat if they couldn't survive after the first three years. They wouldn't lose anything; in fact, by hosting the government aid projects, they could continually receive funding from the Chinese government (for at least three years or even more), which can produce more stable and in cases higher financial gains compared to what they could possibly gain from their home business given the fierce competition and difficult living conditions for the agro-firms in China. Carefully controlling the operational costs could bring even more profits. Earning money from hosting government aid projects is not an uncommon rationale for Chinese companies, and definitely not only the case for agro-firms. This may help explain, at least partially, why sometimes the ATDCs are not seen to actively engage with the local markets or implementing companies expanding agribusiness by, for instance, putting in self-owned capital; for doing agribusiness might not be a prioritized or preferred option to them at all, whereas the project sustainability objective (supposedly realized through agribusiness) is apparently something that's cared about more by the government rather than by the companies. This is also a typical scenario of the 'principal-agent problem'.

The third constraint at the implementer level is the *discretion* issue. In the earlier section, I point out some inherent flaws of Chinese agro-development cooperation in Africa from a *policy design* point of view, namely the multi-objectives, lack of specificity and inadequate consideration of local environment. That said, as already mentioned, it does not exclude the possibility of achieving desired policy outcomes and leaves room for the implementers who might be able to modify the policies through day-to-day practice and experience accumulation—that is, through the execution of positive discretion of the front-line implementers. Some very specific problems facing the ATDCs, for instance the training model and post-training application (Sect. 3.2), are understandably difficult for policymakers to fully predict and take into account beforehand. They are instead easily observed once the project is put into practice and not any demanding tasks for the implementers to solve through communication and collaboration with local partners—indeed, some measures taken by the ATDCs such as that of tripartite translation and bilingual handouts in order to address the language barrier is a positive case of implementer discretion, but surely the discretion is far from fully utilized.

Turning to the investment cases, more discretion by the company implementers themselves is required to determine suitable investment strategies in order to run a successful business. The investment guidance from the government level is admittedly rather limited (and sometimes misleading) particularly considering the state interests and motives behind it, but agro-investment is, after all, a commercial activity that depends fundamentally on company decisions and operations. However, exactly because of the capability and motivation constraints of the implementers, as analysed earlier, the discretion that might possibly offset the flaws of the original policy design is also greatly limited.

Lastly, *multi-organizational cooperation* is also an acute problem in the implementation of China's agricultural development cooperation policy in Africa. As revealed earlier, actors of different types and from different administrative levels constitute a complex 'implementation structure', wherein Chinese government agencies and corporate actors are the key ones. They are supposed to work in tandem with each other both as seen in the quasi-PPP model for the ATDC projects and the state-led agro-investment initiatives. While corporate actors play a leading role on the front lines, the government agencies are supposed to play a supportive role when necessary. In reality, however, the government supportive role is more visible in the pre-implementation phase, such as chairing negotiation with African partners and helping channel finance for companies, but once the projects are started, the government side has seemed to take a rather hands-off attitude.

This is particularly evident when the front-line companies encounter problems in their daily operation, such as the land protests against Wanbao and the discontentment of local partners as seen in the case of the Mozambican ATDC. The companies involved in these cases turned out to be in a rather helpless situation, especially given their general incapability as analysed earlier. Reasons for this lack of cooperation are mutual. From the Chinese government point of view, they tend to regard the daily operation, including problems arising in this process, as solely the responsibility of the companies. They themselves are more a governor or supervisor rather than partner of the companies, and hence present only in diplomatic occasions such as accompanying local African politicians to visit the project sites or the annual inspection of projects. On the other hand, the companies either in the ATDC or in investment projects, when interviewed as to why they did not seek help from Chinese government agencies in the face of difficulties, expressed their hesitance in doing so given the complexity of dealing with government relations, explaining, for instance, that they often gained more criticism and pressure (for example, on their incapability and slow progress) rather than any constructive advices or actual help. This is the case for the relevant government agencies both in China and in their overseas branches in Africa. Because of this, the companies would rather act on their own instead of creating extra trouble for themselves.

5.3 Environment

Environment refers to the setting/context wherein policy implementation takes place, and that could possibly exert some influence/constraints on the implementation process or the implementers' behaviours. For an analytical purpose, the implementation environment can be further differentiated between static environment factors such as natural, political, economic, social, cultural conditions and dynamic environment factors which involve actions and interactions among different actors.

Examples of constraints imposed by *static environment* are many. For instance, as seen in the cases of the ATDCs, although the technology training per se went quite well, the absence of production conditions for local farmers (e.g. infrastructure, tools) and the different farming culture can make the aimed technology transfer a rather vain effort. The local environmental constraints are even more obvious for agro-investment. Factors such as the lack of infrastructure, the shortage of skilled workers, the existence of many long-standing foreign traders, and the complicated land issues all make conducting agribusiness in Africa an extremely challenging enterprise. Given the 'static' nature—that is, relatively stable within a certain period—of this type of environment, in theory it could be possibly taken into consideration either beforehand by the policymakers or later on by the implementers, and therefore the negative effect could to different extents be lessened. However, some prevailing notions (e.g. 'self-orientation', yiwo weizhu) and habitual practice (e.g. taking things for granted without proper prior survey) in Chinese engagement with Africa, not only in terms of agriculture, have made it difficult to avoid such sort of problem.

The constraints imposed by *dynamic environment* tend to be more proactive and also more challenging to the implementers. For instance, in the case of the Mozambican ATDC, politics played out between the two local-governmental agencies, the MINAG and the MCT (Sect. 3.2.1). Both wanted to be the local partner of the Chinese ATDC for their own interests. The MINAG, given its expertise in agriculture, seemed to be the natural choice and indeed participated a lot in the initial stage and even the land of the ATDC was provided by IIAM, the MINAG-affiliated research institute. However, in the end, for unclear reasons, MCT won out and became the formal partner of the ATDC, which inevitably left some resentment between the two ministries over the ATDC issue. The Chinese side, however, knew little about this, only to find the arrangement quite inconvenient because the centre had more direct relevance with MINAG that is also more powerful on many matters. What compounded the situation is that after the three-year Technical Cooperation Stage, the Mozambican government decided to transfer the centre to the MINAG with whom the ATDC had not directly worked. The MINAG took a rather strict attitude towards the ATDC, expressing discontentment about the centre and once insisting on taking over the chair of the ATDC director, which caused considerable, and entirely unexpected, trouble to the Chinese side (Interview 19 October 2015).

A similar case can also be seen in the land conflicts encountered by Wanbao, the private Chinese agro-firm operating in Mozambique. The farmer protest against Wanbao over the land controversy was organized by FONGA (Sect. 4.2.1), a local NGO that had constantly targeted and criticized, and thus had a high level of tension with the local government. As revealed by the NGO director, even FONGA itself didn't think it was the Chinese company to blame, but rather, their own government. They organized the protest more as a weapon to attack and pressure the government. They would even have liked to 'talk and cooperate' with Wanbao on the issue. However, in effect, while the local government largely ignored the situation, dismissing it largely only a 'routine trouble' made by its 'old friend', Wanbao, on the other hand, was directly affected in terms of both disrupting its normal production activity and harming the company's image.

In these two cases, certain similar trends appeared. Politics was playing out among the local countries' internal actors within which the Chinese could possibly play a role, but by and large were sidelined except for the direct negative effects imposed on them. It is admittedly quite a challenge for any foreigners/outsiders to be fully aware of and further able to manipulate such domestic and internal dynamics. However, that doesn't mean there is no room for any action at all, especially when their interests are directly affected. As seen in practice, however, the Chinese actors appeared to behave rather passively, and more importantly, not well equipped to actively engage and effectively deal with such situations. For instance, they couldn't be able to find a good negotiator or even a qualified translator from their team to talk with their partners, not to say their quite limited knowledge of the actual situations and complex dynamics that were going on.

Summary

We have by now examined the three aspects—policy, implementer and environment—that contribute to explain the 'gaps' between expectations and actual results so far of Chinese agro-development cooperation policy in Africa. To sum up, three points are to be raised here. First, it is worth highlighting that all the abovementioned variables as well as the sub-variables cannot be separated in making a sound explanation. For example, a policy with multiple or even competing *objectives* does not necessarily mean that the aims cannot be attained, if the *action plans* can possibly be designed in a more delicate way. The relative ambiguity and lack of specificity as of certain policy *action plans* do not necessarily lead to an implementation failure because the field *implementers* may well conceive of more workable schemes and thus well make up the design flaws of the policymakers. The extent of the *discretion* exerted in that sense, however, will strongly depend on the *capability and motivation* of the implementers involved. And discretion has to be dealt with rather carefully for it may produce undesired results if no proper *policy control* is in place. However, even the most competent and motivated implementers surely won't succeed without effective *collaboration* with one another given the often multi-organizational nature of the implementation process. *Implementation environment* has an inevitable shaping effect on the implementation process; thus, the policymakers should bear that in mind during *policy design*, and also the implementers need to take them into careful consideration in their daily practice. Moreover, there is a higher requirement for the implementers to achieve successful interactions with local partners and even to create a favourable environment, which, again, will have to depend back on the *capability, motivation, discretion and cooperation* of the implementers. In a nutshell, none of these factors alone could fully explain the implementation problem; instead, the problem has to be explained through the synergetic effects of all the relevant factors identified. This is clearly shown in the case of Chinese agro-development cooperation in Africa, where neither the immature policy per se, nor the incompetent implementers, or the unfavourable environment is to blame; it is rather the imperfection of all these three key aspects existing and working together that makes it difficult to achieve satisfactory policy outcomes.

Second, having emphasized the 'synergetic effects' of different factors and indeed as already demonstrated in the analysis above, we could see a (potentially) much greater role of the 'implementer' element. Good policy may not be translated to satisfactory results as expected without qualified and motivated implementers present; on the other hand, well-equipped and effectively stimulated implementers can cope even under certain policy vacuum or evident policy imperfections. The same logic works also in the implementer–environment interactions where the implementers often have a great role to play in connecting, adapting and utilizing the given environment in order to gain the most from it, even it may not seem, at first glance, very favourable (and indeed quite often so) to the policy implementation. In short, the exertion of (positive) discretion and agency by implementers may well offset some of the adverse policy or environment constraints, which thus gives the former a greater weigh in the 'policy–implementer–environment' explanatory triangle. In this vein, at the current stage when SAEs are generally better qualified than many (not all) private agro-firms in China and also (comparatively) more closely aligned to Chinese government's intentions, it might be helpful to engage more of Chinese SAEs in the process of agro-development cooperation with African countries, and gradually extend to more private ones, in order to reduce the 'capability and motivation' risk of the latter and better serve the 'mutual-development' aims.

Last, in spite of all these abovementioned challenges that can be observed from different aspects and levels, it is still too early to give any 'final evaluation' to the Chinese 'package' model of development cooperation. As already noted, China's development cooperation policy, instead of being a deliberately devised and read-made one, is more a policy-in-the-making and meanwhile put into real-life for experiment—something that is typically seen in many areas of China's domestic policies, especially for new policies. Problems and challenges, therefore, are just normal and could be largely regarded acceptable *as long as* constant reflection and quick learning is involved (though it is worth a further research on whether this sort of feedback mechanism is present and to what extent effective in terms of China's development cooperation policy in Africa). Furthermore, the problems observed are also largely 'solvable', particularly on the policy (e.g. through better policy design) and implementer level (e.g. through choosing more SAEs at the current stage as noted earlier).

INTERVIEWS

(Only formal interviews included here [see Methodology in Introduction]. All the informants are well informed of the identity and research purposes of the author; they are all kept anonymous to protect their privacy.)

Interview with one of Wanbao's management team. Interviewed by Lu Jiang. Xaixai, Gaza province, Mozambique. 19 November 2013.

Interview with the Chinese director B of the ATDC in Mozambique. Interviewed by Lu Jiang. [By phone] London, UK. 19 October 2015.

Interview with the Chinese director B of the ATDC in Mozambique. Interviewed by Lu Jiang. Shanghai, China. 23 June 2017.

REFERENCE

Jiang, Lu. 2016. 'Beyond ODA: Chinese Way of Development Cooperation with Africa. The Case of Agriculture'. PhD thesis, London School of Economics and Political Science (LSE).

CHAPTER 6

Conclusion

In this last chapter, I will try to respond to some of the research concerns raised in the Introduction while summarizing China's agricultural development cooperation detailed throughout the book. I will start by a discussion about the historical origin of the current model of—and particularly the mentality behind—Chinese agro-development cooperation with Africa and continue with a brief summary of the manifestation, evaluation and problem diagnosis of the 'package' model. Lastly and returning to the starting point of the book—the transitioning landscape of global IDC—I will give some of my opinions as regards how the whole story of China's contemporary agro-cooperation with Africa fits in this broader context and may have some implications to the latter.

6.1 The Distinctive Mind-Set of 'Mutual Development': What the History Tells…

As emphasized throughout the book, one significant feature that distinguishes Chinese contemporary development cooperation from the Northern donors lies in the idea of 'mutual development', or 'reciprocal benefit', which underpins China's external development cooperation behaviours. While often being disapproved of by the Northern donors (compared to their own DAC model and in particular the claimed recipient-oriented pursuits of ODA), it is indeed more helpful to go deep

© The Author(s) 2020
L. Jiang, *Beyond Official Development Assistance*,
Governing China in the 21st Century,
https://doi.org/10.1007/978-981-32-9507-0_6

into China's past experiences of development cooperation in order to understand why it has been acting in certain ways.[1] The historical review through the case of Chinese agro-development cooperation with Africa (Chapter 2) is such kind of efforts that aim to shed some light on the origin and evolution of 'mutual-development' mentality of China.

The earlier, or 'pure aid', phase of the cooperation between the 1960s and 1970s was driven primarily by political considerations. Those more traditional forms of agricultural aid such as building farms and agro-extension stations were used particularly as part of the diplomatic efforts of the PRC to break the Western blockade and strive for international recognition. Africa-oriented developmental objectives were surely under consideration—for the focal sector of agriculture per se was selected not randomly but almost all at request of the recipient countries of Africa given the sector's special significance to their people's livelihood. Thus, we could see that from the very beginning, the agro-cooperation was dually motivated and mutually beneficial, serving both the development objectives of Africa to enhance agro-productivity and food security, and that of China—though in terms of a more broadly understood 'development' concept that embraces the political facet—to ensure survival and gain acceptance by the international community as a newly established regime.

The foreign aid reforms starting since the early 1980s left an important imprint on the later evolution of Chinese agro-development cooperation practice in Africa. Given the changing environment

---

[1] In addition to the key idea of 'mutual development', some other characteristics of China's contemporary development cooperation models also have their historical roots. The design of the ATDC especially the commercial operation model that is entailed, for instance, while surely taking into account the dimension of promoting Chinese agro-firms to go abroad, is also evidently associated with the previous lessons of Chinese agro-aid in Africa, particularly the lack of project sustainability. This problem did not only largely reduce the developmental impacts of the aid projects, but also cause a great waste of Chinese aid funds. It is, therefore, against this specific background that the designers of ATDC brought sustainability issue to the core and innovatively brought in the business model (Chapter 3). Also, the technology-centric approach to agricultural development cooperation with Africa has a lot to do with China's own successful experience in leveraging agro-technology to boost the growth of the sector (Chapter 2). In terms of experiences with other donors, which are less touched upon in this thesis but could be good examples for the historical imprints, the 'development package' model, for instance, is believed by some scholars to be influenced by Japan's ODA practice in China as well (Bräutigam 2009), and China's insistence on non-interference may well be linked to its earlier negative experiences with the Soviet Union trying to intervene Chinese policy making in the 1950s in exchange for aid to China (Niu 2010).

(and accordingly shifting policy priorities) as well as the experiences and lessons accumulated in the earlier phase, the Chinese government made a series of reform efforts, including adjusting aid scale, enhancing aid performance, and most notably, adopting an increasingly economically pragmatic approach to conducting external development cooperation. Accordingly, in the 'transition period' of the 1980–1990s, Chinese agro-cooperation with Africa underwent a process of consolidation and transformation with a growing emphasis on project efficiency, profitability and sustainability. The notion of mutual development and reciprocal benefit gained greater acknowledgement and reconfirmation at the government level—though in reality it was still the traditional aid forms that prevailed while commercial activities took place only moderately.

It is not until the new period starting from the 2000s that opportunities for *actual* mutual development, especially in *economic* terms, finally mature. Apart from more traditional forms of agro-aid that still remain, two other new models of development cooperation in agriculture also start to emerge, respectively the 'innovative agro-aid model' exemplified by the ATDC project and the 'agribusiness model' that features the use of agro-FDI as a tool to boost the development of African agriculture. Both of these two new modalities entail very strong mutual-development objectives; and different from the previous times, furthermore, the Chinese government has since been more explicitly utilizing development cooperation as an instrument to promote its own development agenda, i.e. the 'Agriculture Going Out' strategy, while helping enhance food security and agricultural development of the partner countries in Africa.

In retrospect, we could see that during the whole course of this six-decade-long cooperation, there have always been clear *self-development* objectives of China involved—more politically driven in the 1960–1970s and from the 1980s on increasingly economically oriented. Therefore, the 'mutual development'—or more pertinently, the sort of 'exchange'—ideology has been at play since the very beginning of Chinese external development cooperation practice; put differently, through development cooperation, China has been attempting not only to help others, but also help itself.

This is deeply rooted in the fact of China being a rather backward, 'Third-World' developing country for most of the time in the last century. It is thus a rational and natural choice for China trying to strike a balance between using the limited resources for domestic development purposes and external development cooperation. Having said that, this process has not been devoid of mistakes and at times even failures. The setback caused by the once over-stretching aid giving, largely motivated by the proletarian internationalism ideology, during the 1970s finally led to a heated debate among Chinese leadership and thereby called a halt to the unrealistic approach to aid provision. It is through this lesson, along with the overarching policy shifts at the turn of the 1980s, that the principle of 'giving aid according to own actual strengths' was able to be approved by the leadership and gradually established; and the biggest reality at the time was—as admitted by Deng Xiaoping—that China was 'still very poor'.

With the Reform and Opening-Up, China's 'actual strengths' (particularly in terms of the country's material power) does have increased tremendously, and accordingly the scale of its foreign development cooperation. However, the fact that tends to be downplayed is that China, until now, is a developing country that has not yet fully completed the industrialization process and still been confronted with a wide range of development challenges—the still vast number of people living below poverty line (given the huge population base), highly imbalanced development across different regions, slow pace of economic structural upgrading along with its accompanied problems, just to name a few. In terms of agriculture, more specifically, despite the great success of the country's agricultural development in the past thirty years, the agro-sector still carries significant, and indeed, rather challenging duties to feed the whole country, support industrial development as well as provide livelihood to almost half of the population who are still living in the rural area, particularly in face of the increasingly tight land constraints. That's partly the reason why the 'Agricultural Going Out' strategy was launched, and notably, why while China is offering agro-technology and finances to support Africa, it's also been trying to make the most of it (e.g. help Chinese agro-firms to seek investment opportunities). The 'mutual-development' logic, therefore, is still valid in the current stage and may remain as a guiding principle until (and perhaps even after) China fully graduates from the developing world.

6.2 'Development Package' and Its Evaluation: The Case of Agriculture

To a large extent, the realistic attitudes towards cooperation objectives as embodied in the 'mutual-development' mentality naturally point to more flexible cooperation modalities, such as the 'development package' model of China. 'Development package', as been manifested by the case of agro-cooperation, can be understood as a mixture of a diversity of technical and economic cooperation forms—ranging from more traditional, ODA type of aid to broader commercial activities, typically trade and investment—with a view to promoting (mutual) development. In essence, it is pragmatic uses of different forms as long as they could possibly serve the expected goals.

This 'pragmaticism' is very much in consistence with the practical-oriented ideology and experience of China's Reform and Opening-Up, and notably Deng's 'black cat, white cat' metaphor.[2] That said, the 'development package' is not something that is proposed out of pure blind-mindedness, but rather, a measure that is still being tested, as a kind of new form of cooperation that not only differs from the DAC model but also China's own previous practices. Against this context, the agricultural sector, which intrinsically entails the possibility for commercial operation, could be seen as a chosen pilot area. It is not guaranteed with better results or effectiveness; indeed, as already revealed earlier (Chapter 5), the package model has so far fallen short of the intended purposes in certain aspects. But still, it can serve as a pool of lessons and experience, and bears the potential to be expanded, after being modified, to other development cooperation areas outside agriculture in the future.

Specifically, in the case of China's current agro-development cooperation with Africa (since the 2000s), three distinctive forms can be observed within the 'development package'. The 'traditional agro-aid model', as the name suggests, remains largely the same as the previous agro-cooperation forms in the past decades during the 1960–1990s, but with a greater focus on the role of agro-technology (Chapter 2). Hundreds of Chinese agro-experts have been sent to different African countries to help with agricultural development plan-making and technical-related issues. Constant exchange and training programs are held both in China and the counterpart countries of Africa. Meanwhile, China has also actively participated in different multilateral cooperation mechanisms such as that with the UN-FAO and OECD-DAC, in order to collectively contribute to the development of African agriculture. In addition, Chinese government continues to support agro-infrastructure

---

[2] The original quote is, 'It doesn't matter whether the cat is black or white, as long as it catches mice'.

building and provide assistance in cash and kind, including emergency food aid, to a number of African countries.

The second form is termed in the book as 'innovative agro-aid model', which is typically exemplified by the Chinese ATDC projects in Africa (Chapter 3). While at first glance the ATDCs look more like a hybrid of the different 'agro-aid' forms adopted before (e.g. farms, agro-technology demonstration/extension stations, experts dispatch), the 'innovative' part lies in the incorporation of corporate actors and commercial operation. The aim of so doing is primarily to fix the problems of project inefficiency and unsustainability as experienced in the past (Chapter 2), thereby to enhance the performance and developmental impacts of these new aid projects; but equally important, the ATDCs are also expected to serve as a platform and entry point for Chinese agro-firms—not only those acting as the implementing agencies but other agro-firms interested in investing in the ATDC-hosting countries as well—to go abroad and engage agribusiness. In actual practice, this combination of traditional aid and innovative business model is realized through the design of two consecutive operational phases of the ATDCs, specifically the three-year Technical Cooperation Stage wherein the centres are fully funded by Chinese government to perform the so-called public-interest functions (e.g. agro-technology demonstration and training) and then the Commercial Operation Stage in which the implementing firms are supposed to be self-funded through market-oriented production while at the same time continuing with the 'public-interest functions'. For now, there have been two dozens or so Chinese ATDCs established across different African countries.

The last form is called 'agribusiness model' (Chapter 4). To certain extent, the 'agribusiness model' could be equalled as regular agricultural investment, but the 'developmental' nature of agriculture and agribusiness as well as some intentional development-oriented efforts involved in many of these investment projects makes it meanwhile also a vital component of the 'development package'. For instance, most of the Chinese agro-firms currently engage in the production stage of the agribusiness value chain and bring with them relatively more advanced agro-equipment and techniques, thus making a direct contribution to the productivity increase in the agricultural sector. The Chinese agribusiness projects in Africa often involve employing and training local smallholder farmers, through plantation production or through contract-farming models, and hence help with creating more jobs and alleviating local poverty. Due to the limited production scale at the current stage, most of these Chinese investment projects, especially those engaged in grain-crop business, serve the local markets only and thus play a positive role in increasing food supplies and enhancing food security of the recipient countries. Furthermore, as revealed in the overall review (Sect. 4.1) as well as the case studies (Sect. 4.2), many of these agribusiness projects have been partially financed by Chinese government through concessional or commercial loans with a clear view to supporting African agriculture. In total, there are around 100 or so Chinese agro-firms who have invested in different countries across the continent and thereby contributed to China's contemporary agro-development cooperation efforts in Africa either individually or through partnering with the Chinese government.

Despite the novelty of the package model and some of its positive results as confirmed by the project-level fieldwork (Sects. 3.2 and 4.2), a number of practical problems have also been observed, which accordingly lead to certain 'implementation gap' of Chinese agro-development cooperation policy in Africa. A systematic explanation is provided (Chapter 5) wherein the explanatory factors are grouped into three levels—the design and control of Chinese agro-development cooperation *policy* with Africa, the motivation and capability (among others) of the Chinese policy *implementers* and especially those front-liners, and the structural influence of the static and dynamic local *environment*. And most prominent problem among the three has seemed to rest on the 'implementers' given their potential role in actively remedying the policy imperfections and effectively responding to the adverse environment. In particular, the lack of strong or true *motivation* of engaging in agro-aid and agribusiness in Africa—for both SAEs and private agro-firms (but perhaps more so for the latter)—and more importantly, the limited *capability* of them in operating agro-aid and agribusiness projects in the African context have accounted for a large part of the 'implementer' problems. These three levels of factors, working together and synergistically, explain the 'implementation gaps' as observed from the field between the expected objectives and actual outcomes of Chinese agro-development cooperation policy with Africa.

6.3 CHINA AND THE TRANSITIONING LANDSCAPE OF GLOBAL IDC

In the Introduction, I have outlined differences in terms of both *general features* (e.g. in geographical allocation, targeted sectors, financing methods, and cooperation forms), and more essentially, some *key principles* concerning aid provision (e.g. concessionality, conditionality and tying status of aid) between the Northern donors and Southern development partners. The 'mutual-development' mentality of China and accordingly its 'development package' modality, which have been much discussed in the book, largely fall into the second, also more debated, group of distinctions. The pursuit of 'mutual-development' forms a strong contrast with the traditional donors who have always tried to make development cooperation an independent agenda (from other political or economic interactions) with claimed purely recipient-oriented development objectives.[3] The 'package' model of development cooperation, furthermore, also clearly goes against the common practice of the North wherein there is always a line carefully maintained between the believed altruistic ODA and the more self-seeking commercial activities such as trade and investment; a mixture of both, either through embedment (e.g. tied aid) or combination (e.g. development package), would thus be easily regarded as inappropriate, if not 'immoral'. These two, therefore, can be seen as among the 'new' elements that China has brought into the global IDC arena and also the challenging ones to the traditional donors more specifically.

What, then, makes these differences between China and the Northern donors? In the previous section, I have tried to trace the origins of Chinese development cooperation thinking and behaviours from its history; and indeed, those of the traditional donors also have their historical roots. First (and at a surface level), the Northern donors had an entirely different starting point when they began to provide external development cooperation to the developing world—most of them were already quite advanced economically back then and enjoyed a period of peace

---

[3] That said, the 'development objectives' as defined by the traditional donors have been kept changing through the past seven decades—first 'economic growth' (through promoting productive sector and infrastructure development as in the 1960s), then 'poverty reduction' (through emphasizing agricultural and social sector development as in the 1970s and 1990s), 'macroeconomic reforms' (as in the 'Structural Adjustment' period in the 1980s) and more recently 'good governance' (as in the late 1990s). This sort of recipient-oriented, but essentially donor-dominated, development objectives as well as their evident lack of consistence, cannot be said to have brought particular benefit to the recipient countries. Moreover, the inconsistence of donor-defined 'development objectives', while reflecting the prominent development challenges and prevailing development thinking at different times, hasn't been devoid of donors' manipulation in order for own political and economic advantages (see, for instance, Hjertholm and White 2000).

and prosperity particularly during the 1960s. This, therefore, made sense of provision of the more concessional, donation-style ODA, as well as their less explicitly expressed motives (compared to the Southern actors like China) of using development cooperation to serve self-benefits of the donors.[4]

At a deeper level, however, part of the reason for traditional donors' reluctance to openly embrace mutual benefits and a broader range of cooperation forms may also lie in the cautiousness deriving from memories of the colonial past. In other words, the donors might try to avoid the possibility, or impression, of being seen as taking advantage again of the recipient countries through offering development cooperation or ODA. The post-WWII development cooperation was from the very beginning portrayed as a fresh form of engagement of the advanced countries with the 'underdeveloped areas'—as the US President Truman emphasized in his inaugural address in 1949 (Chapter 1)—that features 'democratic fair dealing' and not 'old imperialism' any more. The Northern donors have thus tended to behave more cautiously and perhaps also been more sensitive to any 'signs' of neo-colonialism (of themselves and others) in engagement with the recipients. China as well as other Southern actors who are without this sort of 'historical burden', on the other hand, tend to regard the 'win-win' or 'mutual benefit' concept more acceptable, justifiable and also achievable.

The long and almost exclusive preoccupation with ODA[5] and the strict rules applied to it (as well as that to the emerging 'development PPP', see Introduction) can be regarded precisely as the sort of efforts of the Northern donors to pursue certain 'purity' of development

---

[4] This does not exclude, for instance, the *actual practice* of tied aid that used to be widely adopted by Northern donors and started to be reduced (to varying degrees) only from the turn of the new century.

[5] As noted in the Introduction, despite a growing trend, the practice of development PPP among Northern donors is still relatively marginalized compared to that of the traditional ODA model. In addition, the OECD-DAC also uses the concept of 'associated financing' which includes ODA and/or OOF (other official flows) and/or export credit or other transactions (Hynes and Scott 2013, 6), partially to differentiate and facilitate the calculation of other kinds of financial flows into developing countries from ODA. But the volume of 'the other flows' pales in comparison to ODA. In 2017, for instance, the total ODA by DAC members was about $147 billion while the OOF and officially supported export credits were $2.3 billion and $2.1 billion, respectively (OECD.Stat online database).

cooperation. This, however, has seemed rather difficult to maintain due to the inherent contradictions involved.

On top of everything else, despite the claimed altruism, development cooperation provided by Northern donors has never been devoid of broader self-seeking considerations. CDC—the British development finance institution, for instance—has upheld the idea of 'doing good without losing money' from the very beginning of its establishment in the 1940s (CDC's official website). The boundaries between EU's development policy and other areas of external relations (e.g. trade, foreign and security policy) have also become increasingly blurred in the past years (Grimm and Hackenesch 2017, 549). The recent proposals of the Trump Administration to massively cut the country's aid budget and even merge USAID to the Department of State, in line with its 'America First' vision, has expressed more than explicitly how the largest donor in the North (and the world) weigh between domestic needs and that of other countries. The economics and politics[6] of foreign aid, including that of external development cooperation, are just well known; as a result, the claimed recipient-oriented 'development objectives' have often been distorted for the donors' commercial and political advantage (Hjertholm and White 2000; Alesina and Dollar 2000).

Moreover, despite the comprehensive standards and rules written on paper, the genuineness of donors to faithfully comply with them is questionable, let alone the difficulties in enforcing and evaluating implementation of them. Take the untying of aid for example, within technical cooperation and food aid—the 'grey areas' for tied aid[7]—30% and at least 50% of them are reported as tied, respectively. A high level of non-reporting exists for technical cooperation and other likely tied sectors such as infrastructure, transport and energy. And there are large variations in terms of untying and reporting on the tying status of aid among DAC donors; the US aid, for instance, is still extensively tied while Japan represents half of the non-reporting in total (Clay et al. 2009, 56). Similar cases will likely be seen for the PPP model rising in the Northern development circle recently, for the obvious difficulties to effectively define those binding principles (particularly neutrality, additionality, etc.)

---

[6]For the politics of foreign aid and development cooperation, see e.g. Morgenthau (1962), Kapoor (2008), and Van der Veen (2011).

[7]They are exempted from the Recommendation made by OECD-DAC.

as well as that to supervise and assess the results. Some of recent research has already revealed problems such as lack of control over the behaviours of private sector actors in the PPP projects of DFID (ICAI 2015).

It is clear from above that aid in general, and even development cooperation more narrowly, have always been entwined with providers' self-interest pursuits. 'Mutual benefit', therefore, both in political and economic terms, has never been an exclusive mind-set or practice to the Southern actors; it is just long been downplayed in the DAC community. There is hence a need to broaden the understanding and practice of 'international development cooperation'—for development partners from *both the advanced countries and developing world*[8]—through allowing the idea of 'mutual benefit' and accordingly embracing cooperation forms beyond the traditional ODA (in the North) or pure aid (in the South). A couple of reasons that follow may justify this potential initiative.

It is firstly an almost inevitable adjustment in response to the transitioning landscape of IDC. The unsatisfactory effectiveness of ODA by Northern donors (even with the reform process since the 2000s), the increasing visibility of 'emerging donors' along with their distinct models, as well as the growing trend of private sector engagement, all call for a reflection of the existing IDC architecture that has been dominated by traditional actors, modalities and rules for more than seven decades. Southern (and other) development partners, for example, could be encouraged in a more open-minded and constructive manner—not at any potential costs of being imposed of or converged to the Northern standards. There is indeed much space for North–South cooperation in IDC, and also very much to the benefits of the recipients. For instance, while China (given its current comparative advantage in financing and infrastructure) may assist the recipients to *seize* the momentum of growth first, the Northern donors (with their more attention on social infrastructure) could help them to *maintain* that; the two thus are positively complementary to each other. Apart from that, greater attention could also be gradually transferred to innovative IDC thinking, financing methods and cooperation forms, along with more experiment and

---

[8] Though perhaps more transformative and difficult for the former for reasons discussed before.

research conducted in order to address the potential deficiencies and improve the effectiveness of them.

Second, it also relates to the sustainability and scaling up of development finances globally. For *official* development partners from both the North and South, the governments face the same problem as to gaining domestic support for spending money on other countries; apparently, altruism along does not always suffice to convince ordinary people and a diversity of interest groups at home. This is partly the reason why we've kept seeing broken promises of Northern donors to increase aid and even to the very opposite, plans of some to dramatically cut the aid budget. And as noted before, this sort of pressure could be even greater for the Southern actors given their own poor population and development challenges domestically. Allowing 'win-win' between development partners and recipients may hence provide incentives for the former to participate more actively, mobilize resources from diversified channels and on a larger scale, and establish a broad-based and sustained foundation for a country to engage in the undertaking of external development cooperation. This is even more so for the *private* sector actors who are intrinsically profit driven; to encourage more of them and resources from the private sector (rather than the relatively few philanthropy-motivated private Foundations and their donations), it might be necessary to allow for certain space of profits to the participant companies as applied in Chinese 'development package' or some Northern 'development PPP'.

Last but not least, it should also be kept in mind for development partners that it boils down to the recipients—*their own efforts and in particular the political will of their leadership*—in order to see real progress of economic and social development in those countries. IDC or any external assistance, therefore, may work more as a supportive force, either financially or intellectually, but will not be able to change situation of the recipients significantly without endeavours and cooperation from within. This has at least two implications to IDC. First, people should have a reasonable expectation as to what IDC could possibly contribute to the development of a country. The effectiveness of certain projects or programmes is not determined merely by the design of IDC providers— be it in more traditional or more innovative forms. Imposed standards or rules (e.g. greater concessionality or more conditionality), furthermore, wouldn't guarantee better results either.

More essentially, IDC providers should treat recipients as equals, who are with fine judgment and capabilities in terms of choosing development partners, negotiating cooperation terms, and overcoming potential implementation problems. More and more African states, for instance, are trying to end aid dependency and boost their national development through trade and FDI. 'Win-win' scenario, in this vein, does sometimes imply a relative winner and a relative loser; but sometimes it might be a 'necessary satisfice' of certain short-term interests, especially for a latecomer, with a view to gaining development opportunities and greater, long-term benefits in the future—just like what China experienced in its economic 'take-off' stage in the 1980–1990s. 'Ownership' as advocated by the IDC community, therefore, should not be only about more participation or discretion in carrying out a given menu of development initiatives, but also an active and determining role in agenda making and rule setting. The recipient countries have, and if not adequately then should build, their capabilities in the abovementioned respects in order to really 'own' and make the most of external IDC initiatives.

REFERENCES

Alesina, Alberto, and David Dollar. 2000. 'Who Gives Foreign Aid to Whom and Why?' *Journal of Economic Growth* 5 (1): 33–63.
Bräutigam, Deborah. 2009. *The Dragon's Gift: The Real Story of China in Africa*. Oxford: Oxford University Press.
Clay, Edward, Matthew Geddes, and Luisa Natali. 2009. 'Untying Aid: Is It Working? An Evaluation of the Implementation of the Paris Declaration and of the 2001 DAC Recommendation of Untying ODA to the LDCs'. DIIS (Danish Institute for International Studies), Copenhagen.
Grimm, Sven, and Christine Hackenesch. 2017. 'China in Africa: What Challenges for a Reforming European Union Development Policy? Illustrations from Country Cases'. *Development Policy Review* 35 (4): 549–566.
Hjertholm, Peter, and Howard White. 2000. 'Foreign Aid in Historical Perspective: Background and Trends'. In *Foreign Aid and Development: Lessons Learnt and Directions for the Future*, 59–77. London: Routledge.
William, Hynes, and Simon Scott. 2013. 'The Evolution of Official Development Assistance: Achievements, Criticisms, and A Way Forward'. OECD Development Co-operation Working Papers No. 12. OECD Publishing, Paris.
ICAI. 2015. 'Business in Development'. ICAI (Independent Commission for Aid Impact). https://icai.independent.gov.uk/wp-content/uploads/ICAI-Business-in-Development-FINAL.pdf.
Kapoor, Ilan. 2008. *The Postcolonial Politics of Development*. Princeton, NJ: Princeton University Press.

Morgenthau, Hans. 1962. 'A Political Theory of Foreign Aid'. *The American Political Science Review* 56 (2): 301–309.

Niu, Jun. 2010. *Zhonghua Renmin Gongheguo Duiwai Guanxi Shi Gailun, 1949–2000* (Introduction to History of Foreign Relations of the People's Republic of China, 1949–2000). Beijing: Peking University Press.

Veen, Maurits van der. 2011. *Ideas, Interests and Foreign Aid*. Cambridge: Cambridge University Press.

APPENDICES

APPENDIX A: CLASSIFICATIONS OF CROPS AS USED IN THE CHINESE CONTEXT

Staple-food crops			Cash crops				
Grains/ cereals	Beans	Roots and tubers	Fibre crops	Oil crops	Sugar crops	Tropical crops	Others
Rice, wheat, maize, etc.	Soybean, pea, mung bean, etc.	Potato, sweet potato, cassava, yam, etc.	Cotton, etc.	Soybean, palm oil, etc.	Sugarcane, rape, etc.	Rubber, sisal, etc.	Coffee, tea, tabaco, etc.

Notes This is a crop classification that is commonly used in the Chinese context; however, it is not perfectly strict (for there may be some overlap between the two categories). Staple-food crops (liangshi zuowu), as defined by the Chinese government in its official documents, include mainly grains, beans, and root and tuber crops. Staple-food crops are used both for human food (kouliang, e.g. rice and wheat) and animal feed (siliaoliang, e.g. maize and soybeans). Cash crops (jingji zuowu) are those supposed to have more commercial value added and can be used for both food and industrial purposes. Although cash crops can be used for food purposes, some, like oil and sugar crops, are quite indispensable—comparatively speaking, they are not imperative in food security terms. One of the tricky crop types for differentiation is soybean, which is treated more as an oil crop in China although the residue of it, the soybean meal, is also used as important animal feed
Source The author

© The Editor(s) (if applicable) and The Author(s), under exclusive license to Springer Nature Singapore Pte Ltd. 2020
L. Jiang, *Beyond Official Development Assistance,* Governing China in the 21st Century,
https://doi.org/10.1007/978-981-32-9507-0

Appendix B: Overseas Agro-Projects of CNADC

Company	Project/subsidiary	Area	Main business	Other info
Africa				
CSFAC	China-Zambia Friendship Farm (Zambia, 1990)	670 ha	Crop farming (maize, soybean, wheat)	
	Cocoa Factory (Ghana, 1996)	N/A	Cocoa producing, processing and trading	Joint venture (China 45%, Ghana 55%); Not being operational since established and now looking for investors to take over
	Societe Sino-Guineenne Pour La Cooperation Dans Le Developpement Agricole S.A (Guinea, 1996)	N/A	Crop farming, animal husbandry, fishery, agro-processing and trading, technological consulting,	Joint venture (China 80%, Guinea 20%); Used to be *government agro-aid project* and transferred to CSFAC to operate in 1998
	Cooperation Agrotechnique Gabon-Chine (Gabon, 1998)	300 ha	Crop farming, animal husbandry, agro-processing	Joint venture (China 75%, Gabon 25%)
	CSFAC Friendship Farm (Zambia, 1999)	2600 ha	Animal husbandry, vegetable planting	
CAAIC	Zhongken Industry (Zambia, 1994)	3600 ha	Crop farming (maize, wheat), animal husbandry	Transferred from the CSFAC in 2010
	Tanzania Company (Tanzania, 1999)	6900 ha	Sisal planting and processing	Transferred from the CSFAC in 2010 and using the Government Concessional Loans of the EXIM Bank
	CAAIC & Yuanshi Company (Madagascar, 2014)	N/A	Hybrid rice planting	In cooperation with private Yuanshi company and the CADF of the CDB

Company	Project/subsidiary	Area	Main business	Other info
CAIDC	ATDC (South Africa, withdrew in 2018)	N/A	Freshwater aquaculture	*Government agro-aid projects*
	ATDC (Benin)	N/A	Crop and animal farming	
	Maize Co-research Project (Benin)	N/A	Hybrid maize planting	
	Soil Improvement Project (Algeria)	N/A	Soil improvement	
Australia				
CSFAC	Australia Company (1989)	30,000 ha	Animal husbandry	
Eastern Europe				
CAIDC	Ukraine Company	2600 ha	Crop farming (grains except for rice; soybeans and other oil crops) and dairy farming	

Source The author based on company websites and media reports, updated by 2019

Appendix C: Some of the Major M&A Deals by COFCO in Recent Years

Year	Investment targets	Value of M&A
2010	Vineyard and Vine Factory (Chilli)	N/A
2011	Worldbest Biochemicals CassavaProcessing Factory (Thailand)	N/A
2011	99% share of Tully Sugar Factory (Australia)	140 million Australian dollar (around 130 million USD)
2014	51% share of Nidera (The Netherlands)	1.2 billion USD
	Nidera: One of the major international agribusiness and trading companies. It specializes in supply-chain business, connecting commodity producers and users. Procures agro-products from farmers, merchandisers and processors in the major producing areas across the Americas, the FormerSoviet Union, Europe and Australia, and sells to Europe, the Mediterranean basin, the Middle East and Asia. Wheat, maize andsoybeansare among the main crop types that Nidera is handling. The company is also strong in some crop technology aspects and set up extensive storage and logistics networks in its partner countries	
2014	51% share of Noble Agri (Singapore-listed)	1.5 billion USD
	Noble Agri: One of the leading originators ofgrainsand oilseeds, e.g. wheat, maize, barley,soybeansin South America. It is also a top crusher and distributor in the Middle East and Asia. The company also trades some key types of cash crops such ascottn, sugar, coffee and cocoa	
2016–2017	Finished purchase of the total share of Nidera and Noble Agri	N/A

Source The author based on company websites and media reports, updated by 2019

Appendix D: Agricultural Foreign Investments by Chinese Provincial State Farming Enterprises (SFEs)

Reclamation area	Farming enterprise/ group corporation	Investment country	Investment field	Other investment information
The 17 reclamation areas that have completed the conglomeration transformation				
Beijing (Municipality)	Beijing Capital Agribusiness Group	Australia	Animal husbandry	Purchased and managed local farms since 2010
Tianjin (Municipality)	Tianjin State Farms Agribusiness Group Corporation	Bulgaria	Crop farming Animal husbandry	Purchased 100% equity of a local agribusiness firm including 3400 ha of self-owned land, 5700 ha of leased land and related equipment, storage and office facilities in 2014; planned to establish grain warehouses and processing factories in later phase
Shanghai (Municipality)	Bright Food Group Corporation	New Zealand, Australia,	Dairy industry	Conducted four transnational M&A deals since 2009, including Synlait Milk (New Zealand), Weetabix (the UK), Manassen (Australia) and DIVA (France)
Chongqing (Municipality)	Chongqing Agricultural Investment Group Corporation	**Sudan**	Crop farming (Alfalfa, a kind of animal feed)	Gained access to 120,000 ha of land for Alfalfa farming as a way for Sudanese government to pay off its 20 million USD debts to Chinese companies

Reclamation area	Farming enterprise/ group corporation	Investment country	Investment field	Other investment information
Heilongjiang (Province)	Heilongjiang Beidahuang State Farms Agribusiness Group Corporation	Russia, Brazil, Philippines,	Crop farming (soybeans, maize, wheat, rice, vegetables)	Had invested 24 million USD to lease approx. 47,000 ha of foreign land by 2009; the aim was to expand overseas land to 330,000 ha in the future
Jiangsu (Province)	Jiangsu State Farms Agribusiness Group Corporation	*Zambia*	Crop farming (grains and vegetables)	Had managed four overseas farms in Zambia, with land area totalling about 2300 ha since early 1990s
Anhui (Province)	Anhui State Farms Agribusiness Group Corporation	*Zimbabwe*	Crop farming (wheat, maize, soybeans, tobacco)	Took over three overseas farms in Zimbabwe since 2010, cultivating 5000 ha of land by 2013; planned to expand to 50,000 ha in the second phase by 2015; investment volume approx. 240 billion USD
Shanxi (陝西) (Province)	Shanxi State Farms Agribusiness Group Corporation	*Cameroon*	Crop farming (rice, cassava) Animal husbandry (Ostrich)	Gained access to 10,000 ha of virgin land in Cameron for reclamation and farming under a 90-year lease since 2006
Guangdong (Province)	Guangdong Guangken Rubber Group Corporation	Thailand, Malaysia, Singapore, Indonesia, Cambodia, Vietnam,	Crop farming (rubber)	Owned approx. 45,000 ha of overseas rubber plantations in a number of Southeast Asian countries by 2013; developed integrated value chain from seed breeding, planting, processing to trade

APPENDICES 219

Reclamation area	Farming enterprise/ group corporation	Investment country	Investment field	Other investment information
Yunnan (Province)	Yunnan Rubber Industry Group Corporation	Laos, Myanmar	Crop farming (rubber)	Owned approx. 10,000 ha of overseas rubber plantation in Laos and Myanmar by 2011; developed integrated value chain including planting, processing, trade
Hainan (Province)	Hainan Rubber Group Corporation	*Sierra Leone*	Crop farming (rubber and rice)	Planned in 2012 to cultivate 100,000 ha of land for rubber planting and 35,000 ha for rice planting in Sierra Leone; planned to develop integrated value chain including planting, processing, trade
Guangxi (Province)	Guangxi State Farms Agribusiness Group Corporation	Indonesia, Vietnam, Myanmar,	Crop farming (Cassava)	Had invested 200 million USD in several agricultural FDI projects, particularly in Southeast Asia by 2014
Others Gansu, Ningxia, Guangzhou, Kunming, Nanjing				
The 17 reclamation areas that have not undergone conglomeration transformation				
Xinjiang (Autonomous Region)	Xinjiang Production and Construction Corps	Ukraine, *Angola*	Crop farming Animal husbandry	Signed MOU in 2013 with Ukraine KSG Agribusiness firm to co-manage 100,000 ha of farmland on a 50-year lease, with capital input from the Chinese side totalling 2.6 billion USD; invested 160 million USD in building overseas farms in Angola with total area of 13,000 ha

Reclamation area	Farming enterprise/ group corporation	Investment country	Investment field	Other investment information
Inner Mongolia (Autonomous Region)	Hailaer State Farms Agribusiness (Group) Corporation	Russia	Crop farming (rapeseeds, wheat, barley)	Planned to invest 80 million USD in 100,000 ha of land under a 20-year lease in Russia, still in the discussion period by 2013
Hubei (Province)	Lianfeng Overseas Agricultural Development Company	**Mozambique, Zimbabwe,** Australia,	Crop farming Animal husbandry	Had access to approx. 27,000 ha of overseas farms, with investment volume totalling over 130 million USD

Others Liaoning, Jilin, Hubei, Henan, Shandong, Shanxi (山西), Zhejiang, Fujian, Hunan, Jiangxi, Sichuan, Guizhou, Qinghai

Note State farming enterprises emanated from the country's long-standing State Farm and Land Reclamation System. The system, characterized prominently by the running of a large number of state-owned farms all across the country, was formally set up after the founding of the People's Republic of China in 1949, and has since played an essential role in securing adequate supply of agricultural products for the whole population, boosting rural economy and development, and ensuring the stability and prosperity of the frontier regions, among others (Dequan Cheng 2013). With the launch of the Reform and Opening-Up policy in 1978, a series of transformations, both in terms of the production and the management models of the state farms, began to take place. A particularly pertinent point here is the business operation of the state farms and the conglomeration of the reclamation areas (largely in line with the provincial demarcation) (Reclamation areas are specifically identified—largely—as state-run farming areas, each of which can hold a number of state farms. There are now 34 reclamation areas in China), that is, to gradually turn the state farms into enterprise entities, and on the basis of that, transform the entire reclamation area into a group corporation formed up by those enterprises (Zheng 2004; Zhang 2010). This is how the so-called state farming enterprises (SFEs) discussed in the book have come into being. Also, through conglomeration, it is believed that strengths of different state farms can be fully integrated and the newly founded group corporation will be able to achieve a better position in the competition both at home and abroad. Until recently, around half of the total 34 reclamation areas in China have completed their conglomeration transformation

Source The author based on company websites and media reports, updated by 2019

APPENDIX E: SELECTED EXAMPLES OF CHINESE PRIVATE OVERSEAS AGRO-PROJECTS

Fields	Companies	Countries	Crop types	Investment modalities
Grains	Muxue (Chongqing Municipality)	Laos	Grains, coffee, Chinese medicine,	Farm plantation (approx. 100,000 ha) and preliminary processing
	Wanbao (Hubei Province)	Mozambique	Rice	Farm plantation (approx. 20,000 ha) and preliminary processing
Oils	Fudi (Zhejiang Province)	Brazil	Soybeans	Farm plantation (approx. 18,000 ha)
	Julong (Tianjin Municipality)	Indonesia (Liberia, Cameroon, Ghana, Kenya in plan)	Palm oil	Farm plantation (approx. 150,000 ha), processing, trade and logistics
	Huifu (Hebei province)	Brazil, Argentina, Indonesia	Soybeans, palm oil	Farm plantation (approx. 200,000 ha), trade and logistics
Cotton	CACD (Shandong Province)	Zimbabwe	Cotton	Contract farming (100,000 ha) and preliminary processing
Rubber	Gaoshen (Yunnan Province)	Laos, Myanmar	Rubber	Farm plantation (approx. 13,000 ha) and processing

Source The author based on company websites and media reports, updated by 2019

References

Cheng, Dequan. 2013. 'Zhongguo Nongken: nongye "guojiadui" (State Farming System: The Agricultural "National Team")'. http://history.people.com.cn/n/2013/0826/c368432-22699322.html.

Zheng, Yougui. 2004. 'Woguo Nongken Tizhi Gaige Huigu Yu Bianxi: Yi Heilongjiang Hainan Liangsheng Weili (Review and Discussion on the Reform of China's State Farming System: The Cases of Heilongjiang and Hainan Provinces)'. *Zhongguo Jingjishi Yanjiu* (Chinese Economic History Research) 4: 43–51.

Zhang, Q. Forrest. 2010. 'Reforming China's State-Owned Farms: State Farms in Agrarian Transition'.

INTERVIEWS

(Only formal interviews included here [see Methodology in Introduction]. All the informants are well informed of the identity and research purposes of the author; they are all kept anonymous to protect their privacy.)

Interview with the former Chinese ambassador in Rwanda. Interviewed by Lu Jiang. Beijing, China. 23 August 2013.

Interview with the Chinese Economic and Commercial Counsellor of the Embassy of the People's Republic of China in Mozambique. Interviewed by Lu Jiang. Maputo, Mozambique. 9 October 2013.

Interview with the Chinese director A of the ATDC in Mozambique. Interviewed by Lu Jiang. Boane, Maputo province, Mozambique. 18 October 2013.

Interview with a Chinese staff A working at the ATDC in Mozambique. Interviewed by Lu Jiang. Maputo, Mozambique. 4 November 2013a.

Interview with a Chinese staff B working at the ATDC in Mozambique. Interviewed by Lu Jiang. Boane, Maputo province, Mozambique. 4 November 2013b.

Interview with the Chinese director A of the ATDC in Mozambique. Interviewed by Lu Jiang. Boane, Maputo province, Mozambique. 8 November 2013a.

Interview with several Mozambican workers hired by the ATDC in Mozambique. Interviewed by Lu Jiang and Sérgio Chichava. Boane, Mozambique. 8 November 2013b.

© The Editor(s) (if applicable) and The Author(s), under exclusive license to Springer Nature Singapore Pte Ltd. 2020
L. Jiang, *Beyond Official Development Assistance*, Governing China in the 21st Century,
https://doi.org/10.1007/978-981-32-9507-0

Interview with a Mozambican staff working at the MCT. Interviewed by Lu Jiang and Sérgio Chichava. Maputo, Mozambique. 14 November 2013.
Interview with two of Wanbao's management team. Interviewed by Lu Jiang. Xaixai, Gaza province, Mozambique. 18 November 2013.
Interview with a Chinese staff working for Wanbao. Interviewed by Lu Jiang. Xaixai, Gaza province, Mozambique. 19 November 2013a.
Interview with two Mozambican agro-technicians working for Wanbao. Interviewed by Lu Jiang. Xaixai, Gaza province, Mozambique. 19 November 2013b.
Interview with one of Wanbao's management team. Interviewed by Lu Jiang. Xaixai, Gaza province, Mozambique. 19 November 2013c.
Interview with a Chinese staff working for Wanbao. Interviewed by Lu Jiang. Xaixai, Gaza province, Mozambique. 20 November 2013a.
Interview with a Chinese accountant assigned by CADFund to Wanbao. Interviewed by Lu Jiang. Xaixai, Gaza province, Mozambique. 20 November 2013b.
Interview with two of Wanbao's management team. Interviewed by Lu Jiang. Xaixai, Gaza province, Mozambique. 20 November 2013c.
Interview with the director of FONGA. Interviewed by Lu Jiang. Xaixai, Gaza province, Mozambique. 21 November 2013a.
Interview with two of Wanbao's management team. Interviewed by Lu Jiang. Xaixai, Gaza province, Mozambique. 21 November 2013b.
Interview with the chairman of the DPA Gaza. Interview by Lu Jiang and Idalêncio Sitoe. Xaixai, Gaza province, Mozambique. 22 November 2013.
Interview with two female Mozambican farmers. Interview by Lu Jiang and Sérgio Chichava. Xaixai, Gaza province, Mozambique. 20 December 2013a.
Interview with the chairman of RBL-EP. Interview by Lu Jiang and Sérgio Chichava Xaixai, Gaza province, Mozambique. 20 December 2013b.
Interview with a staff working for CAAIC. Interviewed by Lu Jiang. Maputo, Mozambique, 7 January 2014.
Interview with a Chinese working for a private Chinese agro-company in Mozambique. Interviewed by Lu Jiang. Maputo, Mozambique. 29 December 2014.
Interview with a Chinese staff working at the ATDC in Mozambique. Interviewed by Lu Jiang. Boane, Maputo province, Mozambique. 29 December 2014.
Interview with the Chinese manager of CAAIC's Mozambican project. Interviewed by Lu Jiang. Maputo, Mozambique. 10 January 2015.
Interview with a Chinese staff working for Hefeng. Interviewed by Lu Jiang. Buzi, Sofala province, Mozambique. 14 January 2015.
Interview with the farm director of Hefeng. Buzi, Sofala province, Mozambique. 15 January 2015

Interview with a Chinese staff working at the ATDC in South Africa. Interviewed by Lu Jiang and Angela Harding. Gariep Dam, Free State province, South Africa. 29 January 2015.
Interview with a Chinese staff A working at the ATDC in South Africa. Interviewed by Lu Jiang and Angela Harding. Gariep Dam, Free State province, South Africa. 30 January 2015a.
Interview with a Chinese staff B working at the ATDC in South Africa. Interviewed by Lu Jiang and Angela Harding. Gariep Dam, Free State province, South Africa. 30 January 2015b.
Interview with several South African farmers working at one of the six fish farms. Interviewed by Lu Jiang and Angela Harding. Gariep Dam, Free State province, South Africa. 30 January 2015c.
Interview with a Chinese staff working at the ATDC in South Africa. Interviewed by Lu Jiang. [By phone] London, UK. 8 March 2015.
Interview with the Chinese director B of the ATDC in Mozambique. Interviewed by Lu Jiang. [By phone] London, UK. 19 October 2015.
Interview with the Chinese director of the ATDC in Tanzania. Interviewed by Lu Jiang. [By phone] London, UK. 15 November 2015.
Interview with the Chinese director B of the ATDC in Mozambique. Interviewed by Lu Jiang. Shanghai, China. 23 June 2017.

Bibliography

Adem, Seifudein, ed. 2014. *China's Diplomacy in Eastern and Southern Africa*. New York: Routledge.
Agrawal, S. 2007. 'Emerging Donors in International Development Assistance: The India Case'. Working Paper. International Development Research Centre, Canada.
Alden, Chris. 2007. *China in Africa: Partner, Competitor or Hegemon?* London: Zed Books.
———. 2010. 'Resurgent Continent? Africa and the World: Emerging Powers and Africa'. Working Paper. IDEAS, London.
———. 2013. 'China and the Long March into African Agriculture'. *Cahiers Agriculture* 22 (1): 16–21.
Alden, Chris, and Amnon Aran. 2012. *Foreign Policy Analysis: New Approaches*. London: Routledge.
Alden, Chris, and Sérgio Chichava, eds. 2014. *China and Mozambique: From Comrades to Capitalists*. Auckland Park: Fanele.
Alden, Chris, and Daniel Large. 2011. 'China's Exceptionalism and the Challenges of Delivering Difference in Africa'. *Journal of Contemporary China* 20 (68): 21–38.
———. 2015. 'On Becoming a Norms Maker: Chinese Foreign Policy, Norms Evolution and the Challenges of Security in Africa'. *China Quarterly* 221: 123–142.
———. 2019. *New Directions in Africa-China Studies*. Abingdon: Routledge.
Alden, Chris, Daniel Large, and Ricardo Soares de Oliveira, eds. 2008. *China Returns to Africa: A Rising Power and a Continent Embrace*. London: Hurst & Company.

Alesina, Alberto, and David Dollar. 2000. 'Who Gives Foreign Aid to Whom and Why?' *Journal of Economic Growth* 5 (1): 33–63.

Alonso, José. 2012. 'From Aid to Global Development Policy'. Working Paper No. 121. United Nations Department of Economic and Social Affairs (UNDESA). http://www.un.org/esa/desa/papers/2012/wp121_2012.pdf.

Alonso, José, and Jonathan Glennie. 2015. 'What Is Development Cooperation?' Policy Brief. 2016 Development Cooperation Forum Policy Briefs. United Nations Department of Economic and Social Affairs (UNDESA). http://www.un.org/en/ecosoc/newfunct/pdf15/2016_dcf_policy_brief_no.1.pdf.

Amanor, Kojo, and Sérgio Chichava. 2016. 'South–South Cooperation, Agribusiness, and African Agricultural Development: Brazil and China in Ghana and Mozambique'. *World Development* 81: 13–23.

Anderlini, Jamil. 2008. 'China Eyes Overseas Land in Food Push'. *Financial Times*, 8 May. http://www.ft.com/cms/s/0/cb8a989a-1d2a-11dd-82ae-000077b07658.html#axzz42zAYuMoZ.

Anderson, James E. 1979. *Public Policy-Making*. 2nd ed. New York: Holt, Rinehart and Winston.

Anseeuw, Ward et al. 2011. 'Land Rights and the Rush for Land: Findings of the Global Commercial Pressures on Land Research Project'. http://www.landcoalition.org/sites/default/files/documents/resources/ILC%20GSR%20report_ENG.pdf.

Bardach, Eugene. 1977. *The Implementation Game: What Happens After a Bill Becomes a Law*. MIT Studies in American Politics and Public Policy, 1. Cambridge: MIT Press.

Barrett, Susan, and Colin Fudge, eds. 1981. *Policy and Action: Essays on the Implementation of Public Policy*. London: Methuen.

Baynton-Glen, Sarah. 2012. 'China-Africa: Agricultural Potential'. Standard Chartered.

Beausang, F. 2012. *Globalization and the BRICs: Why the BRICs Will Not Rule the World for Long*. London: Palgrave Macmillan.

Benin, Samuel, Adam Kennedy, Melissa Lambert, and Linden McBride. 2010. 'Monitoring African Agricultural Development Processes and Performance: A Comparative Analysis'. https://resakss.files.wordpress.com/2011/06/resakss_aw_ator_2010_web.pdf.

Benmamourn, Mamoun, and Kevin Lehnert. 2013. 'Financing Growth: Comparing the Effects of FDI, ODA, and International Remittances'. *Journal of Economic Development* 38 (2): 43–65.

Berman, Paul. 1978. 'The Study of Macro- and Micro-Implementation'. The RAND Paper Series. https://www.rand.org/content/dam/rand/pubs/papers/2008/P6071.pdf.

———. 1980. 'Thinking About Programmed and Adaptive Implementation: Matching Strategies to Situations'. In *Why Policies Succeed or Fail?* (Mann and Ingram Eds.).

Besharati, Neissan Alessandro. 2013. 'South African Development Partnership Agency (SADPA): Strategic Aid or Development Packages for Africa?' (SAIIA) South African Institute of International Affairs.
Binder, Andrea, Markus Palenberg, and Jan Martin Witte. 2007. 'Engaging Business in Development'. GPPi Research Paper Series No. 8. Global Public Policy Institute, Berlin.
BMZ. 2005. 'Public Private Partnership (PPP) in German Development Cooperation'. Federal Ministry for Economic Cooperation and Development, Berlin.
Bräutigam, Deborah. 1998. *Chinese Aid and African Development: Exporting Green Revolution*. New York: Palgrave Macmillan.
———. 2009. *The Dragon's Gift: The Real Story of China in Africa*. Oxford: Oxford University Press.
———. 2010. 'China, Africa and the International Aid Architecture'. Working Paper 107. African Development Bank Group. https://www.afdb.org/fileadmin/uploads/afdb/Documents/Publications/WORKING%20107%20%20PDF%20E33.pdf.
———. 2011. 'Aid "with Chinese Characteristics": Chinese Foreign Aid and Development Finance Meet the OECD-DAC Aid Regime'. *Journal of International Development* 23 (5): 752–764.
———. 2016. *Will Africa Feed China?* Oxford: Oxford University Press.
Bräutigam, Deborah, and Sigrid-Marianella Ekman. 2012. 'Rumours and Realities of Chinese Agricultural Engagement in Mozambique'. *African Affairs* 111 (444): 483–492.
Bräutigam, Deborah, and Xiaoyang Tang. 2009. 'China's Engagement in African Agriculture: "Down to the Countryside"'. *The China Quarterly* 199 (September): 686–706.
———. 2012a. 'An Overview of Chinese Agricultural and Rural Engagement in Ethiopia'. Discussion Paper 1185. IFPRI (International Food Policy Research Institute). https://deborahbrautigam.files.wordpress.com/2014/02/ifpri-ethiopia-dp.pdf.
———. 2012b. 'An Overview of Chinese Agricultural and Rural Engagement in Tanzania'. Discussion Paper 1214. IFPRI (International Food Policy Research Institute). http://ebrary.ifpri.org/cdm/ref/collection/p15738coll2/id/127148.
Brazilchina.net. 2014. 'Kunnan Chongchong Zhongguo Nongqi Chongqing Liangshi Jituan Mengduan Baxi? (Too Many Difficulties: Does CGG's Dream Shattered in Brazil?)'. http://www.bxqw.com/userlist/hbpd/newshow-31065.html.
Brighi, Elisabetta, and Christopher Hill. 2012. 'Implementation and Behaviour'. In *Foreign Policy: Theories, Actors, Cases* (Smith et al. Eds.).

Brown, Chris, and Kirsten Ainley. 2009. *Understanding International Relations*. Basingstoke: Palgrave Macmillan.

Burges, Sean. 2014. 'Brazil's International Development Co-operation: Old and New Motivations'. *Development Policy Review* 32 (3): 355–374.

Burnside, Craig, and David Dollar. 2000. 'Aid, Policy and Growth'. *The American Economic Review* 90 (4): 847–868.

CAAIC (China-Africa Agriculture Investment Co. Ltd.). n.d. 'Gongsi Jianjie (Company Profile)'. Accessed 26 March 2016. http://www.caaic.com.cn/Article_List.aspx?columnID=1.

Cabral, Lídia, Giuliano Russo, and Julia Weinstock. 2014. 'Brazil and the Shifting Consensus on Development Co-Operation: Salutary Diversions from the "Aid-Effectiveness" Trail?' *Development Policy Review* 32 (2): 179–202.

CACD (China-Africa Cotton Developement Ltd.). n.d. 'China-Africa Cotton Mozambique Limited'. Accessed 31 May 2019a. http://www.ca-cotton.com/en/company/c/.

———. n.d. 'Introduction'. Accessed 31 May 2019b. http://www.ca-cotton.com/en/aboutus/a/.

Cai, Kevin G. 1999. 'Outward Foreign Direct Investment: A Novel Dimension of China's Integration into the Regional and Global Economy'. *The China Quarterly* 160 (December): 856–880.

Cai, Lingming. 1991. 'Mupoli Nongchang Gaige Ji (Reforms of the Mupoli Farm)'. *Guoji Jingji Hezuo* (International Economic Cooperation) 8: 42–44.

———. 1992. 'Woguo Dui Feizhou de Nongye Yuanzhu (China's Agricultural Aid to Africa)'. *Guoji Jingji Hezuo* (International Economic Cooperation) 2: 43–44.

CAIDC (China Agriculture International Development Co. Ltd.). n.d. 'Gongsi Jianjie (Company Profile)'. Accessed 14 May 2013. http://www.caidco.com/index.php?a=content&id=347.

CAITEC (Chinese Academy of International Trade and Economic Cooperation). 2018. *Guoji Fazhan Hezuo Zhilu: 40 Nian Gaige Kaifang Dachao Xia de Zhongguo Duiwai Yuanzhu* (Road of International Development Cooperation: China's Foreign Aid in the Four-Decade Waves of Reform and Opening-Up). Beijing: China Commerce and Trade Press.

Camara, Morro. 2004. 'The Impact of Programme Versus Project Aid on Fiscal Behaviour in The Gambia'.

Carlsnaes, Walter. 2002. 'Foreign Policy'. In *Handbook of International Relations* (Carlsnaes et al. Eds.).

———. 2012. 'Actors, Structures, and Foreign Policy Analysis'. In *Foreign Policy: Theories, Actors, Cases* (Smith et al. Eds.).

———. 2013. 'Foreign Policy'. In *Handbook of International Relations* (Carlsnaes et al. Eds.).

Carlsnaes, Walter, Thomas Risse-Kappen, and Beth A. Simmons. 2002. *Handbook of International Relations*. 1st ed. London: Sage.
———. 2013. *Handbook of International Relations*. 2nd ed. London: Sage.
CCP (China's Communist Party). 2007. 'Guanyu Jiji Fazhan Xiandai Nongye Zhashi Tuijin Shehui Zhuyi Xin Nongchun Jianshe de Ruogan Yijian ("No. 1 Document of the CCP")'. http://news.xinhuanet.com/politics/2007-01/29/content_5670478.htm.
———. 2008. 'Guanyu Tuijin Nongcun Gaige Fazhan Ruogan Zhongda Wenti de Jueding (Decisions on Several Key Issues of Promoting the Rural Reform)'. http://www.gov.cn/jrzg/2008-10/19/content_1125094.htm.
———. 2010. 'Guanyu Jiada Tongchou Fazhan Lidu Jinyibu Hangshi Nongye Nongcun Fazhan Jichu de Ruogan Yijian ("No. 1 Document of the CCP")'. http://theory.people.com.cn/GB/10898856.html.
———. 2014. 'Guanyu Quanmian Shenhua Nongcun Gaige Jiakuai Tuijin Nongye Xiandaihua de Ruogan Yijian ("No. 1 Document of the CCP")'. http://www.gov.cn/jrzg/2014-01/19/content_2570454.htm.
CCTV.com. 2018. 'Zhongfei Nongye Hezuo: "shouren Yiyu Buru Shouren yiyu" (China-South Africa Agricultural Cooperation: Teaching Others How to Fish Is Better Than Giving Them Fishes)', 26 July. http://sannong.cctv.com/2018/07/26/ARTIzbS3iLbcbeSRBwCHQnxL180726.shtml.
Cen, Boning. 2010. 'Tansuo Zhongfei Nongye Hezuo Xinmoshi (Exploring New Models of China-Africa Agricultural Cooperation)'. *Nongjing* (Agriculture Economics Magazine).
Chanana, D. 2009. 'India as an Emerging Donor'. *Economic and Political Weekly* 44.
———. 2010. 'India's Transition to Global Donor: Limitations and Prospects'. *Real Instituto Elcano* 123.
Chandy, Laurence. 2011. Reframing Development Cooperation. In *The 2011 Brookings Blum Roundtable Policy Briefs*. Washington, DC: The Brookings Institute. https://www.brookings.edu/wp-content/uploads/2016/07/2011_blum_reframing_development_cooperation_chandy.pdf.
Chandy, Laurence, and Homi Kharas. 2011. 'Why Can't We All Just Get Along? The Practical Limits to International Development Cooperation'. *Journal of International Development* 23 (5): 739–751.
Chang, Bao. 2011. 'CGG Is Setting Up a Soybean Base in Brazil'. *China Daily*. http://usa.chinadaily.com.cn/business/2011-11/24/content_14154127.htm.
Chaturvedi, Sachin. 2008. 'Emerging Patterns in Architecture for Management of Economic Assistance and Development Cooperation: Implications and Challenges for India'. Working Paper.
———. 2012. 'India's Development Partnership: Key Policy Shifts and Institutional Evolution'. *Cambridge Review of International Affairs* 25 (4): 557–577.

Chaturvedi, Sachin, Anuradha Chenoy, Deepta Chopra, Anuradha Joshi, and Khush Lagdhyan. 2014. 'Indian Development Cooperation: The State of the Debate'. Working Paper No. 95. Evidence Report. IDS (Institute of Development Studies), Sussex.

Chen, Cheng. 2006. 'Wuyuan Wuhui Feizhouqing (Unregretful Affections with Africa)'. 23 June. http://news.sohu.com/20060623/n243887468.shtml.

Chen, Xiangyang. 2009. 'Xinshiqi Zhongguo Dawaijiao de Fangxiang (Directions of China's Great Diplomacy in the New Era)'. *Liaowang Xinwen Zhoukan* (Outlook Weekly).

Chen, Xiaochen. 2013. 'Gengyun Feizhou: Tansangniya Zhongguo Jianma Nongchang de Zhenshi Gushi (Farming in Africa: The Real Story of Chinese Sisal Farm in Tanzania)'. http://finance.sina.com.cn/roll/20130521/0127 15526584.shtml.

Chen, Yangyong. 2009. 'Jiangzemin "zouchuqu" zhanlue de Xingcheng Jiqi Zhongyao Yiyi (Formulation and Implications of Jiang Zemin's "Going Out" Strategy)'. *Dangde Wenxian* (The Party's Documents) 127 (1): 63–69.

Chen, Yanjuan, Lu Qin, and Yan Deng. 2012. 'Zhongguo Dui Angela Nongye Touzi de Xianzhuang, Wenti Yu Duice (China's Agricultural Investment in Angola: Current Situations, Problems and Countermeasures)'. *Duiwai Jingji Shiwu* (Economic Relations and Trade) 12.

Cheng, Dequan. 2013. 'Zhongguo Nongken: nongye "guojiadui" (State Farming System: The Agricultural "National Team")'. http://history.people.com.cn/n/2013/0826/c368432-22699322.html.

Cheng, Guoqiang. 2013. *Quanqiu Nongye Zhanlue: Jiyu Quanqiu Shiye de Zhongguo Liangshi Anquan Kuangjia* (Global Agricultural Strategy: China's Food Security Framework Based on a Global Perspective). Zhongguo fazhan chubanshe (China Development Press).

Cheng, Rongdong, and Xuelei Bai. 2018. 'Yangguang Xinwen Jujiao Hubei Hefeng Feizhou Zhongtian (CNR News Foduses on Hubei Hefeng's Farming in Africa)', 15 August. http://www.cnr.cn/hubei/yaowen/20180815/t20180815_524332005.shtml.

Chichava, Sérgio. 2008. 'Mozambique and China: From Politics to Business'. IESE (Instituto de Estudos Sociais E Económicos) Discussion Paper.

———. 2013. 'Xai-Xai Chinese Rice Farm and Mozambican Internal Political Dynamics: A Complex Relation'. LSE IDEAS Africa Programme Occational Paper 2. http://s3.amazonaws.com/china_resources/17484/2013-07-24_09_26_57_-0400_Sergio-Chichava---Occasional-Paper-2.pdf.

Chichava, Sérgio, Jimena Duran, and Lu Jiang. 2014. 'The Chinese Agricultural Technology Demonstration Centre in Mozambique: A Story of a Gift'. In *China and Mozambique: From Comrades to Capitalists* (Alden and Chichava Eds.).

Chichava, Sérgio, and Natalia Fingermann. 2015. 'Chinese and Brazilian Agricultural Models in Mozambique. The Case of the Chinese Agricultural Technology Demonstration Centre and of the Brazilian ProALIMENTOS Programme'. China and Brazil in Africa Agriculture Project. Future Agricultures.

Chin, Gregory. 2012. 'China as a "Net Donor": Tracking Dollars and Sense'. *Cambridge Review of International Affairs* 25 (4): 579–603.

Chin, Gregory, and B. Michael Frolic. 2007. 'Emerging Donors in Development Assistance: The Case of China'. Working Paper. International Development Research Centre, Canada.

Chin, Gregory, and Fahimul Quadir. 2012. 'Introduction: Rising States, Rising Donors and the Global Aid Regime'. *Cambridge Review of International Affairs* 25 (4): 493–506.

China.com.cn. 2012. 'Mali Tanglian youdian "tian" (The Malian Association Is a Bit Sweet)'. http://finance.china.com.cn/roll/20120618/810592.shtml.

China-DAC (The China-DAC Study Group). 2009. 'The China-DAC Study Group: Sharing Experiences and Promoting Learning About Growth and Poverty Reduction in China and African Countries'. http://www.oecd.org/china/44390151.pdf.

———. 2011. 'Economic Transformation and Poverty Reduction: How It Happened in China, Helping It Happen in Africa'. http://www.oecd.org/officialdocuments/publicdisplaydocumentpdf/?cote=DCD(2011)4&docLanguage=En.

Chinese Embassy in Tanzania. 2011. 'China's Food Aid to Africa and Agricultural Cooperation with African Continent'. http://www.fmprc.gov.cn/mfa_eng/wjb_663304/zwjg_665342/zwbd_665378/t851124.shtml.

Clarke, Michael. 1979. 'Foreign Policy Implementation: Problems and Approaches'. *British Journal of International Studies* 5 (2): 112–128.

Clarke, Michael, and Brian White. 1989. *Understanding Foreign Policy: The Foreign Policy Systems Approach.* Aldershot: Edward Elgar.

Clay, Edward, Matthew Geddes, and Luisa Natali. 2009a. 'Untying Aid: Is It Working? An Evaluation of the Implementation of the Paris Declaration and of the 2001 DAC Recommendation of Untying ODA to the LDCs'. DIIS (Danish Institute for International Studies), Copenhagen.

———. 2009b. 'Untying Aid: Is It Working? Evaluation of the Paris Declaration'. DIIS (Danish Institute for International Studies). https://www.oecd.org/dac/evaluation/dcdndep/44375975.pdf.

CLET (China Light Industrial Corporation for Foreign Economic and Technical Co-operation). n.d. 'Foreign Investment Projects of CLETC'. Accessed 29 March 2016. http://www.cletc.com/364-929-10283.aspx.

CNADC (China National Agricultural Development Group Co. Ltd.). 2015. 'Zhongken Gongsi: Xinzhanlue Zhutui Nongye "zouchuqu" bufa (CSFAC:

New Strategy Promotes Agricultural "Going Out")'. *CNADC (China National Agricultural Development Group Co. Ltd.) News*, 18 February. http://www.zgnfb.com/news-5803.html.

———. 2017. 'Woguo Yuanzhu Nanfei Nongye Jishu Shifan Zhongxin Jishu Hezuoqi Xiangmu Shunli Yijiao (China-Aided South African ATDC Successfully Transferred to South Africa After the Technical Cooperation Stage)'. *Zhongguo Nongfa (CNADC)*, 22 September. http://zgnfb.com/jqckj/news/9/37/111-1.shtml.

———. n.d. 'Gongsi Jianjie (Company Profile)'. Accessed 19 May 2014a. http://www.cnadc.com.cn/jtgk/qygk/qyjj/.

———. n.d. 'Qiye Jianjie (Company Profile)'. Accessed 19 May 2014b. http://www.cnadc.com.cn/jtgk/qygk/qyjj/index.asp.

CNFC (China National Fishery Co. Ltd.). n.d. 'Gongsi Jianjie (Company Profile)'. Accessed 26 March 2016. http://www.cofc.com.cn/cn/about.aspx?TypeId=10338.

Comnews (Run by China's Ministry of Commerce). 2014. 'Guoji Liangcang Bicang, Dadou Hangye Ruhe Yingdui Weiji? (How Can Soybean Companies Cope with "Market Corner" Crisis Imposed by International Traders)', 16 April. http://www.chinadaily.com.cn/hqcj/gjcj/2014-06-16/content_11840743.html.

Cook, Seth, Jixia Lu, Henry Tugendhat, and Dawit Alemu. 2016. 'Chinese Migrants in Africa: Facts and Fictions from the Agri-Food Sector in Ethiopia and Ghana'. *World Development* 81: 61–70.

Cooper, Andrew F., and Asif B. Farooq. 2015. 'Emerging Donors: The Promise and Limits of Bilateral and Multilateral Democracy Promotion'. *Cambridge Review of International Affairs* (Online), 1–22.

Cooper, Richard. 1972. 'Trade Policy Is Foreign Policy'. *Foreign Policy* 9: 18–36.

Cotula, Lorenzo, Sonja Vermeulen, Rebeca Leonard, and James Keeley. 2009. 'Land Grab or Development Opportunity? Agricultural Investment and International Land Deals in Africa'. https://www.google.com.hk/url?sa=t&rct=j&q=&esrc=s&source=web&cd=1&ved=0ahUKEwj6v9iSnpfVAhUFwBQKHaZUBuQQFggkMAA&url=http%3a%2f%2f-www%2efao%2eorg%2f3%2fa-ak241e%2epdf&usg=AFQjCNHkljuMWiuA7EQjCKqNez-HSfdMDw.

CSFAC (China State Farms Agribusiness Co. Ltd.). n.d. 'Gongsi Jianjie (Company Profile)'. Accessed 24 May 2014. http://csfagc.cn/lm.asp?lm=23&artid=51.

Currie-Alder, Bruce. 2016. 'The State of Development Studies: Origins, Evolution and Prospects'. *Canadian Journal of Development Studies* 37 (1): 5–26.

Dai, Chunning, ed. 2009. *Zhongguo Duiwai Touzi Xiangmu Anli Fenxi: Zhongguo Jinchukou Yinhang Haiwai Touzi Xiangmu Jingxuan* (Chinese

Foreign Investment: Case Selection of Overseas Investment Projects of the EXIM Bank of China). Beijing: Tsinghua University Press.

Davies, Joanne. 2011. 'Washington's Growth and Opportunity Act or Beijing's "Overarching Brilliance": Will African Governments Choose Neither?' *Third World Quarterly* 32 (6): 1147–1163.

Deleon, Peter. 1999. 'The Missing Link Revisited: Contemporary Implementation Research'. *Review of Policy Research* 16 (3–4): 311–338.

Deng, Xiaoping. 1978. 'Shixian Sihua, Yongbu Chengba (Realise the Four Modernisation, Never Be the Hegemon)'. In *Deng Xiaoping Wenxuan* (The Selected Works of Deng Xiaoping). Vol. 2. http://cpc.people.com.cn/GB/64184/64185/66611/4488666.html.

———. 1980. 'Muqian de Xingshi He Renwu (The Current Situations and Tasks)'. In *Deng Xiaoping Wenxuan* (The Selected Works of Deng Xiaoping). Vol. 2. http://cpc.people.com.cn/GB/64184/64185/66611/4488647.html.

Department of State of the US. n.d. 'Marshall Plan, 1948'. Accessed 31 May 2019. https://history.state.gov/milestones/1945-1952/marshall-plan.

Derthick, Martha. 1972. *New Towns In-Town: Why a Federal Program Failed*. Washington, DC: Urban Institute.

Devex. 2011. 'Bilateral Donor Agencies Open for Partnerships: A Closer Look at 5 Leaders in Development Partnerships'. https://pages.devex.com/rs/685-KBL-765/images/Devex_Reports_Biateral_Donor_Agencies_A_Closer_Look_at_5_Development_Leaders.pdf.

DFID. 2011. 'The Engine of Development: The Private Sector and Prosperity for Poor People'. Department for International Development, London.

Diao, Xinshen, Peter Hazell, and James Thurlow. 2010. 'The Role of Agriculture in African Development'. *World Development* 38 (10): 1375–1383.

Ding, Dong. 2014. 'Zhongguo Nongken Dazao Guoji Da Liangshang (China's State Farming System Aims to Develop into International Food Trader)'. http://www.chinanews.com/cj/2014/04-10/6046032.shtml.

Dreher, Axel, and Andreas Fuchs. 2015. 'Rogue Aid? An Empirical Analysis of China's Aid Allocation'. *Canadian Journal of Economics* 48 (3): 988–1023.

Dreher, Axel, Andreas Fuchs, Roland Hodler, Bradley Parks, Paul Raschky, and Michael J. Tierney. 2016. 'Aid on Demand: African Leaders and the Geography of China's Foreign Assistance'. Working Paper. AidData.

Dreher, Axel, Andreas Fuchs, Bradley Parks, Austin M. Strange, and Michael J. Tierney. 2015. 'Apples and Dragon Fruits: The Determinants of Aid and Other Forms of State Financing from China to Africa'. Working Paper 15. AidData.

Dreher, Axel, Peter Nunnenkamp, and Rainer Thiele. 2011. 'Are "New" Donors Different? Comparing the Allocation of Bilateral Aid Between Non-DAC and DAC Donor Countries'. *World Development* 39 (11): 1950–1968.

Easterly, William. 2003. 'Can Foreign Aid Buy Growth?' *Journal of Economic Perspectives* 17 (3): 23–48.

———. 2006. *The White Man's Burden: Why the West's Efforts to Aid the Rest Have Done So Much Ill and So Little Good*. New York: Penguin Press.

EC (European Commission). 2005. 'The Crisis in African Agriculture: A More Effective Role for EC Aid?' http://practicalaction.org/docs/advocacy/the_crisis_in_african_agriculture.pdf.

ECA of the UN (Economic Commission for Africa of the United Nations Economic and Social Council). 2007. 'Africa Review Report on Agriculture and Rural Development'. https://sustainabledevelopment.un.org/content/documents/eca_bg2.pdf.

ECCO in Mozambique (Economic and Commercial Counsellor's Office of the Embassy of the People's Republic of China in Mozambique). 2007. 'Zhongguo Yuanzhu Mosangbike Nongye Jishu Shifan Zhongxin Xiangmu Kexingxing Kaocha Yuanman Jieshu (The Feasibility Study on China-Aided Agriculture Technology Demonstration Centre in Mozambique Finishes)'. http://mz.mofcom.gov.cn/article/zxhz/200706/20070604767242.shtml.

ECCO in Tanzania (Economic and Commercial Counsellor's Office of the Embassy of the People's Republic of China in Tanzania). 2004a. 'Tan Zhengfu Gongkai Zhaobiao Chushou Lufu Shuidao Nongchang (Tanzanian Government Invites a Bid for Lufu Rice Farm)'. http://tz.mofcom.gov.cn/aarticle/jmxw/200408/20040800261893.html.

———. 2004b. 'Tan Zhengfu Gongkai Zhaobiao Chushou Mubalali Nongchang (Tanzanian Government Invites a Bid for Mubalali Farm)'.

Economic Information. 2015. 'Luoshi Zhongyao Yihao Wenjian, Zhengcexing Xinyong Baoxian Zhichi nongye "zouchuqu" (Realizing CCP's No. 1 Document: Policy-Oriented Insurance Supports Agricultural "Going Out")'. *Jingji Cankao Bao* (Economic Information), 20 March. http://news.xinhuanet.com/fortune/2015-03/20/c_127601043.htm.

ECOSOC of the UN. 2008. 'Background Study for the Development Cooperation Forum: Trends in South-South and Triangular Development Cooperation'. United Nations Economic and Social Council.

Eicher, Carl. 2003. 'Flashback: Fifty Years of Donor Aid to African Agriculture'. https://rmportal.net/framelib/donor-aid-to-african-agriculture.pdf.

Elmore, Richard F. 1979. 'Backward Mapping: Implementation Research and Policy Decisions'. *Political Science Quarterly* 94 (4): 601–616.

———. 1985. 'Forward and Backward Mapping: Reversible Logic in the Analysis of Public Policy'. In *Policy Implementation in Federal and Unitary Systems: Questions of Analysis and Design* (Hanf and Toonen Eds.), 33–70.

Emmerij, Louis. 2002. 'Aid as a Flight Forward'. *Development and Change* 33 (2): 247–259.

European Commission. 2014a. 'A Stronger Role of the Private Sector in Achieving Inclusive and Sustainable Growth in Developing Countries'. http://ec.europa.eu/transparency/regdoc/rep/1/2014/EN/1-2014-263-EN-F1-1.Pdf.

———. 2014b. 'Synthesis of Budget Support Evaluations: Analysis of the Findings, Conclusions and Recommendations of Seven Country Evaluations of Budget Support'.
EXIM Bank of China. 2013. 'Zhongguo Jinchukou Yinhang "liangyou" daikuan Yewu Jieshao ("Two Preferential Loans" of the EXIM Bank of China)'. http://www.chinca.org/cms/html/files/2013-12/16/201312161029 48872930302.pdf.
FAO (Food and Agriculture Organization of the United Nations). 2002. 'FAO Rice Information: Mozambique'. http://www.fao.org/docrep/005/y4347e/y4347e17.htm#TopOfPage.
———. 2003. 'Food Security: Concepts and Measurement'. Trade Reforms and Food Security: Conceptualizing the Linkages. http://www.fao.org/docrep/005/y4671e/y4671e06.htm#fnB21.
———. 2010. 'The State of Food Insecurity in the World: Addressing Food Insecurity in Protracted Crises'. http://www.fao.org/docrep/013/i1683e/i1683e.pdf.
———. 2013. 'Trends and Impacts of Foreign Investment in Developing Country Agriculture: Evidence from Case Studies'. http://www.fao.org/fileadmin/user_upload/newsroom/docs/Trends%20publication%2012%20 November%202012.pdf.
———. 2014. 'Responsible Agricultural Investments in Developing Countries: How to Make Principles and Guidelines Effective'. https://www.google.com.hk/url?sa=t&rct=j&q=&esrc=s&source=web&cd=1&ved=0ahUKEwjo-MznnJfVAhUI7xQKHZH2AnMQFggpMAA&url=http%3a%2f%2fwww%2eregeringen%2ese%2f49bb90%2fcontentassets%2f5edb15744f844f-c590e478ef4f42bdea%2fresponsible-agricultural-investments-in-developing-countries&usg=AFQjCNF1hCe-r3yHYiDCUWFAQWHv3G4udw.
FAO of Hubei (Foreign Affairs Office of Hubei Provincial People's Government). 2012. 'Hubeisheng Yu Waiguo Dijie Youhao Chengshi Xiangqing (Twinned Foreign Cities with Hubei Province)'. http://www.fohb.gov.cn/swzx/show/648.aspx.
Fischer, Frank, Gerald Miller, and Mara S. Sidney, eds. 2007. *Handbook of Public Policy Analysis: Theory, Politics, and Methods*. Public Administration and Public Policy 125. Boca Raton: CRC/Taylor & Francis.
FOCAAC (Forum on China-Africa Agricultural Cooperation). 2010. 'Zhongfei Nongye Hezuo Luntan Beijing Xuanyan (Beijing Declaration of Forum on China-Africa Agricultural Cooperation)'. http://www.moa.gov.cn/ztzl/zfnyhzlt/ltdt/201008/t20100813_1618055.htm.
FOCAC (Forum on China Africa Cooperation). 2000. 'Programme for China-Africa Cooperation in Economic and Social Development'. Ministry of Foreign Affairs of the People's Republic of China, Beijing. https://www.focac.org/eng/zywx_1/zywj/t606797.htm.

———. 2003. 'The Forum on China-Africa Cooperation Addis Ababa Action Plan (2004–2006)'. Ministry of Foreign Affairs of the People's Republic of China, Beijing. https://www.focac.org/eng/zywx_1/zywj/t606801.htm.

———. 2006. 'The Forum on China-Africa Cooperation Beijing Action Plan (2007–2009)'. Ministry of Foreign Affairs of the People's Republic of China, Beijing. https://www.focac.org/eng/zywx_1/zywj/t280369.htm.

———. 2009. 'The Forum on China-Africa Cooperation Sharm El-Sheikh Action Plan (2010–2012)'. Ministry of Foreign Affairs of the People's Republic of China, Beijing. https://www.focac.org/eng/zywx_1/zywj/t626387.htm.

———. 2012. 'The Forum on China-Africa Cooperation Beijing Action Plan (2013–2015)'. Ministry of Foreign Affairs of the People's Republic of China, Beijing. https://www.focac.org/eng/zywx_1/zywj/t954620.htm.

———. 2015. 'The Forum on China-Africa Cooperation Johannesburg Action Plan (2016–2018)'. Ministry of Foreign Affairs of the People's Republic of China, Beijing. https://www.focac.org/eng/zywx_1/zywj/t1327961.htm.

———. 2018. 'The Forum on China-Africa Cooperation Beijing Action Plan (2019-2021)'. Ministry of Foreign Affairs of the People's Republic of China, Beijing. https://www.focac.org/eng/zywx_1/zywj/t1594297.htm.

Freeman, Duncan, Jonathan Holslag, and Steffi Weil. 2008. 'China's Foreign Farming Policy: Can Land Provide Security?' Asia Papers. Brussels Institute of Contemporary China Studies. http://www.farmlandgrab.org/wp-content/uploads/2008/11/freeman-holslag-and-weil-2008-chinas-foreign-farmong-policy-biccs-asia-paper-vol-3-9.pdf.

Freemantle, Simon, and Jeremy Stevens. 2011. 'China's Food Security Challenge: What Role for Africa?' Standard Bank.

Fu, Xiaohan. 2008. '"Duiwai Jingji Jishu Yuanzhu de Baxiang Yuanze" juece de Cengci Fenxi (Level Analysis of the Decision-Making on "The Eight Principles of Foreign Economic and Technical Assistance")'. *Lishi Jiaoxue* (History Teaching) 2: 95–98.

Fuchs, Andreas, and Krishana Vadlamannati. 2013. 'The Needy Donor: An Empirical Analysis of India's Aid Motives'. *World Development* 44: 110–128.

Führer, Helmut. 1996. *The Story of Official Development Assistance: A Story of the Development Assistance Committee and the Development Co-operation Directorate in Dates, Names and Figures*. Paris: OECD Publishing.

Gadzala, Aleksandra W., ed. 2015. *Africa and China: How Africans and Their Governments Are Shaping Relations with China*. Lanham: Rowman & Littlefield.

Ganho, Ana Sofia. 2013. '"Friendship" Rice, Business, or "Land-Grabbing"? The Hubei-Gaza Rice Project in Xaixai'. LDPI (The Land Deal Politics Initiative) Working Paper 32. http://www.iss.nl/fileadmin/ASSETS/iss/Research_and_projects/Research_networks/LDPI/LDPI_WP_32.pdf.

Gao, Guixian, Yueji Zhu, and Deyi Zhou. 2014. 'Zhongfei Nongye Hezuo de Kunjing Diwei He Chulu (Difficulties, Status and Solutions of China-Africa Agricultural Cooperation)'. *Zhongguo Ruan Kexue* (China Soft Science) 1: 36–42.

Goggin, Malcolm L., A. O. M. Bowman, J. P. Lester, and L. J. O'Toole. 1990. *Implementation Theory and Practice: Toward a Third Generation*. Glenview: Scott, Foresman/Little, Brown Higher Education.

Goldstein, Andrea, Nicolas Pinaud, Helmut Reisen, and Xiaobao Chen. 2006. 'China and India: What's in It for Africa?' Report. OECD Development Centre. http://www.oecd.org/development/pgd/36259343.pdf.

Government of India. 2003. 'Budget 2003–04: Speech of Jaswant Singh, Minister of Finance'.

Gradl, Christina, Subathirai Sivakumaran, and Sabha Sobhani. 2010. 'The MDGs: Everyone's Business—How Inclusive Business Models Contribute to Development and Who Supports Them'. UNDP (United Nations Development Programme).

Gray, Patty. 2011. 'Looking "The Gift" in the Mouth: Russia as Donor'. *Anthropology Today* 27 (2): 5–8.

Grimm, S. 2011. 'South Africa as a Development Partner in Africa'. Policy Brief 11. Centre for Chinese Studies, Stellenbosch.

Grimm, Sven, and Christine Hackenesch. 2017. 'China in Africa: What Challenges for a Reforming European Union Development Policy? Illustrations from Country Cases'. *Development Policy Review* 35 (4): 549–566.

Grobbelaar, Neuma. 2014. 'Rising Powers in International Development: The State of the Debate in South Africa'. IDS (Institute of Development Studies), Sussex. https://www.google.com.hk/url?sa=t&rct=j&q=&esrc=s&source=web&cd=2&ved=0ahUKEwi_49jAzNDUAhXOLlAKHVq8B-0wQFgguMAE&url=https%3a%2f%2fopendocs%2eids%2eac%2euk%-2fopendocs%2fbitstream%2f123456789%2f4305%2f1%2fER91%2520Rising%2520Powers%2520in%2520International%2520Development%2520The%2520State%2520of%2520the%2520Debate%2520in%-2520South%2520Africa%2epdf&usg=AFQjCNFsE7Gc4j-5_TZwO9Rlmvw6ODqAGg.

Grobbelaar, Neuma, and Yunnan Chen. 2014. 'Understanding South Africa's Role in Achieving Regional and Global Development Progress'. IDS (Institute of Development Studies), Sussex. https://opendocs.ids.ac.uk/opendocs/bitstream/handle/123456789/3880/PB64%20Understanding%20South%20Africa's%20Role%20in%20Achieving%20Regional%20and%20Global%20Development%20Progress.pdf?sequence=3.

Gu, Jiing, Chuanhong Zhang, Alcides Vaz, and Langton Mukwereza. 2016. 'Chinese State Capitalism? Rethinking the Role of the State and Business in Chinese Development Cooperation in Africa'. *World Development* 81: 24–34.

Gunn, Lewis A. 1978. 'Why Is Implementation So Difficult?' *Management Services in Government* 33: 169–176.
Guo, Kaixuan. 2018. 'Guokaihang Zhaokai Zhichi Nongye "Zouchuqu" Yinqi Hezuo Tuidonghui (CDB Holds Bank-Company-Cooperation Meeting to Support Agricultural "Going Out")'. *Xinhua News*, 30 September. http://www.xinhuanet.com/money/2018-09/30/c_129964279.htm.
Guo, Shuhong. 2005. 'Zhongfei Nongye Hezuo Qianli Fenxi Yu Celue Yanjiu (Potential Analysis and Strategy Research on China-Africa Agricultural Cooperation)'. *Shijie Nongye* (World Agriculture) 317 (9): 31–34.
Haan, Arian. 2011. 'Will China Change International Development as We Know It?' *Journal of International Development* 23: 881–908.
Han, Changfu. 2018. 'Tuidong Zhongfei Nongye Hezuo Zaishang Xin Taijie (Step Up China-Africa Agricultural Cooperation)'. Ministry of Agriculture and Rural Affairs of the People's Republic of China, 1 September. http://www.moa.gov.cn/xw/zwdt/201809/t20180901_6156672.htm.
Han, Xiangshan. 2003. 'Feizhou Nongye Kaifa Dayou Kewei (Agricultural Cooperation with Africa Is of Great Potential)'. *Xiya Feizhou* (West Asia and Africa) 1: 62–65.
Han, Yan. 2011. 'Fazhan Huli Gongying de Zhongfei Nongye Hezuo (Develop Reciprocal China-Africa Agricultural Cooperation)'. *Guoji Jingji Hezuo* (International Economic Cooperation) 5: 33–37.
Hanf, Kenneth. 1978. 'Introduction'. In *Interorganizational Policy Making: Limits to Coordination and Central Control* (Hanf and Scharpf Eds.).
Hanf, Kenneth, and Fritz Wilhelm Scharpf, eds. 1978. *Interorganizational Policy Making: Limits to Coordination and Central Control.* Vol. 1. Sage Modern Politics Series. London: Sage.
Hanson, Henrik, and Finn Tarp. 2000. 'Aid Effectiveness Disputed'. *Journal of International Development* 12 (3): 375–398.
Harding, Angela. 2014. 'New and Interrelated Facets of Land Acquisition: The Case of the Chinese Investments in South Africa (Master's thesis, Unpublished)'. University of Pretoria.
Hargrove, E. C. 1975. *The Missing Link: The Study of the Implementation of Social Policy.* Washington, DC: Urban Institute.
Harry S. Truman. 1949. 'Truman's Inaugural Address'. https://www.trumanlibrary.org/whistlestop/50yr_archive/inagural20jan1949.htm.
Harsch, Earnest. 2004. 'Agriculture: Africa's "Engine for Growth"'. *Africa Recovery*. http://www.un.org/en/africarenewal/vol17no4/174ag.htm.
Hausmann, Jeannine, and Erik Lundsgaarde. 2015. 'Turkey's Role in Development Cooperation'. Working Paper. Centre for Policy Research at United Nations University.
Hay, Colin. 2002. *Political Analysis.* Basingstoke: Palgrave.

He, Fan, and Zhizhong Yao. 2013. *Zhongguo Duiwai Touzi: Lilun Yu Wenti* (Chinese Foreign Investment: Theories and Problems). Shanghai: Shanghai University of Finance & Economics Press.

Hill, Christopher, and Michael Smith. 2011. *International Relations and the European Union*. Oxford University Press.

Hill, Michael, and Peter L. Hupe. 2002. *Implementing Public Policy: Governance in Theory and Practice*. London: Sage.

Hjern, Benny. 1982. 'Implementation Research: The Link Gone Missing'. *Journal of Public Policy* 2 (3): 301–308.

Hjern, Benny, and Chris Hull. 1982. 'Implementation Research as Empirical Constitutionalism'. *European Journal of Political Research* 10 (2): 105–115.

Hjern, Benny, and David O. Porter. 1981. 'Implementation Structures: A New Unit of Administrative Analysis'. *Organization Studies* 2 (3): 211–227.

Hjertholm, Peter, and Howard White. 2000. 'Foreign Aid in Historical Perspective: Background and Trends'. In *Foreign Aid and Development: Lessons Learnt and Directions for the Future*, 59–77. London: Routledge.

Hood, Christopher. 1976. *The Limits of Administration*. London: Wiley.

Hu, Junhua. 2011. 'Zhongfang Jituan Ni Touzi 1.5yi Yuan Cangu Baxi Matou (Chinatex Plans to Invest 150 Million RMB in Building a Seaport in Brazil)'. http://money.163.com/11/0505/02/738N2HHS00253B0H.html.

Huang, Jikun. 2010. 'Liushinian Zhongguo Nongye de Fazhan He Sanshinian Gaige Qiji (Sixty Years of Chinese Agricultural Development and Thirty Years of the Reform Miracle)'. *Agro-Technology Economy* (Nongye Jishu Jingji) 1: 4–18.

Huang, Peizhao. 2002. 'Zhongfei Nongye Hezuo Dayou Kewei (China-Africa Agricultural Cooperation Has Great Potential)'. *People's Daily*, 5 October.

Hudson, Valerie M. 2007. *Foreign Policy Analysis: Classic and Contemporary Theory*. 1st ed. Lanham: Rowman & Littlefield.

———. 2012. 'The History and Evolution of Foreign Policy Analysis'. In *Foreign Policy: Theories, Actors, Cases* (Smith et al. Eds.).

ICAI. 2015. 'Business in Development'. ICAI (Independent Commission for Aid Impact). https://icai.independent.gov.uk/wp-content/uploads/ICAI-Business-in-Development-FINAL.pdf.

IDS Online Databases. n.d. 'International Development Statistics'. Accessed 31 May 2019. http://www.oecd.org/development/stats/idsonline.htm.

Ierley, Doug. 2002. 'Private Capital Flows as a Springboard for World Bank Reform'. *Journal of International Law* 23 (1).

Ingram, George, Anne E. Johnson, and Helen Moser. 2016. 'USAID's Public-Private Partnerships: A Data Picture and Review of Business Engagement'. Brookings. https://www.brookings.edu/wp-content/uploads/2016/07/WP94PPPReport2016Web.pdf.

Inoue, Cristina, and Alcides Vaz. 2012. 'Brazil as "Southern Donor": Beyond Hierarchy and National Interests in Development Cooperation?' *Cambridge Review of International Affairs* 25 (4): 507–534.
IOB. 2013. 'Public-Private Partnerships in Developing Countries'. 378. IOB Study. Policy and Operations Evaluation Department (IOB) of Ministry of Foreign Affairs of the Netherlands.
Jiang, Huajie. 2013. 'Nongji Yuanfei (1971–1983): Zhongguo Yuanfei Moshi Yu Chengxiao de Gean Yanjiu (Agricultural Technological Aid to Africa 1971–1983: A Case Study of the Modalities and Effectiveness of Chinese Aid to Africa)'. *Waijiao Pinglun* (Foreign Affairs Review) 1: 30–49.
Jiang, Lu. 2015. 'Chinese Agricultural Investment in Africa: Motives, Actors and Modalities'. Occasional Paper 223. Foreign Policy Programme. SAIIA (South African Institute of International Affairs).
———. 2016. 'Beyond ODA: Chinese Way of Development Cooperation with Africa. The Case of Agriculture'. PhD thesis, London School of Economics and Political Science (LSE).
Jiang, Lu, Angela Harding, Ward Anseeuw, and Chris Alden. 2016. 'Chinese Agricultural Technology Demonstration Centres in Southern Africa: The New Business of Development'. *Public Sphere*.
Jiang, Yunzhang. 2014. 'Guangfang Baogao Dingdiao Nongye Haiwai Touzi (Official Report Set Tones for Agricultural Overseas Investment)'. http://www.eeo.com.cn/2014/0507/260161.shtml.
Jiao, Jian. 2013. 'Zhongguo Liangshi Anquan Baogao (Chinese Food Security Report)'. *Caijing Zazhi* (Financial Magazine). http://news.ifeng.com/shendu/cj/detail_2013_12/09/31912251_0.shtml.
Justiça Ambiental. 2013. '"Wambao Agriculture" os recentes e reais impactos de mais uma bolada dos dragões em nome do desenvolvimento ("Wambao Agriculture" Recent and Actual Impacts of Another Hefty Dragons in the Name of Development)'. Justiça Ambiental. http://www.verdade.co.mz/ambiente/39110--wambao-agriculture-os-recentes-e-reais-impactos-de-mais-uma-bolada-dos-dragoes-em-nome-do-desenvolvimento.
Kajisa, Kei, and Ellen Payongayong. 2013. 'Extensification and Intensification Process of Rainfed Lowland Rice Farming in Mozambique'. JICA Research Institute Working Papers 61. https://jica-ri.jica.go.jp/publication/assets/JICA-RI_WP_No.61_2013.pdf.
Kapoor, Ilan. 2008. *The Postcolonial Politics of Development*. Princeton, NJ: Princeton University Press.
Kharas, Homi. 2007. 'Trends and Issues in Development Aid'. Wolfensohn Center for Development at Brookings.
———. 2009. 'Action on Aid: Steps Toward Making Aid More Effective'. Wolfensohn Center for Development at Brookings.
Kickert, Walter, Erik-Hans Klijn, and Joop Koppenjan, eds. 1997. *Managing Complex Networks: Strategies for the Public Sector*. London: Sage.

Kilama, Eric. 2016. 'The Influence of China and Emerging Donors Aid Allocation: A Recipient Perspective'. *China Economic Review* 38: 76–91.

Kim, Soyeun, and Simon Lightfoot. 2011. 'Does "DAC-Ability" Really Matter? The Emergence of Non-DAC Donors: Introduction to Policy Arena'. *Journal of International Development* 23 (5): 711–721.

Kondoh, Hisahiro. 2015. 'Convergence of Aid Models in Emerging Donors? Learning Processes, Norms and Identities, and Recipients'. Working Paper. JICA Research Institute, Tokyo.

Kong, Jiemin. 2010. 'Zhongnongfa Jituan CFO Zhang Peijun: Houji Bofa (Interview with CFO of CNADC)'. http://www.chinaacc.com/new/635_6 52_201011/11su437990814.shtml.

Kragelund, Peter. 2008. 'The Return of Non-DAC Donors to Africa: New Prospects for African Development? Peter Kragelund, 2008'. *Development Policy Review* 26 (5): 555–584.

———. 2010. 'The Potential Role of Non-traditional Donors' Aid in Africa, International Centre for Trade and Sustainable Development'. Issue Paper 11. International Centre for Trade and Sustainable Development.

———. 2011. 'Back to BASICs? The Rejuvenation of Non-traditional Donors' Development Cooperation with Africa'. *Development and Change* 42 (2): 587–607.

———. 2015. 'Towards Convergence and Cooperation in the Global Development Finance Regime: Closing Africa's Policy Space?' *Cambridge Review of International Affairs* 28 (2): 246–262.

Kulaklikaya, Musa, and Rahman Nurdun. 2010. 'Turkey as a New Player in Development Cooperation'. *Insight Turkey* 12 (4): 131–145.

Lagerkvist, Johan. 2013. 'As China Returns: Perceptions of Land Grabbing and Spatial Power Relations in Mozambique'. *Journal of Asian and African Studies*, 1–16.

Lancaster, Carol. 2007. 'The Chinese Aid System'. Centre for Global Development.

Lawson, Marian L. 2013. 'Foreign Assistance: Public-Private Partnerships (PPPs)'. Congressional Research Service. https://www.fas.org/sgp/crs/misc/R41880.pdf.

Leite et al. 2014. 'Brazil's Engagement in International Development Cooperation: The State of the Debate'. Evidence Report No. 59. Institute of Development Studies, Brighton.

Lengauer, Sara. 2011. 'China's Foreign Aid Policy: Motive and Method'. *Culture Mandala* 9 (2).

Lewis, David, and Helen Wallace. 1984. *Policies into Practice: National and International Case Studies in Implementation*. London: Heinemann Educational.

Li, Jia. 2012. 'Zhongguo Duiwai Yuanzhu "wutiaojianxing" de Yuanyin Fenxi (Reason Analysis of the Unconditionality of Chinese Foreign Aid)'. http://blog.sina.com.cn/s/blog_c45684f30102v7k7.html.

Li, Jiali. 2005. 'Dui Jiaqiang Zhongfei Nongye Hezuo de Ruogan Sikao (On Strengthening China-Africa Agricultural Cooperation)'. *Shijie Nongye* (World Agriculture) 313 (5): 11–14.

———. 2010. 'Sino-Africa Agricultural Cooperation Experience Sharing'. Foreign Economic Cooperation Center of Chinese Ministry of Agriculture, Beijing. http://www.iprcc.org/userfiles/file/Li%20Jiali-EN.pdf.

Li, Xiaoyun, Zhanfeng Guo, and Jin Wu. 2011. 'Zhongguo nongye fazhan dui feizhou de qishi (Experiences and Lessons for Africa from China's Success in Agricultural Development)'. *Xiya Feizhou* (West Asia and Africa) 8: 77–92.

Li, Xiaoyun, Gubo Qi, Lixia Tang, and Jin Wu. 2010. *Xiaonong wei jichu de nongye fazhan: zhongguo yu feizhou de bijiao yanjiu* (Smallholder-Based Agricultural Development: A Comparative Analysis of Chinese and African Experiences). Beijing: Shehui kexue wenxian chuban she (Social Sciences Academic Press).

Li, Xiaoyun, Lixia Tang, Gubo Qi, and Haimin Wang. 2013. 'What Can Africa Learn from China's Experience in Agricultural Development'. *IDS Bulletin* 44 (4): 31–41.

Li, Xiaoyun, and Jin Wu. 2009. 'Zhongguo Duifei Yuanzhu de Shijian Jingyan Yu Mianlin de Tiaozhan (A Study on China's ODA to Africa)'. *Zhongguo Nongye Daxue Xuebao Shehui Kexue Ban* (China Agricultural University Journal of Social Sciences Edition) 26 (45–54).

Liang, Hongyu, and Cheng 'an Wang. 1995. 'Woguo Kaishi Gaige Duiwai Yuanzhu Fangshi (China Starts to Reform the Modalities of Foreign Aid)'. *Guoji Shangbao* (International Business Daily), 6 June.

Lindblom, Charles E. 1959. 'The Science of "Muddling Through"'. *Public Administration Review* 19 (2): 79–88.

Lindquist, Evert A., and John Wanna. 2015. 'Is Implementation Only About Policy Execution?: Advice for Public Sector Leaders from the Literature'. In *New Accountabilities, New Challenges* (Wanna, Lindquist and Marshall Eds.).

Lipsky, Michael. 1980. *Street-Level Bureaucracy: Dilemmas of the Individual in Public Services*. Publications of Russell Sage Foundation. New York: Russell Sage.

Liu, Dalong. 2011. 'Zongshu: Zhongguo Yu Mosangbike Kaizhan Nongye Hezuo Qianjing Guangkuo (Overview: China-Mozambique Agricultural Cooperation Has Great Prospects)'. Xinhua News Agency. http://news.xinhuanet.com/world/2011-09/19/c_131147121.htm.

Liu, Yanbo, and Min Liu. 2016. 'Six Experiences of Qingdao Ruichang in Investing African Agriculture (Qingdao Ruichang Touzi Feizhou Nongye Liuda Jingyan)'. 6 September. https://www.imsilkroad.com/news/p/6348.html.

Liu, Zhijie. 2000. 'Zhongken Jituan Canyu Feizhou Nongye Kaifa Jie Shuoguo (CSFAC Group Bears Fruits in Participating Agricultural Development in Africa)'. *People's Daily (Overseas Edition)*, 19 October. http://www.people.com.cn/GB/paper39/1716/277533.html.

Lu, Jixia, Qian He, and Xiaoyun Li. 2015. 'Zhongguo Yuanfei Nongye Zhuanjia Paiqian Xiangmu de Kechixuxing Chutan (Sustainability of Chinese Agro-Expert Dispatch Programme)'. *Shijie Nongye* (World Agriculture) 432 (4).
Lu, Ting-en. 2003. 'Guanyu Shenru Kaizhan Nongye Touzi Yu Hezuo de Jidian Kanfa (Opinions on Further Developing Agricultural Investment and Cooperation)'. *Xiya Feizhou* (West Asia and Africa) 1: 9–13.
Ma, Jiantang. 2012. 'Kexue Tiaokong Wen Wujia, Wenzhong Qiujin Mo Fazhan (Stabilising the Prices and Seeking for Development)'. *Qiushi* 2. http://www.qstheory.cn/zxdk/2012/201202/201201/t20120112_134627.htm.
Ma, Zhigang, Qi Wang, Zhihong Tian, and Xueling Zhai. 2014. 'Zhichi Nongye Duiwai Touzi Shouduan Fangshi de Tantao (Supporting Measures of China's Agricultural Foreign Investment)'. *Shijie Nongye* (World Agriculture) 2.
Mann, Dean E., and Helen M. Ingram, eds. 1980. *Why Policies Succeed or Fail? Vol. 8. Yearbooks in Politics and Public Policy*. London: Sage.
Manning, Richard. 2006. 'Will "Emerging Donors" Change the Face of International Co-operation?' *Development Policy Review* 24 (4): 371–385.
Mao, Zedong. 1997. 'Guanyu Sange Shijie Huafen Wenti (On the Classification of the Three Worlds)'. In *Maozedong Wenji* (The Collected of Mao Tse-Tung's Works). Vol. 8. Beijing: People's Publishing House. http://www.99lib.net/book/621/19954.htm.
Marks, Stephen. 2008. 'China and the Great Global Landgrab'. *Pambazuka News*, 11 December. http://www.pambazuka.net/en/category.php/africa_china/52635.
Marsh, David, and Gerry Stoker. 2010. *Theory and Methods in Political Science*. 3rd ed. Political Analysis. Basingstoke and New York: Palgrave Macmillan.
Martel, Leon. 1979. *Lend-Lease, Loans, and the Coming of the Cold War: A Study of the Implementation of Foreign Policy*. Westview Special Studies in International Relations. Boulder, CO: Westview Press.
Mason, Jannifer. 2002. *Qualitative Researching*. 2nd ed. London: Sage.
Matland, Richard E. 1995. 'Synthesizing the Implementation Literature: The Ambiguity-Conflict Model of Policy Implementation'. *Journal of Public Administration Research and Theory* 5 (2): 145–174.
May, Peter J. 2012. 'Policy Design and Implementation'. In *The Sage Handbook of Public Administration*, 292–304.
McCormick, Dorothy. 2008. 'China & India as Africa's New Donors: The Impact of Aid on Development'. *Review of African Political Economy* 35 (115): 73–92.
McEwan, Cheryl, and Mawdsley, Emma. 2012. 'Trilateral Development Cooperation: Power and Politics in Emerging Aid Relationships'. *Development and Change* 43 (16): 1185–1209.

Meng, Qingtao. 2013. 'Zhongguo Yuanzhu Feizhou Yiwang (Recalling the History of Chinese Aid in Africa)'. *Qingxi Zhonghua* 2. https://www.qxzh.zj.cn/magazine/article/876.html.

Meyers, Marcia K., and Vibeke Lehmann Nielsen. 2012. 'Street-Level Bureaucrats and the Implementation of Public Policy'. In *The Sage Handbook of Public Administration*, 305–318.

Min, Baohua, and Jie Han. 2012. 'Goujian Mosangbike de Guojia Liangcang: Wanbao Liangyou Youxian Gongsi Shishi "zouchuqu" zhanlue Jishi (Building Mozambique's National Grain Storage: Wanbao implementing "Going Out" Strategy)'. *Xiangyang Ribao* (Xiangyang Daily), 18 December.

Mlachila, Montfort, and Misa Takebe. 2011. 'FDI from BRICs to LICs: Emerging Growth Driver?' Working Paper. IMF.

MMO Notícias. 2014. 'Polícia Acusada de Impedir Marcha de Camponeses Em Xai-Xai (Police Accused of Preventing March of Peasants in Xai -Xai)'. *MMO Notícias*, 21 March. http://noticias.mmo.co.mz/2014/05/policia-acusada-de-impedir-marcha-de-camponeses-em-xai-xai.html.

MOA and EXIM Bank of the PRC (Ministry of Agriculture and the Export and Import Bank of the People's Republic of China). 2008. 'Agreement on Co-supporting Agricultural "Going Out"'.

MOA of the PRC (Ministry of Agriculture of the People's Republic of China). 2008. 'Nongyebu Bangongting Guanyu Xiezhu Xuanba Dierpi Yuanfei Gaoji Nongye Zhuanjia de Han (Ministry of Agriculture on Assisting to Select the Second Batch of Senior Agricultural Experts)'.

———. 2010. 'Capability Building'. http://www.moa.gov.cn/ztzl/zfnyhzlt/zhongguo/201008/t20100806_1613799.htm.

———. 2013. '834 Jia Nongye Chanyehua Guojia Zhongdian Longtou Qiye Mingdan (List of National Leading Companies of Agricultural Industrialization)'. http://finance.sina.com.cn/nongye/nyhgjj/20130227/000014665798.shtml.

———. 2017. 'Report on Chinese Overseas Agricultural Investment and Cooperation'. Ministry of Agriculture, Beijing.

MOC and MOA of the PRC (Ministry of Commerce and Ministry of Agriculture of the People's Republic of China). 2011. *Guanyu Cujin Yuanfei Nongye Jishu Shifan Zhongxin Xiangmu Kechixu Fazhan de Zhidaoyijian* (Guidance on Promoting the Sustainable Development of the Agriculture Technology Demonstration Centre Project in Africa).

———. 2012. *Yuanfei Nongye Jishu Shifanzhong Xinjiance Pingjia Banfa (Shixing)* (Supervision and Evaluation Measures of the Agriculture Technology Demonstration Centre in Africa [Under Trial]).

MOC of the PRC (Ministry of Commerce of the People's Republic of China). 2010. 'Zhongguo Yu Feizhou Jingmao Guanxi Baogao (China-Africa Economic and Trade Relations Report)'.

———. 2011. 'Statistical Bulletin of China's Outward Foreign Direct Investment'.

———. 2013. 'Zhongguo Yu Feizhou Jingmao Guanxi Baogao (China-Africa Economic and Trade Relations Report)'.

———. 2015. *Duiwai Yuanzhu Chengtao Xiangmu Guanli Banfa (Shixing)* (Regulations on Foreign Aid Complete Projects). http://www.scio.gov.cn/xwfbh/xwbfbh/wqfbh/33978/34188/xgzc34194/Document/1469217/1469217.htm.

MOF and MOC of the PRC (Ministry of Finance and Ministry of Commerce of the People's Republic of China). 2011. *Guanyu Zuohao 2011nian Duiwai Jingji Jishu Hezuo Zhuanxiang Zijin Shenbao Gongzuo de Tongzhi* (On Applying for the Special Fund for Foreign Economic and Technological Cooperation in 2011). http://www.mofcom.gov.cn/article/b/bf/201104/20110407525027.shtml.

———. 2012. *Guanyu Zuohao 2012nian Duiwai Jingji Jishu Hezuo Zhuanxiang Zijin Shenbao Gongzuo de Tongzhi* (On Applying for the Special Fund for Foreign Economic and Technological Cooperation in 2012). http://www.mofcom.gov.cn/article/cwgongzuo/huiyjl/201207/20120708225224.shtml.

MOFA of the PRC (Ministry of Foreign Affairs of the People's Republic of China). n.d. 'Chairman Mao Zedong's Theory on the Division of the Three World and the Strategy of Forming an Alliance Against an opponent'. https://www.fmprc.gov.cn/mfa_eng/ziliao_665539/3602_665543/3604_665547/t18008.shtml.

———. n.d. 'The Third Wave of Establishing Diplomatic Relations with Other Countries'. Ministry of Foreign Affairs of the People's Republic of China, Beijing. Accessed 22 January 2016. http://www.fmprc.gov.cn/mfa_eng/ziliao_665539/3602_665543/3604_665547/t18014.shtml.

MOFET of the PRC (Ministry of Foreign Economy and Trade of the People's Republic of China). 1983. 'Diliuci Quanguo Yuanwai Gongzuo Huiyi Wenjian (The Sixth National Conference on Foreign Aid)'. Beijing.

———. 1984. 'Guanyu Gonggu Jiancheng Jingyuan Chengtao Xiangmu Chengguo de Yijian (On Consolidating the Effects of Complete Projects of Foreign Economic Aid)'. Beijing.

Mold, Andrew. 2009. *Policy Ownership and Aid Conditionality in the Light of the Financial Crisis: A Critical Review*. OECD Publishing. http://www.keepeek.com/Digital-Asset-Management/oecd/development/policy-ownership-and-aid-conditionality-in-the-light-of-the-financial-crisis_9789264075528-en#.WPWLnhJ95E4.

Momani, Bessma, and Crystal Ennis. 2012. 'Between Caution and Controversy: Lessons from the Gulf Arab States as (Re-)Emerging Donors'. *Cambridge Review of International Affairs* 25 (4): 605–627.

Morgenthau, Hans. 1962. 'A Political Theory of Foreign Aid'. *The American Political Science Review* 56 (2): 301–309.
Mosley, Paul, and Marion J. Eeckhout. 2000. 'From Project Aid to Programme Assistance'. In *Foreign Aid and Development: Lessons Learnt and Directions for the Future*, 101–119. London: Routledge.
Moyo, Dambisa. 2010. *Dead Aid: Why Aid Is Not Working and How There Is Another Way for Africa*. London: Penguin Press.
Mu, Dong. 2013. 'Ji Zanbiya Zhongken Nongchang Nvchangzhang Lili (Documenting Lili, the Owner of Zhongken Farm)'. Xinhua News. 12 September 2013. http://news.xinhuanet.com/overseas/2013-09/12/c_117340064.htm.
Muresan, Arina. 2012. 'Agricultural Development and "Land Grabs": The Chinese Presence in the African Agricultural Sector'. Consultancy Africa Intelligence (CAI).
Mwase, Nkunde, and Yongzheng Yang. 2012. 'BRICs' Philosophies for Development Financing and Their Implications for LICs'. Working Paper. IMF.
Naim, Moises. 2009. 'Rogue Aid'. *Foreign Policy*. https://foreignpolicy.com/2009/10/15/rogue-aid/.
NBS of the PRC (National Bureau of Statistics of the People's Republic of China). 2011. 'Tongji Dazhongxiaowei Xing Qiye Huafen Fangfa (Classifications of Large/Medium/Small/Micro-Sized Enterprises)'. http://www.stats.gov.cn/statsinfo/auto2073/201310/t20131031_450691.html.
NDRC and CDB of the PRC (National Development and Reform Commission and the China Development Bank). 2005. 'Guanyu Jinyibu Jiaqiang Dui Jingwai Touzi Zhongdian Xiangmu Rongzi Zhichi Youguan Wenti de Tongzhi (On Further Strengthening the Financial Support to the Strategic Overseas Investment Projects)'.
NDRC and EXIM Bank (National Development and Reform Commission and the Export and Import Bank of China). 2004. 'Guanyu Dui Guojia Guli de Jingwai Touzi Zhongdian Xiangmu Geiyu Xindai Zhichi Zhengce de Tongzhi (On Providing Financial Support to Strategic Overseas Investment Projects)'.
NDRC and MIIT of the PRC (National Development and Reform Commission and Ministry of Industry and Information Technology of the People's Republic of China). 2011. 'Shipin Gongye Fazhan Shierwu Guihua (The 12th Five-Year Plan of the Food-Processing Industry)'. http://www.sdpc.gov.cn/zcfb/zcfbghwb/201201/W020140221370687309930.pdf.
NDRC and MOC of the PRC (National Development and Reform Committee and Ministry of Commerce of People's Republic of China). 2013. *Guanyu Yinfa Guli Kaizhan Jingwai Nongye Touzi Hezuo Zhidao Yijian de Tongzhi* (Suggestions on Overseas Agricultural Investment and Cooperation).
NEPAD (New Partnership for Africa's Development). 2003. 'Comprehensive Africa Agriculture Development Programme 2003'.

———. 2013. 'Agriculture in Africa: Transformation and Outlook'. http://www.nepad.org/resource/agriculture-africa-transformation-and-outlook.
Ning, Bo. 2012. 'Hubei Hefeng Touzi 10yi Mosangbike Kaifa Nongye (Hefeng from Hubei Province Invests 1 Billion RMB in Mozambican Agriculture)'. *Xiaogan Ribao* (Xiaogan Daily), 5 June. http://szb.xgrb.cn:9999/epaper/xgrb/html/2012/06/05/01/01_102.htm.
Niu, Jun. 2010. *Zhonghua Renmin Gongheguo Duiwai Guanxi Shi Gailun, 1949–2000* (Introduction to History of Foreign Relations of the People's Republic of China, 1949–2000). Beijing: Peking University Press.
Niu, Qichang. 2013. 'Haiwai Nongchang de Zhongguo Shenying (The Chinese in Overseas Farms)'. *Jingji Daobao* (Economic Herald), 25 September. http://paper.dzwww.com/jjdb/data/20130925/html/2/content_2.html.
Observer. 2013. 'Woguo Haiwai Liangshi Jidi Shoudi Shuidao Yunhui (The First Batch of Rice Grown Overseas Were Shipped Back to China)'. http://www.guancha.cn/Industry/2013_12_15_192762.shtml.
OECD. 1978. *Recommendation on Terms and Conditions of Aid (from the 1978 DAC Chair Report on Development Co-operation)*. OECD.
———. 1985. *Twenty-Five Years of Development Cooperation. A Review: Efforts and Policies of the Members of the Development Assistance Committee*. Paris: OECD.
———. 2008. 'Is It ODA?' www.oecd.org/dac/stats.
———. 2016. *Development Co-operation Report 2016: The Sustainable Development Goals as Business Opportunities*. Paris: OECD Publishing. http://dx.doi.org/10.1787/dcr-2016-en.
———. 2017. 'Development Aid at a Glance: Africa'. http://www.oecd.org/dac/stats/documentupload/Africa-Development-Aid-at-a-Glance.pdf.
OECD-DAC. 2007. 'Reporting Directives for the Creditor Reporting System Corrigendum on Programme-Based Approaches'. http://www.oecd.org/dac/stats/44479916.pdf.
———. 2013. 'Converged Statistical Reporting Directives for the Creditor Reporting System (CRS) and the Annual Dac Questionnaire—Addendum 2'. OECD. http://www.oecd.org/dac/stats/documentupload/DCD-DAC(2013)15-ADD2-FINAL-ENG.pdf#page=5.
Omilola, Batatunde, and Frank Van Lerven. 2014. 'Accelerating Poverty and Hunger Reduction in Africa: Progress and Policy Prescriptions'. UNDP. http://www.za.undp.org/content/dam/south_africa/docs/mdgs/Accelerating%20Poverty%20and%20Hunger%20Reduction%20in%20Africa-Progress%20and%20Policy%20Prescriptions.pdf.
Opoku-Mensah. 2009. 'China and the International Aid System: Challenges and Opportunities'. Working Paper. Aalborg University: Research Centre on Development and International Relations.
O'Toole, Laurence J. 2000. 'Research on Policy Implementation: Assessment and Prospects'. *Journal of Public Administration Research and Theory* 10 (2): 263–288.

Ottaviani, Jacopo, Andrea Fama, Isacco Chiaf, and Cecilia Anesi. 2013. 'China Accused of Stealth Land Grab over Mozambique's Great Rice Project'. http://www.theecologist.org/News/news_analysis/2177709/china_accused_of_stealth_land_grab_over_mozambiques_great_rice_project.html.

Özkan, M., and B. Akgün. 2010. 'Turkey's Opening to Africa'. *The Journal of Modern African Studies* 48 (4).

Palumbo, Dennis James, and Donald J. Calista, eds. 1990. *Implementation and the Policy Process: Opening Up the Black Box*. New York: Greenwood Press.

Pang, Lijing. 2015. 'Shiye Haiwai Touzi Chaoyong (A Wave of Foreign Investment)'. 13 July. http://www.eeo.com.cn/2015/0205/272190.shtml.

Parsons, Wayne. 1996. *Public Policy: An Introduction to the Theory and Practice of Policy Analysis*. Cheltenham: Edward Elgar.

Paulo, Sebastian, and Helmut Reisen. 2010. 'Eastern Donors and Western Soft Law: Towards a DAC Donor Peer Review of China and India?' *Development Policy Review* 28 (5): 535–552.

People.cn. 2012. 'Zhongcheng Jituan: Rang Tianmi de Shiye Zaofu Yu Feizhou Renmin (The COMPLANT: Sweet Career Benefits African People)'. People. cn, 12 November. http://finance.people.com.cn/n/2012/1112/c351563-19555158.html.

———. 2013. 'Guokaihang Hubei Fenhang Zhichi Nongye "zouchuqu" xingcheng "wanbao moshi" (CDB Hubei Supports "Agricultural Going Out" and Forms "Wanbao" Model)'. People.cn, 14 March. http://finance.people.com.cn/bank/n/2013/0314/c202331-20786349.html.

People's Congress of the PRC. 2001. 'Guomin Jingji Yu Shehui Fazhan Wunian Jihua (Five-Year Plan of the National Economy and Social Development)'.

———. 2006. 'Guomin Jingji Yu Shehui Fazhan Wunian Jihua (Five-Year Plan of the National Economy and Social Development)'.

———. 2011. 'Guomin Jingji Yu Shehui Fazhan Wunian Jihua (Five-Year Plan of the National Economy and Social Development)'.

People's Daily. 2013. 'Gengyun Mengxiang de Haiwai Youzi (The Overseas Chinese Seeking for Dreams)'. *People's Daily (Overseas Edition)*, 21 September. http://paper.people.com.cn/rmrbhwb/html/2013-09/21/content_1301448.htm.

Pereira, Javier. 2015. 'Leveraging AID: A Literature Review on the Additionality of Using ODA to Leverage Private Investments'. UKAN (UK Aid Network).

Peters, B. Guy. 2001. *The Politics of Bureaucracy*. 5th ed. London: Routledge.

———. 2014. 'Implementation Structures as Institutions'. *Public Policy and Administration* 29 (2): 131–144.

Peters, B. Guy, and Jon Pierre. 2012a. 'The Role of Public Administration in Governing'. In *The Sage Handbook of Public Administration* (Peters and Pierre Eds.), 1–12.

———, eds. 2012b. *The Sage Handbook of Public Administration*. 2nd ed. London: Sage.

Pompa, Claudia. 2013a. 'Understanding Challenge Funds'. London: Overseas Development Institute. https://www.odi.org/sites/odi.org.uk/files/odi-assets/publications-opinion-files/9086.pdf.

———. 2013b. 'Understanding Challenge Funds'. Overseas Development Institute.

Power, Marcus, and Ana Cristina Alves, eds. 2012. *China and Angela: A Marriage of Convenience?* Cape Town: Pambazuka Press.

Power, Marcus, Giles Mohan, and May Tan-Mullins. 2012. *China's Resource Diplomacy in Africa*. New York: Palgrave Macmillan.

Pülzl, Helga, and Oliver Treib. 2007. 'Implementing Public Policy'. In *Handbook of Public Policy Analysis: Theory, Politics, and Methods*.

Qi, Haishan. 2012. 'Jilinsheng Zai Haiwai Touzi Yu 4yi Jianshe Nongchang (Jilin Province Invested More Than 400 Million RMB in Building Overseas Farms)'. Xinhua News Agency. http://news.xinhuanet.com/fortune/2012-11/22/c_113761449.htm?_fin.

Qin, Lu. 2016. 'Yuanfei Nongye Jishu Shifan Zhongxin: Chengxiao, Wenti He Zhengce Jianyi (ATDC in Africa: Effectiveness, Problems and Policy Suggestions)'. *Guoji Jingji Hezuo* (International Economic Cooperation) 8. http://www.fecc.agri.cn/yjzx/yjzx_zxxx/201709/t20170901_295884.html.

Quadir, Fahimul. 2013. Rising Donors and the New Narrative of 'South–South' Cooperation: What Prospects for Changing the Landscape of Development Assistance Programmes? *Third World Quarterly* 34 (2): 321–338.

Rakhmangulov, M. 2010. 'Establishing International Development Assistance Strategy in Russia'. *International Organization Research Journal* 5 (5): 50–67.

Rampa, Francesco, Sanoussi Bilal, and Elizebeth Sidiropoulos. 2012. 'Leveraging South–South Cooperation for Africa's Development'. *South African Journal of International Affairs* 19 (2): 247–269.

Ren, Jie. 2014. 'Zhongfei Mianye Daidong Mosangbike Miannong Zengshou (China Africa Cotton Company Promotes Income Increase of Mozambican Farmers)'. http://gb.cri.cn/42071/2014/06/18/7551s4581935.htm.

Ripley, Randall B., and Grace A. Franklin. 1982. *Bureaucracy and Policy Implementation*. The Dorsey Series in Political Science. Homewood, IL: Dorsey Press.

Robledo, Carmen. 2015. 'New Donors, Same Old Practices? South-South Cooperation of Latin American Emerging Donors'. *Bandung: Journal of Global South* 2 (3).

Roussel, Lauren. 2013. 'The Changing Donor Landscape in Nicaragua: Rising Competition Enhances Ownership and Fosters Cooperation'. *Journal of International Development* 25 (6): 802–818.

Rowlands, Dane. 2008. 'Emerging Donors in International Development Assistance: A Synthesis Report'. Working Paper. International Development Research Centre, Canada.

———. 2012. 'Individual BRICS or a Collective Bloc? Convergence and Divergence Amongst "Emerging Donor" Nations'. *Cambridge Review of International Affairs* 25 (4): 629–649.

Rubinstein, Carl. 2009. 'China's Eye on African Agriculture'. *Asian Times*, 2 October. http://www.atimes.com/atimes/China_Business/KJ02Cb01.html.

Rudincová, Kateřina. 2014. 'New Player on the Scene: Turkish Engagement in Africa'. *Bulletin of Geography* 25.

Runde, Daniel, Holly Wise, Anna Saito Carson, and Cleanor Coates. 2011. 'Seizing the Opportunity in Public-Private Partnerships: Strengthening Capacity at the State Department, USAID, and MCC'. Center for Strategic & International Studies. https://csis-prod.s3.amazonaws.com/s3fs-public/legacy_files/files/publication/111102_Runde_PublicPrivatePartnerships_Web.pdf.

Sabatier, Paul. 1986. 'Top-Down and Bottom-Up Approaches to Implementation Research: A Critical Analysis and Suggested Synthesis'. *Journal of Public Policy* 6 (1): 21–48.

———. 1988. 'An Advocacy Coalition Framework of Policy Change and the Role of Policy-Oriented Learning Therein'. *Policy Sciences* 21 (2): 129–168.

Sabatier, Paul, and Daniel Mazmanian. 1979. 'The Conditions of Effective Implementation: A Guide to Accomplishing Policy Objectives'. *Policy Analysis* 5 (4): 481–504.

———. 1980. 'The Implementation of Public Policy: A Framework of Analysis'. *Policy Studies Journal* 8 (4): 538–560.

Sachs, Jeffrey. 2005. *The End of Poverty: Economic Possibilities for Our Time*. New York: Penguin Press.

Saetren, Harald. 2005. 'Facts and Myths About Research on Public Policy Implementation: Out-of-Fashion, Allegedly Dead, But Still Very Much Alive and Relevant'. *Policy Studies Journal* 33 (4): 559–582.

Sato, Jin, Hiroaki Shiga, Takaaki Kobayashi, and Hisahiro Kondoh. 2011. '"Emerging Donors" from a Recipient Perspective: An Institutional Analysis of Foreign Aid in Cambodia'. *World Development* 39 (12): 2091–2104.

Sautman, Barry, and Hairong Yan. 2010. 'Chinese Farms in Zambia: From Socialist to "Agro-Imperialist"'. *African and Asian Studies* 9: 307–333.

Sauvy, Alfred. 1952. 'TROIS MONDES, UNE PLANÈTE'. *L'Observateur*, 14 August.

Scharpf, Fritz Wilhelm. 1978. 'Interorganizational Policy Studies: Issues, Concepts and Perspectives'. In *Interorganizational Policy Making: Limits to Coordination and Central Control* (Hanf and Scharpf Eds.). Sage.

Scoones, Ian, Kojo Amanor, Arilson Favareto, and Gubo Qi. 2016. 'A New Politics of Development Cooperation? Chinese and Brazilian Engagements in African Agriculture'. *World Development* 81.

Scoones, Ian, Lídia Cabral, and Henry Tugendhat, eds. 2013. *China and Brazil in African Agriculture*. IDS (Institute of Development Studies).

Shen, Junlin. 2017. 'Ruichang Mianye: Rang 100wan Feizhouren Shouyi (Ruichang Cotton Company: Benefiting 1 Million African People)'. *Qingdao Ribao* (Qingdao Daily), 9 June. http://www.qdbofcom.gov.cn/n32208327/ n32208334/n32208552/n32208553/170609160637403446.html.

Shi, Lin, ed. 1989. *Dangdai zhongguo de duiwai jingji hezuo* (Foreign Economic Cooperation of Contemporary China). Beijing: Zhongguo shehui kexue chubanshe (China Social Science Press).

Shu, Yun. 2009. 'Jiuzheng Yu Guoli Bufu de Duiwai Yuanzhu: Zhongguo Waiyuan Wangshi (Correcting the Aid-Giving That Is Incompatible with the State Strength: Memories of Chinese Foreign Aid)'. *Tongzhou Gongjin* 1: 40–44.

Shushan, Debra, and Christopher Marcoux. 2011. 'The Rise (and Decline?) of Arab Aid: Generosity and Allocation in the Oil Era'. *World Development* 39 (11): 1969–1980.

Silva, Sara, Ari Kokko, and Hanna Norberg. 2015. 'Now Open for Business: Joint Development Initiatives Between the Private and Public Sectors in Development Cooperation 1'. Expertgruppen för biståndsanalys (EBA), Stockholm.

Singer, J. David. 1961. 'The Level-of-Analysis Problem in International Relations'. *World Politics* 14 (1): 77–92.

SINOSURE. n.d. 'A Brief Introduction of Investment Insurance: Overseas Investment Insurance'. Accessed 27 March 2016. http://www.sinosure.com. cn/sinosure/english/products_introduction01.htm.

Six, Clemens. 2009. 'The Rise of Postcolonial States as Donors: A Challenge to the Development Paradigm?' *Third World Quarterly* 30 (6): 1103–1121.

Smaller, Carin, Wei Qiu, and Yalan Liu. 2012. 'Farmland and Water: China Invests Abroad'. IISD (International Institute for Sustainable Development).

Smith, Kimberly, Talita Fordelone, and Felix Zimmermann. 2010. 'Beyond the DAC—The Welcome Role of Other Providers of Development Co-operation'. DCD Issues Brief. OECD. https://www.oecd.org/dac/ 45361474.pdf.

Smith, Steve, and Michael Clarke. 1985. *Foreign Policy Implementation*. London: Allen & Unwin.

Smith, Steve, Amelia Hadfield, and Tim Dunne. 2012. *Foreign Policy: Theories, Actors, Cases.* 2nd ed. Oxford University Press.

Smith, Thomas. 1973. 'The Policy Implementation Process'. *Policy Sciences* 4 (2): 197–209.

Soest, Jaap van. 1978. *The Start of International Development Cooperation in the United Nations 1945–1952*. Assen: Van Gorcum Press.

Sohu News. 2018. 'Zhongguo Nongye Zoujin Feizhou (China's Agriculture Expands to Africa)'. *Sohu News*. 4 September. https://www.sohu. com/a/251848387_782515.

Song, Hongyuan. 2014. 'Nongye "zouchuqu", Qiye Ruhe Zouwen Zouhao? (How Can Companies Perform Well in Agricultural "Going Out")'. http:// gb.cri.cn/44571/2014/05/04/3005s4527758.htm.

Song, Hongyuan, Xiao Xu, Xueling Zhai, Xuegao Xu, Li Wang, and Hailong Xia. 2012. 'Kuoda Nongye Duiwai Touzi, Jiakuai "zouchuqu" zhanlue (Expand Agricultural Foreign Investment and Hasten the Implementation of "Going Out" Strategy)'. *Jingji Yanjiu Cankao* (Economic Research Review) 2444 (28).
Spring, Anita. 2009. 'Chinese Development Aid and Agribusiness Entrepreneurs in Africa'. Repositioning African Business and Development for the 21st Century. International Academy of African Business and Development.
State Council of the PRC (People's Republic of China). 1996. 'Zhongguo de Liangshi Wenti (China's Food Issue)'. http://www.scio.gov.cn/zfbps/ndhf/1996/Document/307978/307978.htm.
———. 2008. 'Guojia Liangshi Anquan Zhongchangqi Guihua Gangyao 2008–2020 (Medium/Long-Term Plan of China's Food Security 2008–2020)'. http://www.gov.cn/jrzg/2008-11/13/content_1148414.htm.
———. 2011. 'China's Foreign Aid'. State Council of the People's Republic of China. http://news.xinhuanet.com/english2010/china/2011-04/21/c_13839683.htm.
———. 2014. 'China's Foreign Aid'. State Council of the People's Republic of China. http://english.gov.cn/archive/white_paper/2014/08/23/content_281474982986592.htm.
State Planning Committee of the PRC (People's Republic of China). 1991. 'Guanyu Jiaqiang Haiwai Touzi Xiangmu Guanli de Yijian (On Strengthening the Management of Overseas Investment)'. http://www.cn21.com.cn/managetools/zcfg/tz/050925.htm.
Stoker, Robert Phillip. 1991. *Reluctant Partners: Implementing Federal Policy*. Pitt Series in Policy and Institutional Studies. Pittsburgh, PA: University of Pittsburgh Press.
Sun, Helen Lei. 2011. 'Understanding China's Agricultural Investments in Africa'. Occasional Paper No. 102. SAIIA (South African Institute of International Affairs). http://www.saiia.org.za/occasional-papers/understanding-chinas-agricultural-investments-in-africa.
Sun, Lihua. 2019. 'Mosangbike: Wanbo Mosang Nongyeyuan Shuidao Xiying Fengshou (Mozambique: Wanbao Agricultural Park Has a Rice Harvest)'. *Sohu News*. 3 April. http://www.sohu.com/a/305718995_201960.
Sun, Yi. 2007. 'Zhongzan Nongye Hezuo Qianjing Guangkuo (Attractive Prospect on China-Zambia Agricultural Cooperation)'. *Jingji Ribao* (Economic Daily). 7 November. http://wap.cnki.net/touch/web/Newspaper/Article/JJRB200711070083.html.
Sun, Yihou. 1996. 'Shilun yingxiang nongye yuanzhu xiangmu xiaoyi de zhuyao yinsu (Main Factors Affecting the Effectiveness of Agricultural Foreign Aid Projects)'. *Guoji jingji hezuo* (International Economic Cooperation) 7: 54–56.
Sun, Yun. 2014. 'Africa in China's Foreign Policy'. Africa Growth Initiative Publications. Brookings. http://www.brookings.edu/~/media/research/files/papers/2014/04/africa-china-policy-sun/africa-in-china-web_cmg7.pdf.

Sun, Zifa. 2012. 'Zhongguo Haiyou 1.28yi Pinkun Renkou (China Still Has a Poor Population of 128 Million')'. http://www.chinanews.com/gn/2012/03-12/3737442.shtml.

Tang, Lixia, Xiaoyun Li, and Gubo Qi. 2014. 'Zhongguo Dui Feizhou Nongye Yuanzhu Guanli Moshi de Yanhua Yu Chengxiao (Evolution and Effectiveness of the Management Modalities of Chinese Agricultural Aid to Africa)'. *Guoji Wenti Yanjiu* (International Studies) 6: 29–40.

Tang, Shihua, and Huan Wang. 2011. 'Zhongliang Jituan: Zhishao Touzi 100yi Meiyuan Haiwai Shougou (COFCO: Will Invest at Least 10 Billion USD in Overseas M&As)'. http://www.yicai.com/news/2011/11/1181724.html.

Tang, Xiaoyang. 2013. 'Zhongguo Dui Feizhou Nongye Yuanzhu Xingshi de Yanbian Jiqi Xiaoguo (Evolution and Effectiveness of the Forms of Chinese Agricultural Aid to Africa)'. *Shijie Jingji Yu Zhengzhi* (World Economics and Politics) 5: 55–69.

Tang, Zhengping. 2002. 'Qianjing Guangkuo de Zhongfei Nongye Hezuo (China-Africa Agricultural Cooperation Has Bright Prospects)'. *Xiya Feizhou* (West Asia and Africa) 2: 13–17.

Tan-Mullins, May, Giles Mohan, and Marcus Power. 2010. 'Redefining "Aid" in the China-Africa Context'. *Development and Change* 41 (5): 857–881.

Tarnoff, Curt. 1989. 'The Private Enterprise Initiative of the Agency for International Development'. Congressional Research Service. https://babel.hathitrust.org/cgi/pt?id=pur1.32754077272585;view=1up;seq=7.

Tarp, Finn, ed. 2000. *Foreign Aid and Development: Lessons Learnt and Directions for the Future*. London: Routledge.

Thurow, Roger. 2008. 'Agriculture's Last Frontier: African Farmers, U.S. Companies Try to Create Another Breadbasket With Hybrids'. *The Wall Street Journal*. http://www.wsj.com/articles/SB121185343060221769.

Tian, Tian. 2014. 'Zhongliang Jituan, Zhongchuliang Jituan Quanqiu Fanwei Nei Xunzhao Xinde Liangshi Jinkou Yuan (COFCO and CGRC Search for Sources of Grains Around the Globe)'. http://www.xiaomai.cn/html/news/20140224/335558.html.

Tian, Yu, and Guohui Zheng. 2014. 'Liu Shenli Yu Mosangbike Nongyebu Buzhang Jiuxing Huitan Qieshi Tuijin Zhongmo Hezuo (Liu Shenli Talks with Mozambique's Minister of Agriculture, Discussing China-Mozambican Cooperation)'. *CNADC (China National Agricultural Development Group Co. Ltd.) News*, 28 July. http://www.zgnfb.com/news-5281.html.

Timmis, Hannah. 2018. 'Lessons from Donor Support to Technical Assistance Programmes'. K4D Helpdesk Report. Institute of Development Studies, Brighton, UK. https://assets.publishing.service.gov.uk/media/5ab0e81140f0b62d854a9bc5/Lessons_from_donor_support_to_technical_assistance_programmes.pdf.

Troilo, Pete. 2011. 'PPPs in the Developing World'. Devex. https://www.devex.com/news/ppps-in-the-developing-world-76370.

Trubek, David. 2012. 'Reversal of Fortune? International Economic Governance, Alternative Development Strategies, and the Rise of the BRICS'. Working Paper.

Tugendhat, Henry, and Dawit Alemu. 2016. 'Chinese Agricultural Training Courses for African Officials: Between Power and Partnerships'. *World Development* 81 (May): 71–81.

Turki, Benyan. 2014. 'The Kuwait Fund for Arab Economic Development and Its Activities in African Countries, 1961–2010'. *Middle East Journal* 68 (3): 421–435.

UNCTAD (United Nations Conference on Trade and Development). 2009. 'World Investment Report 2009: Transnational Corporations, Agricultural Production and Development'. http://unctad.org/en/Docs/wir2009_en.pdf.

———. 2014. 'World Investment Report 2014: Transnational Corporations, Agricultural Production and Development'. http://unctad.org/en/PublicationsLibrary/wir2014_en.pdf.

UNDP. 2016. 'Strategy Note: UNDP's Private Sector and Foundations Strategy for the Sustainable Development Goals 2016–2020'. UNDP (United Nations Development Programme).

USAID. 2015. 'Partnering for Impact: USAID and the Private Sector 2014–2015'. https://www.usaid.gov/sites/default/files/documents/15396/usaid_partnership%20report_FINAL3.pdf.

———. 2016. 'Global Development Alliance Annual Program Statement (GDA APS)'. https://www.usaid.gov/sites/default/files/documents/15396/GDA%20APS_APS-OAA-16-000001_2016_0.pdf.

Van Meter, Donald S., and Carl E. Van Horn. 1975. 'The Policy Implementation Process A Conceptual Framework'. *Administration & Society* 6 (4): 445–488.

Vaz, Alcides, and Cristina Inoue. 2007. 'Emerging Donors in International Development Assistance: The Brazil Case'. Working Paper. International Development Research Center, Canada.

Veen, Maurits van der. 2011. *Ideas, Interests and Foreign Aid*. Cambridge: Cambridge University Press.

Vickers, Brendan. 2012. 'Towards a New Aid Paradigm: South Africa as African Development Partner'. *Cambridge Review of International Affairs* 25 (4): 535–556.

Villanger, Espen. 2007. 'Arab Foreign Aid: Disbursement Patterns, Aid Policies and Motives'. *Forum for Development Studies* 34 (2): 223–256.

Walz, Julie, and Vijaya Ramachandran. 2011. 'Brave New World: A Literature Review of Emerging Donors and the Changing Nature of Foreign Assistance'. Working Paper 273. Centre for Global Development, Washington, DC.

Wan, Baorui. 2011. 'Guanyu Nongye "zouchuqu" wenti (On the Issue of "Agricultural Going Out")'. *Jingji Yanjiu Cankao* (Economic Research Review) 2380 (36): 19.

———. 2012. 'Jiakuai Shishi Nongye "zouchuqu" zhanlue (Quickening the Implementation of Agricultural Going Out Policy)'. *Renmin Ribao* (People's Daily), 5 June. http://paper.people.com.cn/rmrb//html/2012-06/05/nw.D110000renmrb_20120605_1-07.htm.

Wanbao. n.d. 'Gongsi Jieshao (Company Profile)'. Accessed 8 February 2016. http://en.wblyjt.com/?comContentId=8f102a02-541d-4fff-bf4d-c1161890 03ff.

Wang, Chao. 2014. 'Firm That Cottoned on to a Good Deal'. China Daily Africa. http://africa.chinadaily.com.cn/weekly/2014-06/13/content_1758 4808.htm.

Wang, Chenyan. 2008. 'Dui Feizhou Nongye Yuanzhu Xin Xingshi de Tansuo (Exploring New Forms of Agricultural Aid to Africa)'. *Guoji Jingji Hezuo* (International Economic Cooperation) 4: 35–38.

Wang, Xiaobing, and Adam Ozanne. 2010. 'Two Approaches to Aid in Africa: China and the West'.

Wang, Yuhan. 2013. 'Wo Gongsi Yu Yuanshi Guoji Gongsi Qianshu Touzi Madajiasijia Zajiaoshuidao Xiangguan Xieyi (CAAIC Signed Agreement with Yuanshi on Hybrid Rice Project in Madagascar)'. *CNADC (China National Agricultural Development Group Co. Ltd.) News*, 28 November. http://www.zgnfb.com/news-4701.html.

Wanna, John, Evert A. Lindquist, and Penelope Marshall. 2015. *New Accountabilities, New Challenges*. Acton: ANU Press.

Wendt, Alexander. 1987. 'The Agent-Structure Problem in International Relations Theory'. *International Organization* 41 (3): 335–370.

WFP (World Food Programme). 2015. 'Contributions to WFP: Comparative Figures and Five-Year Aggregate Ranking'. http://documents.wfp.org/stellent/groups/public/documents/research/wfp232961.pdf.

White, Howard. 1996. 'Evaluating Programme Aid: Introduction and Synthesis'. *IDS Bulletin* 27 (4). IDS (Institute of Development Studies), Sussex.

Will, Magret. 2013. *Contract Farming Handbook: A Practical Guide for Linking Small-Scale Producers and Buyers Through Business Model Innovation*. Bonn and Eschborn: GIZ. http://www.unidroit.org/english/documents/2013/study80a/bibliogr-references/s-80a-will-contract.pdf.

William Hynes, and Simon Scott. 2013. 'The Evolution of Official Development Assistance: Achievements, Criticisms and A Way Forward'. OECD Development Co-operation Working Papers No. 12. OECD Publishing, Paris.

Wily, Liz. 2011. 'The Tragedy of Public Lands: The Fate of the Commons Under Global Commercial Pressure'. http://www.landcoalition.org/sites/default/files/documents/resources/WILY_Commons_web_11.03.11.pdf.

———. 2012. 'Rights to Resources in Crisis: Reviewing the Fate of Customary Tenure in Africa'. http://www.rightsandresources.org/documents/files/doc_4699.pdf.

Windhoff-Héritier, Adrienne. 1980. *Politikimplementation*. Hain.

Winter, Søren C. 1990. 'Integrating Implementation Research'. In *Implementation and the Policy Process*.
———. 2012. 'Implementation: Introduction'. In *The Sage Handbook of Public Administration* (Peters and Pierre Eds.), 255–263.
Wolfe, Braude, Pearl Thandrayan, and Elizabeth Sidiropoulos. 2008. 'Emerging Donors in International Development Assistance: The South Africa Case'. Working Paper. International Development Research Center, Canada.
Woods, Ngaire. 2008. 'Whose Aid? Whose Influence? China, Emerging Donors and the Silent Revolution in Development Assistance'. *International Affairs* 84 (6): 1205–1221.
World Bank. 2013. 'Growing Africa: Unlocking the Potential of Agribusiness'. The World Bank. http://siteresources.worldbank.org/INTAFRICA/Resources/africa-agribusiness-report-2013.pdf.
———. n.d. 'Arable Land (Hectares Per Person)'. Accessed 27 March 2016. http://data.worldbank.org/indicator/AG.LND.ARBL.HA.PC.
Xalma, C. 2010. 'Report on South-South Cooperation in Ibero-America'. SEGIB Studies No. 5. Madrid.
Xiangyang Government. 2013. 'Wanbao Liangyou Yu Zhongfei Fazhan Jijin Qianyue, Hezuo Touzi Kaifa Wanbao Feizhou Mosangbike Nongye Xiangmu (Wanbao and CADFund Signed Agreement to Co-operate in Agricultural Project in Mozambique)'. http://www.xiangyang.gov.cn/news/xyxw/xyyw/201309/t20130916_438735.shtml.
Xiao, Zongzhi, and Derong Zhang. 2002. 'Zhongguo Wushi Duonian Lai de Duiwai Jingji Jishu Yuanzhu Pingxi (On China's Economical & Technical Assistance to Foreign Countries during 50 Years or More)'. *Beijing Keji Daxue Xuebao Kehui Kexue Ban* (Journal of University of Science and Technology Beijing/Social Sciences Edition) 18 (4): 80–83.
Xinhua News Agency. 2010. 'Hui Liangyu Zai Zhongfei Nongye Hezuo Luntan Bimushi Shang de Jianghua (Hui Liangyu's Speech on the Closing Ceremony of Forum on China-Africa Agricultural Cooperation)'. http://news.xinhuanet.com/2010-08/12/c_12440117.htm.
Xu, Jifeng, and Lu Qin. 2011. 'Zhongguo Yuanzhu Feizhou Nongye Jishu Shifan Zhongxin Kechixu Fazhan Jianyi (Suggestions on the Sustainable Development of Chinese Agriculture Technology Demonstration Centre in Africa)'. *Shijie Nongye* (World Agriculture) 12: 87–99.
Xu, Juan. 2013. 'Guojia Kaifa Yinhang Qingdao Fenhang Zhuli qiye "zouchuqu" (CDB Qingdao Supports Enterprises to "Go Out")'. People.cn, 30 July. http://society.people.com.cn/n/2013/0730/c1008-22379126.html.
Xu, Xiuli, Xiaoyun Li, Gubo Qi, Lixia Tang, and Langton Mukwereza. 2016. 'Science, Technology, and the Politics of Knowledge: The Case of China's Agricultural Technology Demonstration Centers in Africa'. *World Development* 81: 82–91.

Xu, Xiuli, and Lili Xu. 2011. 'Guoji Fazhan Huayu de Chongsu: Zhongguo Yu Feizhou Guojia Nongye Hezuo de Fangshi Yu Fansi (Reshaping the International Development Discourse? The Modalities of China-Africa Agricultural Cooperation and Its Implications)'. *Zhongguo Nongye Daxue Xuebao Shehui Kexue Ban* (China Agricultural University Journal of Social Sciences Edition) 28 (4): 26–33.

Yang, Hongxi, and Kaiming Chen. 2010. 'Zhongguo Duiwai Yuanzhu: Chengjiu Jiaoxun He Liangxing Fazhan (Chinese Foreign Aid: Achievement, Lessons and Benign Development)'. *Guoji Zhanwang* (World Outlook) 1: 46–56.

Yang, Shaopin. 2012. 'Zhongguo Nongye Jiakuai shishi "zouchuqu" (Hasten the Implementation of China's "Agricultural Going Out" Strategy)'. http://money.163.com/12/0822/12/89GTIALO00254S3A.html.

Yang, Yi, Zhigang Ma, Qi Wang, Lili Zhang, and Yan Dong. 2012. 'Zhongguo Nongye Duiwai Touzi Hezuo de Xianzhuang Fenxi (Status Analysis of China's Agricultural Foreign Investment and Cooperation)' 404 (12): 107–112.

Ye, Xingqing. 2007. 'Zhongguo Nongye yiying "zouchuqu" (Chinese Agriculture Should Also "Go Out")'. *Liaowang (Outlook)*, no. 20: 50.

Younis, Musab, Jennifer Constantine, Akansha Yadav, Elise Wach, Lizbeth Navas-Aleman, and Alex Shankland. 2013. 'Rising Powers in International Development: An Annotated Bibliography'. IDS (Institute of Development Studies), Sussex.

Yu, Haomiao, and Ruijuan Chang. 2014. 'Qiye Dui Feizhou Nongye Touzi de Silu (Thoughts on Companies' Agricultural Investment in Africa)'. *Shijie Nongye* (World Agriculture) 421 (5): 174–176, 187.

Yu, Wenjing. 2014. 'Nongken "zouchuqu" bufa Jiakuai (The State Farming System Has Hastened Its Pace to "Go Out")'. http://finance.china.com.cn/roll/20140410/2323715.shtml.

Yu, Wenjing, and Yu Wang. 2015. 'The Contribution Rate of Technology Advances to Agricultural Development Is to Be Above 56% (Woguo Nongye Jishu Jinbu Gongxianlv Jiang Chaoguo 56%)'. *Xinhua News Agency*, 27 December. http://news.xinhuanet.com/fortune/2015-12/27/c_1117592182.htm.

Yu, Yuanyuan. 2014. 'Tansang Jianma Xiangmu Qishilu (Learning from Tanzanian Sisal Farm)'. *CNADC (China National Agricultural Development Group Co. Ltd) News*, 10 October. http://www.zgnfb.com/news-5461.html.

Yuan, Jirong. 2013. 'Zhongguo Jianma Nongchang Zaofu Tansangniya (Chinese Sisal Farm Benefits Tanzania)'. http://world.people.com.cn/n/2013/0206/c1002-20444180.html.

Yun, Wenju. 1998. 'Zhongfei hezuo kaifa nongye de zhanlue xuanze (Strategic Choices of China-Africa Agricultural Cooperative Development)'. *Zhongguo ruan kexue* (China Soft Science) 12: 96–102.

———. 2000a. '21 shiji de zhongfei nongye hezuo (Sino-Africa Agricultural Cooperation in the 21st Century)'. *Xiya Feizhou* (West Asia and Africa) 5: 38–42.

———. 2000b. 'Cong guoji yuanzhu de fazhan kan zhongguo duifei nongye yuanzhu (The Development of International Aid and China's Agricultural Aid to Africa)'. *Xiya Feizhou* (West Asia and Africa) 2: 17–23.

Zha, Daojiong. 2010. 'Guoji Zhengzhi Yanjiu Yu Zhongguo de Liangshi Anquan (China's Food Security: An International Politics Perspective)'. *Guoji Zhengzhi Yanjiu* (International Politics Quarterly) 31 (2).

Zhai, Xueling. 2006. 'Woguo Nongye "zouchuqu" de Wenti Ji Duice (Problems and Countermeasures of China's Agricultural "Going Out")'. *Guoji Jingji Hezuo* (International Economic Cooperation) 7: 7–10.

Zhang, Hao. 2014. '"Nongfa Xi" cheng Yangqi Gaige Xianxingjun (The CNADC System Becomes the Pioneers Among China's SOEs)'. http://www.nbd.com.cn/articles/2014-07-22/850366.html.

Zhang, Q. Forrest. 2010. 'Reforming China's State-Owned Farms: State Farms in Agrarian Transition'.

Zhang, Qingmin. 2009. 'Liushinian Lai Xinzhongguo Waijiao Buju de Fazhan (Development of the Overall Diplomatic Arrangement of the New China in the Past Six Decades)'. *Waijiao Pinglun* (Foreign Affairs Review) 4: 32–42.

Zhang, Xiaojun, and Xi Zhang. 2015. 'Hubei Nongken Chengdan Haiwai Yuanzhu Xiangmu Jihaiwai Nongye Hezuo Kaifa Xiangmu Jianjie (Foreign Aid and Overseas Agricultural Exploitation Projects Undertaken by Hubei Bureau of State Farm and Land Reclamation)'. http://www.hubeifarm.com/hwkf/gzjl/3876.htm.

Zhang, Yanbing, Jing Gu, and Yunnan Chen. 2015. 'China's Engagement in International Development Cooperation: The State of the Debate'. IDS (Institute of Development Studies).

Zhang, Yu. 2008. 'Zhongguo Nongken Haiwai Tuohuang (Chinese State-Farming Companies Explore Overseas)'. http://zzwz.qikan.com/ArticleView.aspx?titleid=zzwz20080816.

Zhang, Yunhua. 2009. 'Canyu Haiwai Nongye Kaifa de Jiyu Yu Duice (Opportunities and Countermeasures of Participating in Overseas Agricultural Exploration)'. *Nongcun Gongzuo Tongxun* (Rural Work Newsletter) 9.

Zhang, Zhe. 2010. 'Zhongken Nongchang Chanpin Zhan Dangdi 20% (Products of Zhongken Farm Occupies 20% of Local Market)'. http://news.sina.com.cn/c/sd/2010-04-08/144520032529_3.shtml.

Zhao, Xiaohui, and Junjie Tao. 2011. 'Nongyebu Yu Guojia Kaifa Yinhang 18ri Qianshu Guihua Hezuo Beiwanglu (Ministry of Agriculture and CDB Signed MOU on 18th)'. Xinhua New Agency. http://www.gov.cn/jrzg/2011-02/18/content_1805743.htm.

Zheng, Yougui. 2004. 'Woguo Nongken Tizhi Gaige Huigu Yu Bianxi: Yi Heilongjiang Hainan Liangsheng Weili (Review and Discussion on the Reform of China's State Farming System: The Cases of Heilongjiang and Hainan Provinces)'. *Zhongguo Jingjishi Yanjiu* (Chinese Economic History Research) 4: 43–51.

Zhou, Baogen. 2010. 'Cong Duiwai Jingmao Shijiao Kan Ruhe Tigao Woguo Yuanwai Xiangmu de Youxiaoxing (How to Increase the Effectiveness of Chinese Foreign Aid Projects: From the Foreign Economic and Commercial Point of View)'. *Hongqi Wengao* 19.

Zhou, Cui. 2018. 'CDB: Strengthening China-Africa Cooperation Through Channelling Financial and Intellectual Resources (Guokaihang: Rongzi Rongzhi Zhutui Zhongfei Shenhua Hezuo)'. 21 September 2018. http://www.financialnews.com.cn/yh/sd/201809/t20180921_146550.html.

Zhou, Deyi, Ruifu Chang, and Yunlai Xiao, eds. 2011. *Zhongfei Nongye Hezuo Moshi Chuangxin Yanjiu* (Research on Agricultural Cooperative Model Innovations Between China and Africa). Beijing: Zhongguo nongye kexue jishu chubanshe (China Agricultural Science and Technology Press).

Zhou, Enlai. 1964. 'The Eight Principles of Foreign Economic and Technical Cooperation'. In *Selected Works of Zhou Enlai in Diplomacy*. Beijing: Central Party Literature Press.

Zhou, Hong. 2008. 'Zhongguo Duiwai Yuanzhu Yu Gaige Kaifang 30 Nian (China's Foreign Aid and 30 Years of Reform)'. *Shijie Jingji Yu Zhengzhi* (World Economics and Politics) 11: 33–43.

Zhou, Jianjun, and Qiang Wang. 1997. 'Xin Xingshi Xia Dui Feizhou Nongye Yuanzhu de Tantao (Agricultural Aid to Africa Under the New Circumstances)'. *Guoji Jingji Hezuo* (International Economic Cooperation) 3: 9–11.

Zhou, Li. 2008. 'Liangshi Zhuquan, Liangshi Zhengzhi Yu Renlei Kechixu Fazhan (Food Sovereignty, Food Politics and Human Sustainable Development)'. *Shijie Huanjing* (World Environment) 7.

Zhou, Yuegui. 2014. 'Dadan Dao Laowo zuo "nongchangzhu" (Become "Farm Owners" in Laos)'. http://www.asean-china-center.org/2014-08/08/c_133542070.htm.

Zhu, Zhenlei. 2013. 'Zhongfei Nongtou Yu Sudan Nongyebu Qianshu Nongye Hezuo Kuangjia Xieyi (CAAIC Signed Framwork Agreement on Agricultural Cooperation with Sudanese Ministry of Agriculture)'. *CNADC (China National Agricultural Development Group Co. Ltd.) News*, 23 April. http://www.zgnfb.com/news-4095.html.

Zimmermann, Felix, and Kimberly Smith. 2011. 'More Actors, More Money, More Ideas for International Development Co-operation'. *Journal of International Development* 23 (5): 722–738.

Index

A
Additionality, 16, 18, 106, 208
African agriculture, 1, 18, 19, 26, 58, 65, 70, 88, 108, 109, 169, 201, 203, 205
African Union (AU), 20
Agribusiness, 19, 22, 25, 46, 49–51, 58, 71, 74, 82, 83, 95, 96, 98, 100, 106, 107, 109, 113, 116, 118, 125, 128, 131, 132, 135, 137, 138, 151, 157–159, 162, 163, 166–169, 181, 185, 186, 188–192, 194, 204, 205, 217
Agribusiness investment, 20, 58, 106, 185
Agribusiness model, 22, 25, 26, 46, 54, 58, 65, 66, 105, 106, 109, 114, 116, 126, 127, 133, 162, 165, 169, 172, 173, 181, 184, 187, 188, 201, 204
Agribusiness opportunities, 74, 184
Agribusiness value chain, 53, 75, 127, 128, 139, 165, 204

Agricultural cooperation, 1, 25, 54, 65, 106, 107, 111, 133, 185
Agricultural development cooperation, 24, 42, 54, 57, 58, 105, 109, 193, 199, 200
Agricultural FDI, 107, 111, 112, 117
'Agricultural Going Out' strategy, 58, 202
Agricultural infrastructure, 56
Agricultural officials, 79
Agricultural raw materials, 18, 112, 113
Agricultural sector, 18, 19, 36, 40, 53, 54, 56, 83, 105–107, 109, 113, 127, 129, 154, 162, 173, 191, 203, 204
Agricultural technicians, 78
Agricultural trade, 21, 54, 123
Agricultural vocational education systems, 19, 55
Agriculture, 2, 18–20, 35, 53, 54, 86, 99, 105, 109, 113, 114, 116, 125, 127, 138, 141, 162, 164, 166, 194, 200–204

264   INDEX

'Agriculture Going Out', 113, 116, 122, 123
'Agriculture Going Out' policy, 54, 70, 107, 109, 110, 115, 123, 124, 128
'Agriculture Going Out' strategy, 106, 123, 201
Agriculture Leads to Prosperity, 20
Agriculture-related companies, 112, 116
Agriculture Technology Demonstration Centres (ATDCs), 19, 23, 25, 55, 57, 65, 66, 70–75, 86
Agro-aid, 37–40, 49–51, 57, 66, 71, 115, 116, 200, 201, 204, 205
Agro-cooperation, 1, 2, 21, 22, 26, 86, 182–184, 187, 199–201, 203
Agro-development cooperation, 19, 21, 22, 24–26, 36, 38, 48, 53, 54, 109, 114, 115, 126, 182, 183, 185, 187, 188, 191, 192, 196, 197, 199, 200, 203, 205
Agro-experts, 19, 49, 52, 55, 140, 143
Agro-FDI, 58, 107, 109, 113, 124, 156, 201
Agro-industrial parks, 120, 128
Agro-infrastructure, 20, 38, 109, 203
Agro-investment, 23, 50, 58, 83, 92, 96, 98, 107, 115, 117, 122, 124–130, 132, 160, 165, 169, 171, 184, 185, 192–194
Agro-processing, 20, 21, 57, 67, 113, 117, 120, 121, 124, 131, 139, 144, 214
Agro-technology extension, 54, 94, 188
Agro-technology research, 74
Agro-technology transfer, 58, 76, 78, 95, 96, 137, 140, 166, 189, 190
Aid, 2, 4–15, 19–21, 36–40, 42–49, 51, 54–57, 66, 71, 72, 74, 75, 95, 96, 98, 105, 116, 127, 134, 182–184, 186, 191, 192, 200–204, 206–211
Aid performance, 42, 44, 45, 51, 201
Aid scale, 42–44, 201
Altruism, 208, 210
Angola, 69, 116, 117, 120, 121, 131, 219
Asian Relations Conference, 6
ATDC Guidance, 70, 75, 184
ATDC in Mozambique, 76, 77, 82, 93, 166
ATDC in South Africa, 86, 87

B

Bandung Conference, 6, 36
Beira, 131, 160, 161, 167
Boane, 23, 76, 77, 79, 81, 84, 86, 134
Book structure, 24
Brazil, 3, 6, 7, 9, 10, 14, 17, 107, 167, 218, 221
Brazil, Russia, India, China and South Africa (BRICS), 6
Budget support, 10
Buenos Aires Action Plan, 10
Bureau of State Farms and Land Reclamation (BSFLR), 77, 133, 152
Busan Declaration, 17
Business introduction, 66, 71, 74–76, 82, 91, 96, 100
Business model, 14, 17, 73, 75, 200, 204
Buzi, 23, 151–156

C

Capabilities, 40, 55, 58, 72, 73, 111, 123, 129, 144, 148, 155, 156, 166, 186, 188, 190, 191, 193, 196, 197, 205, 210, 211
Capability building, 10, 19, 99

INDEX 265

Cash-crop projects, 116
Cash crops, 108, 110–112, 115, 132, 162, 165, 213
Cassava, 67, 119, 121, 131, 213, 216, 218, 219
CDB Hubei, 138
Central SAEs, 114, 118, 129, 131
Challenge funds, 16
China-Africa Agricultural Investment Co., Ltd. (CAAIC), 23, 118, 129, 133, 157–159, 164, 168, 172, 214
China-Africa Cotton Company, 130, 132
China-Africa Cotton Development Co., Ltd. (CACD), 130, 133, 160–162, 164, 166, 168, 172, 221
China-Africa Development Fund (CADFund), 120, 127, 138, 145, 157, 158, 160, 162, 164, 165
China Agriculture International Development Co Ltd. (CAIDC), 87, 92, 93, 96, 215
China Development Bank (CDB), 18, 119, 120, 122, 124, 127, 136, 138, 139, 160, 214
China Export & Credit Insurance Corporation (SINOSURE), 122, 125
China National Agricultural Development Corporation (CNADC), 87, 92, 114, 157, 158, 164
China National Cereals, Oils and Foodstuffs Corporation Co., Ltd. (COFCO), 114, 216
China National Complete Plant Import & Export Corporation (COMPLANT), 51, 116, 118, 132

China's agro-development cooperation, 21, 35, 49, 54, 76, 106, 162, 183, 185
China State Farms Agribusiness Corporation (CSFAC), 50, 51, 118, 131, 214, 215
Chinese Agriculture Technology Demonstration Centre (ATDC), 22, 25, 67, 76, 94, 134, 160, 166, 194, 204
Chinese agro-experts, 19, 45, 50, 51, 79, 89, 93, 203
Chinese Communist Party (CCP), 123, 124, 133
Chinese community, 82, 131, 168, 190
Chinese experts, 40, 45, 49, 50, 78, 80–83, 88, 95
Chinese Ministry of Agriculture (MOA), 37, 55, 76, 84, 125, 126
Chinese state-owned enterprises (SOEs), 51, 116
Cold War, 6, 15, 36, 39
Collaborative teaching, 79
College students, 79, 89
Colombo Plan, 6
Colonial past, 2, 9, 37, 41, 207
Combination, 2, 3, 47, 57, 129, 135, 136, 154, 159, 165, 204, 206
Combined form, 130
Commercial Operation Stage, 73–75, 77, 85, 98, 186, 204
Commonwealth Development Corporation (CDC), 16, 208
Communist Party of China (CPC), 41, 52, 124
Company-Government Cooperation, 114
Comparative case study, 22
Complete projects, 38, 54, 56
Comprehensive African Agriculture Development Programme (CAADP), 20

266 INDEX

Concessionality, 10–13, 39, 206, 210
Concessional terms, 10
Conditionality, 11, 13, 206, 210
Congo-Brazzaville, 37, 38, 49
Consolidation, 48, 49, 54, 201
Contract and responsibility system (CRS), 44, 51
Contract-farming, 121, 129, 130, 139, 142, 143, 154, 159–161, 165, 172, 204, 221
Contract- farming, 154
Cooperation forms, 2, 3, 10, 15, 26, 35, 46, 48, 105, 203, 205, 207, 209
Corporate actors, 17, 57, 58, 66, 107, 133, 186, 187, 193, 204
Cotton, 21, 25, 68, 81, 110, 112, 118–120, 123, 130, 132, 133, 135, 153, 154, 160, 161, 164, 166, 172, 216, 221
COVEC, 69, 120, 131
Crop-farming companies, 116
Crop-farming projects, 116
CSR, 58

D

DAC donors, 5, 6, 8–17, 59, 208
DAC members, 3, 5, 11, 13, 207
DAP Gaza, 149
Demonstration, 16, 43, 66, 70, 74, 81, 89, 93, 120, 133, 189, 204
Demonstration and training, 70, 74, 78, 80, 88, 90, 204
Demonstration role, 80
Demonstration Stage, 141
Deng, Xiaoping, 41, 42, 46, 52, 202
Department For International Development (DFID), 209
Developed countries, 2, 4, 48
Developing country, 6–8, 10, 11, 26, 44, 47, 51, 56, 201, 202, 207
Development assistance, 4, 6, 19

Development Assistance Committee (DAC), 4, 5
Development cooperation models, 3, 7, 13, 22, 181, 200
Development cooperation providers, 2, 3
Development Cooperation Reports, 14, 15
Development finance institutions (DFIs), 16, 18, 208
Development finances, 3, 210
Development objectives, 2, 17, 47, 70, 109, 200, 201, 206, 208
Development package, 3, 7, 12, 17–19, 21, 22, 25, 26, 35, 47, 54, 59, 105, 181, 200, 202–204, 206, 210
Development PPP, 15–18, 73, 207, 210
Development status, 13, 39, 46
Discretion, 51, 58, 188, 192, 193, 196, 197, 211
Display, 23, 70, 74
Domestic origin, 21
Dynamic environment, 194

E

Economic infrastructure, 9
Economic sectors, 9
Emerging donors, 7, 209
English, 79, 80, 89, 90, 141
Environment, 20, 26, 41, 53, 92, 94, 96, 107, 110, 113, 128, 137, 149, 161, 167, 170, 182, 185, 188, 190, 192, 194, 196, 197, 200, 205
Ethiopia, 55, 56, 67, 72, 117, 120
European Economic Community, 4
European Recovery Programme, 4
Exchange, 20, 23, 40, 41, 53, 55, 86, 87, 91, 92, 124, 125, 132, 137, 141, 148, 149, 200, 201, 203

Experiences, 13–15, 26, 53, 79, 172, 200, 201
Experiment, 1, 3, 19, 38, 52, 70, 189, 197, 209
Expert dispatch, 55
Export-Import Bank of China (EXIM Bank), 11, 18, 47, 118, 119, 122, 124, 127, 214
Extension, 38, 55, 56, 66, 70, 74, 83, 85, 88, 94, 99, 119–121, 204
External assistance, 4, 210
External development cooperation, 1, 5, 13, 18, 21, 22, 25, 26, 39, 44, 48, 199, 201, 206, 208, 210

F
Farming culture, 95, 141, 166, 194
Farm/plantation production, 129
Fieldwork, vii, viii, 23, 25, 69, 74, 75, 77, 79, 83–85, 92, 121, 137–139, 141, 143–145, 154, 156, 157, 166, 167, 181, 191, 205
Financial institutions, 15, 18, 20
Financial sustainability, 97
Financing, 9, 13, 15, 16, 25, 48, 73, 97, 98, 108, 123, 126, 127, 130, 133, 138, 154, 160, 162, 163, 205, 207, 209
Flexibility, 105
FONGA, 147, 149, 151, 195
Food aid, 12, 57, 204, 208
Food and Agricultural Organization (FAO), 56, 135, 170–172
Food-crop, 131
Food security, 19, 20, 53, 58, 70, 71, 111, 112, 133, 165, 172, 200, 201, 205, 213
Foreign aid, 6, 40–42, 44
Foreign aid reforms, 25, 36, 41, 42, 46–48, 65, 200, 208
Foreign Economic Cooperation Centre, 122

Forum on Agricultural Cooperation with Africa (FOCAAC), 54, 107, 109
Forum on China-Africa Cooperation (FOCAC), 19–21, 53–57, 66, 76, 107, 127, 157
'Four Principles of Conducting Economic and Technical Cooperation with African Countries', 46
Free State, 23, 86–90
Freshwater aquaculture, 68, 88, 215

G
Gabon, 56, 117, 214
Gaps, 26, 182, 196
Gariep Dam, 23, 86, 87
Gates Foundation, 14, 81
Gaza Province of Mozambique, 95, 133
Ghana, 38, 49, 56, 117, 214, 221
'Global South', 7
'Going Out', 125, 191
'Going Out' strategy, 47, 52, 107, 122
Governmental actors, 58, 116, 188
Government–Company Cooperation, 72
Government Medium/Long-term Concessional Loan, 47, 127
Grain and Cotton Import Quota System ('Import Quota System'), 112, 113, 126, 185
Grain crops, 58, 110–112, 115, 129
Grain industry, 112
Grains, 67, 68, 112, 123, 130, 168, 213, 215, 216, 218, 221
Grant element, 11
Grants, 9–11, 17, 39, 43
Grants model, 16
Green Super Rice, 81
Guinea, 37, 38, 49, 50, 52, 117
Guinea-Bissau, 106

H

Hefeng, 23, 84, 120, 133, 151–157, 163, 164, 167, 190
Hefeng Oil & Grains Co., Ltd. ('Hefeng'), 151
Historical origin, 199
Historical review, 24, 35, 200
Historical trajectory, 21, 26, 35, 65
History(ies), 4, 6, 13, 21, 35, 40, 206
Hubei BSFLR, 83, 136, 153
Hubei province of China, 77, 83, 84, 96, 115, 133–136, 138, 139, 151, 152, 154, 220
Hu, Jintao, 52, 76, 134
Humanitarian food aid, 20

I

Ideologies, 13, 26, 39, 42, 201–203
Implementation gaps, 21, 173, 182, 183, 205
Implementer, 26, 73, 160, 182–188, 190–194, 196, 197, 205
Implementing companies, 73, 74, 82, 186, 191, 192
In-class teaching, 79
India, 3, 6, 7, 9–11, 13, 14, 17, 167
Indian Technical & Economic Cooperation (ITEC), 10
Informants, vii, 23, 77, 100, 145, 164, 173, 198
Infrastructure, 14, 20, 45, 56, 57, 74, 105, 108, 109, 136, 137, 146, 158, 163, 166, 168, 194, 208, 209
Innovative agro-aid model, 22, 25, 26, 57, 58, 65, 76, 100, 109, 173, 181, 187, 188, 201, 204
Institutional structures, 25, 35
Instituto de Investigação Agrária de Moçambique (IIAM), 77, 80, 194

International development cooperation (IDC), 1–7, 13, 14, 17–19, 22, 24, 26, 35, 58, 199, 206, 209–211
Interviews, 23, 24, 39, 70, 77–86, 88–92, 94–98, 100, 130–132, 134–137, 139–141, 143–149, 152–160, 163–165, 168, 173, 189–191, 195, 198
Investment, 16, 17, 20, 23, 25, 39, 43, 47, 48, 83, 84, 92, 96–98, 106–110, 112, 114–117, 124–129, 133, 137, 138, 146, 151–154, 157–160, 162, 163, 165, 166, 169, 171, 185, 186, 188, 190–193, 202–204, 206, 218, 220

J

Jiang, Zemin, 52
Jilin Overseas Agricultural Exploration Group Corporation (JOAEC), 126
Joint venture, 45, 46, 50, 75, 99, 153, 157, 160, 214

L

Land constraints, 95, 112, 128, 169, 202
Land deals, 128
Land issue, 137, 146, 169, 171, 172, 182, 185, 194
Land ownership, 98
Land tenure, 170, 171
Least Developed Countries (LDCs), 8, 11, 12, 43
LEGs model, 16
Lianfeng, 82, 83, 85, 96, 98, 134–137, 139, 153, 167

INDEX   269

Lianfeng Overseas Agricultural Development Company ('Lianfeng'), 77, 133
Liberia, 38, 67, 72, 96, 120, 221
Loans, 9–11, 13, 14, 16, 17, 39, 43, 118, 119, 124, 125, 138, 141, 160, 205
Local language(s), 79, 80
Local SAEs, 114, 115
Logic, 13, 17, 21, 26, 65, 197, 202

M

Madagascar, 38, 49, 51, 118, 120, 130
Maize, 67, 68, 78, 81, 110–112, 131, 144, 213, 214, 218
Mali, 37, 38, 40, 49, 50, 56, 69, 71, 117, 118, 132, 160
Management, 20, 35, 40, 45, 49–51, 56, 58, 73, 75, 77, 79, 85, 86, 88, 91–93, 99, 114, 129, 136, 137, 140, 146–148, 161, 164, 172, 184, 185, 189, 190, 220
Management cooperation, 46, 75, 99
Managerial sustainability, 92, 97
Maputo, 23, 76, 77, 83, 84, 131, 134, 137, 144, 146, 153, 154, 167
Market, 2, 11, 14, 16, 19, 43, 47, 49, 51, 52, 58, 75, 82, 83, 91, 96–98, 109, 110, 113, 123, 126, 127, 131, 132, 137, 144–146, 156, 157, 159–163, 166–170, 190–192, 204, 205
Market and Profit, 144, 166
Marshall, George C., 4
'Marshall Plan', 4
Mauritania, 37, 38, 49, 56, 69, 107, 117
Mergers and acquisitions (M&A), 110, 128, 129
Methodological, 21, 22

Ministério de Agricultura (MINAG), 76–78, 194, 195
Ministério de Ciência e Tecnologia (MCT), 76–78, 80, 85, 86, 194
Ministry of Agriculture (MOA), 39, 51, 55, 56, 58, 70, 71, 73–76, 107, 108, 112, 117, 122–124, 187
Ministry of Commerce (MOC), 38, 58, 70–76, 107, 110, 112, 117, 122–126, 128, 187
Mixed-ownership companies, 116
Modalities, 1, 3, 5, 8, 11, 13, 17, 19, 21, 23, 25, 35, 38, 45, 52, 74, 105, 106, 126, 133, 172, 181, 201, 202, 209
Motivation, 1, 36, 51, 58, 188, 191, 193, 196, 197, 205
Mozambique, vii, 22, 23, 25, 56, 66, 67, 76, 78, 82–84, 86, 94–96, 98, 100, 106, 115–117, 119, 120, 130–134, 136, 138, 139, 144–146, 151, 152, 154, 156, 159–161, 163–168, 171, 190, 195, 221
Multilateral cooperation, 20, 56, 203
Multi-organizational cooperation, 188, 193
Mutual benefit, 17, 46, 48, 207, 209
Mutual development, 3, 18, 22, 26, 42, 46–48, 54, 57, 58, 65, 70, 100, 105, 106, 109, 114, 162, 182, 183, 197, 199–202, 206

N

National Development and Reform Commission (NDRC), 110, 112, 122–124, 126, 128
Neo-colonialism, 207
Neutrality, 16, 18, 208
Nigeria, 38, 56, 69, 120, 131

Non-conditionality, 12, 14, 39
Non-DAC donors, 5, 7, 8
Non-governmental organizations (NGOs), 2, 14, 24, 147, 149, 186, 189, 195
Non-tying, 39
Northern donors, 2, 8, 12–16, 18, 22, 24, 35, 44, 47, 56, 106, 199, 206–210
North–South divide, 3, 4
North, the, 2, 3, 48, 206, 208–210

O

OECD-DAC, 4, 7, 9, 11, 12, 56, 203
Official aid, 2, 3, 36
Official development assistance (ODA), 2, 3, 5, 6, 9–12, 14–17, 26, 36, 39, 105, 199, 200, 203, 206, 207, 209
Organization for Economic Cooperation and Development (OECD), 4, 11, 14, 15, 56
Overseas agro-resources, 124, 132
Ownership, 11, 99, 115, 129, 187, 211

P

Package model, 21, 59, 173, 181, 182, 197, 199, 203, 205, 206
Paris Declaration, 11
Participant observation, 23, 24
People's Republic of China (PRC), 1, 6, 9, 10, 36–39, 41, 43–45, 47, 52, 55, 56, 58, 70–75, 107, 108, 112, 117, 124–126, 128, 136, 163, 200, 220
Plantation farming, 139, 141, 142, 165
Point Four Programme, 4
Policy, 6–8, 13, 14, 18–21, 26, 41, 42, 44, 46, 52–54, 59, 65, 107, 110, 111, 117, 122, 124, 125, 127, 128, 132, 139, 161, 168, 181–188, 191–194, 196, 197, 200–202, 205, 208
Policy control, 183, 185, 186, 191, 196
Policy design, 183–185, 192, 193, 196, 197
Portuguese, 79, 80, 151
Post-training application, 94, 192
Practical challenges, 162, 172, 181
Pragmatic approach, 201
Pragmaticism, 46, 105, 203
Preferential Buyer's Credit, 127
Preferential Export Buyers' Credit, 47
President Truman, 2, 4, 207
Private sector actors, 2, 3, 14–16, 209, 210
Processing, 20, 21, 40, 52, 56, 88, 92, 110, 113, 118–121, 123, 127, 128, 136, 144, 156, 158–161, 163, 165, 166, 214, 216–219, 221
Processing facilities, 155, 156, 161
Process-tracing, 22
Production and processing, 24, 25, 67, 123, 133, 139, 153, 154, 160, 165, 188
Production models, 121, 126, 129, 130, 139, 154, 165, 172, 189
Productive sector, 9, 19, 206
Profitability, 42, 44, 50, 98, 100, 113, 116, 152, 154, 157, 201
Profits, 85, 95, 97, 98, 129, 146, 159, 161–164, 167–169, 186, 189, 192, 210
Programme-based approaches (PBA), 10
Project Construction Stage, 74
Project sustainability, 66, 71, 76, 85, 92, 96, 97, 100, 116, 183, 184, 186, 192, 200
Proletarian internationalism, 39, 42, 202

INDEX 271

Provincial governments, 40, 51, 77, 96, 117, 133, 148, 152, 153
Public-interest functions, 66, 71, 74, 75, 97, 98, 204
Public policy implementation (PPI), 26, 182
Public–private cooperation, 14, 17, 18, 24, 187
Public–Private Partnership (PPP), 3, 14, 16, 18, 58, 73, 98, 106, 193, 208, 209
Public sector actors, 14
Pure aid, 26, 36, 39, 46, 48, 65, 105, 200, 209
Purity, 39, 207

Q
Qualitative, 22, 181
Qualitative interviewing, 23
Qualitative methods, 22

R
RBL-EP, 136, 137, 140, 146–149, 189
Recipient countries, 3, 4, 11, 13, 17, 40, 45, 47, 55, 57, 70–72, 129, 131, 132, 200, 205–207, 211
Recipient(s), 2, 6, 11, 14, 18, 40, 44, 48, 55, 73, 75, 89, 109, 187, 199, 206–210
Reciprocal benefit, 46, 48, 58, 199, 201
Reform, 1, 3, 11, 17, 21, 42, 44–46, 48, 49, 51, 75, 182, 201, 209
Reform and Opening-Up, 202, 203
Reform and Opening-Up policy, 41, 52, 220
Replacement aid, 37, 38, 40, 48
Research, vii, 7, 14, 19, 22–24, 35, 56, 70, 72, 80, 81, 84, 90, 92, 95, 100, 108, 109, 141, 153, 173, 181, 194, 197, 198, 209, 210
Research concerns, 21, 24, 25, 199
Rice, 24, 25, 37, 40, 50, 56, 67, 68, 78, 79, 81, 82, 84, 95, 108, 110–112, 115, 119–121, 123, 126, 130, 131, 133, 135, 137, 140, 141, 144–146, 152–159, 161, 164, 166–168, 172, 213, 215, 218, 219, 221
Risk-reducing model, 16
Rubber, 108, 110, 112, 115, 119, 130, 213, 218, 219, 221

S
SDIETC Group, 120, 132
Second World War (WWII), 2, 4, 207
Seed-industry, 128
Seed production, 83
Seed testing, 81, 82, 95
Self-sufficiency rate (SSR), 111
Senegal, 38, 106
Sierra Leone, 38, 40, 49, 51, 71, 95, 118, 119, 130, 219
SINOLIGHT, 116, 118, 132
Sisal, 50, 129, 130, 132, 213
Smallholder farmers, 55, 78, 80, 88–90, 94, 95, 129, 155, 204
Social infrastructure, 9, 209
Social sectors, 9, 43, 206
Sofala, 23, 84, 151, 152, 154, 156, 160, 161, 172
South Africa, vii, 6, 7, 9, 10, 17, 22, 23, 25, 68, 76, 86, 88, 90–92, 94–96, 100, 144
Southern actors, 2, 3, 8, 10, 12, 13, 17, 207, 209, 210
Southern countries, 6, 12, 48
Southern development partners, 1, 3, 7–14, 17, 24, 206

South-South Cooperation (SSC), 2, 6, 8, 56
South, the, 2, 6, 9, 10, 35, 209
Soviet, 36, 41
Soviet Union, 5, 6, 37, 39, 41, 200, 216
Soybean industry, 113
Soybeans, 68, 108, 112, 113, 121, 213, 215, 216, 218, 221
Special Program for Food Security (SPFS), 20
Spill-over, 162
Spill-over effects, 58, 106, 162
State farming enterprises (SFEs), 77, 114, 115, 118, 121, 135, 217, 220
State farming system, 134, 139
State-owned agricultural enterprises (SAEs), 84, 87, 106, 112, 114, 115, 121, 125, 126, 130, 197, 205
State-owned enterprises (SOEs), 2, 14, 18, 44, 45, 50, 51, 121, 127, 131, 132, 158, 164, 185, 191
Static environment, 194
Sub-Sahara Africa, 37
Sugar, 21, 38, 40, 49, 50, 110, 112, 118, 132, 213
Sugarcane, 38, 40, 49–51, 108, 118, 130, 132, 152–154, 213
Suggestions, 122, 124, 126, 128
Suggestions on Overseas Agricultural Investment and Cooperation (Suggestions), 122, 123
Supermarkets, 24, 82, 131, 144, 146, 156, 157, 167
Supporting Programs for Food Security, 56
Sustainability, 42, 44, 45, 55, 71, 72, 75, 92, 97, 181, 190, 200, 201, 210

T
Taiwan, 37, 38
Tanzania, 37, 40, 49–51, 68, 96, 107, 116–119, 121, 129, 130, 132, 160
Tanzanian, 52, 129
Technical assistance, 2, 6, 10, 19, 20, 38, 39, 54, 56, 74, 105
Technical cooperation, 12, 45, 49–51, 75, 83, 85, 92, 184, 208
Technical Cooperation Stage (TCS), 74–76, 80, 85, 87, 88, 91, 92, 97, 99, 186, 195, 204
Technical support, 39, 45, 49, 56, 83, 87, 96
Technical sustainability, 97, 99
Technical transfer, 66, 100
Technician Cooperation among Developing Countries (TCDC), 10
Technology transfer, 20, 78, 82, 88, 93–95, 158, 166, 186, 194
Third World, 36, 41, 42, 201
Tied aid, 12, 17, 47, 206, 208
Togo, 38, 51, 68, 72, 118
Trade, 17, 20, 39, 46–48, 52, 111, 123, 168, 203, 206, 208, 211, 218, 219, 221
Traditional agro-aid model, 25, 54, 57, 65, 203
Traditional donors, 3, 21, 206, 207
Training, 19, 24, 39, 45, 49, 55, 56, 58, 70, 74, 78–81, 85, 88, 89, 93–95, 106, 129, 137, 140–143, 155, 159, 189, 194, 203, 204
Training model, 78, 94, 99, 192
Training Stage, 140
Transformation, 48–50, 108, 109, 201, 220
Translator, 79, 80, 89, 143, 190, 195
Transnational agro-companies, 128

Trial and error, 59, 183
Trump Administration, 208
Turkey, 3, 7, 9, 11, 17
Two concessional loans, 47, 49, 127
Tying status of aid, 13, 206, 208

U
UN Chapter, 4, 39
UNFAO, 20
United Nations (UN), 2, 4, 8–12, 15, 19, 41, 56, 57
United States Agency for International Development (USAID), 15, 208
United States (US), 2, 4, 15, 37, 41, 107
Unsustainability, 45, 49, 51, 204
Untying of aid, 208

V
Value Chain, 88, 126–128, 161, 165, 166, 218, 219
Value for money, 72
Vegetables, 67, 68, 78, 81, 82, 111, 130, 131, 135, 218
Vocational education, 55, 56

W
Wanbao, 23, 84, 95, 120, 133, 135–149, 152, 154, 156, 158–160, 163–168, 171, 172, 189, 193, 195

Win-win, 26, 65, 173, 186, 207, 210, 211
World Bank, 4, 109, 111, 169, 170, 172
World Food Program, 57
World Trade Organization (WTO), 54, 113

X
Xi, Jinping, 52, 57
Xinjiang Production and Construction Corps, 69, 131

Y
Yu, Zhengsheng, 133

Z
Zaire, 38, 49
Zambia, 37, 56, 68, 72, 96, 116–120, 131, 144, 160, 218
Zhao, Ziyang, 45, 46, 54
Zhou, Enlai, 37, 39, 46
Zimbabwe, 116, 144

Printed by Printforce, the Netherlands